Praise for

END CREDIT

T0037314

"A hilarious and brutally honest memoir about life could only be told by someone who escaped."
—Judd Apatow, producer of *Girls* and *Bridesmaids* and director of *The 40-Year-Old Virgin*

"I love Patty Lin. I think she's one of the most talented writers I've ever met. And she's also a great person. True, she does have a few food issues that made ordering lunch each day a bit of an ordeal, but she's got a heart of gold. And we had a blast writing together."
—Paul Feig, creator of *Freaks and Geeks* and director of *Bridesmaids*

"Patty Lin has given us more than just a story about walking away from Hollywood to save her soul. This is also a critique of . . . the ways a first-generation Asian American woman must compromise herself for a laugh-track version of happiness and success."
—Gina Frangello, author of *Blow Your House Down*

"A wise, funny, whip-smart, and very moving book, *End Credits* takes us behind the scenes at some of the best-known TV shows of the last twenty-five years. A beautifully written book and a fascinating story. Patty Lin's debut shows brilliance and the promise of more. A stunner."
—Rob Roberge, author of *Liar*

"*End Credits* is masterfully written and reminds us that the end of one chapter is the beginning of another."
—Karen Duffy, author of *Wise Up*

"Patty Lin is a force of nature—I'm not sure there's anything she can't do—and her story will no doubt inspire readers everywhere."
—Susie Luo, author of *Paper Names*

"Patty Lin is one f*%king brave lady! What do you do when you have what everyone in the world wants, but it's not what's in your heart? It takes courage to trust yourself and walk away. This book is more than just a showbiz memoir, it's the story of a beautiful, creative soul getting back to who she really is."
—Emily Spivey, writer for *Saturday Night Live* and *Parks and Recreation*

"A compulsively readable, totally riveting fly-on-the-wall perspective on the cutthroat television industry that manages to be hilarious and heartfelt at the same time. A beautiful memoir—I loved every single moment."
—Alisha Fernandez Miranda, author of *My What If Year*

END CREDITS

How I Broke Up with Hollywood

A Memoir

Patty Lin

Zibby Books
New York

End Credits: How I Broke Up with Hollywood

Copyright © 2023 by Patty Lin

"You & Me & The Bottle Makes 3 Tonight" by Scotty Morris
© 1998 Big Bad Voodoo Music (ASCAP) admin. by Wixen Music Publishing, Inc. All Rights Reserved. Used by Permission.

Library of Congress Control Number: 2023934632
Paperback ISBN: 978-1-958506-06-6
Hardcover ISBN: 979-8-9852828-8-7
eBook ISBN: 979-8-9862596-0-4

Book design by Ursula Damm
Cover design by Emily Mahon
www.zibbybooks.com

Printed in the United States of America

10 9 87654321

For Sweetie

Author's Note

Ever since I retired from television writing at the ripe age of thirty-eight, people have asked me: "Why would you quit such a cool career?" Especially if they know I worked on popular shows like *Friends, Freaks and Geeks, Desperate Housewives,* and *Breaking Bad.* It's impossible to answer this question over the course of a cocktail party conversation. Where would I even begin? There were the grueling hours, the egotistical bosses, the politics and dysfunction, the ways in which TV writing is more like making widgets than creating art. . . . There's just too much to explain. And, really, who wants to get into that when you're trying to relax and enjoy a mojito?

For a long time, I couldn't even talk about it because the memories were too painful. But it's hard to move on when you haven't fully processed what you've been through. So I started writing about it— and I kept writing until all those dark moments were out in the light. Now when someone asks, "Why'd you quit?" I don't have to squeeze a saga into a sound bite. I can just hand them this book.

I've tried to portray the events in this memoir accurately, to the best of my recollection. Others who were present might recall things differently, but this is my experience of what happened. Many of the conversations took place a very long time ago, and when I couldn't remember the exact words that were spoken, I did my best to capture their essence. For readability, in some cases I compressed events or altered the order in which they occurred; some people were made into composite characters and some were omitted altogether. Some of the names have been changed and some have not. They know who they are.

Contents

1

American Junk

Growing up in the Midwest in the 1970s, I never imagined having a career in television, even though I watched a tremendous amount of it. After school, I would plant myself on the couch next to my older brother, Harry, and we'd stare at the TV for hours while polishing off a jumbo-sized bag of Doritos and a two-liter bottle of Coke. We were latchkey kids: our Taiwanese immigrant parents, both working full-time jobs to provide us with a better life than they had, were simply too busy to think about how American junk food and sitcoms might be warping our bodies and brains. We watched so many *Brady Bunch* reruns that I was able to identify each episode even before the first line of dialogue. I'd hear the opening music, see the pan across Tiger's doghouse, and blurt, "This is the one where Jan gets glasses!" Like a savant.

As a kid, I had only a vague awareness that the Bradys weren't real, and that writers were behind the scenes creating these characters and their groovy world. It certainly didn't occur to me that an Asian American girl from Downers Grove, Illinois, could ever grow up to become such a writer.

When I started kindergarten, the teachers took one look at me and put me into a remedial speech-therapy program—never mind the fact that English was my first and only language. The only other kid in the program was a girl with a heavy lisp. They took me out after a few weeks when they realized I had no trouble speaking and was, in fact, verbally precocious.

Many Taiwanese immigrants made their kids go to Chinese school on the weekends, but our parents didn't, partly because they wanted us to assimilate—which is why they gave us English names—and partly because they couldn't be bothered. Survival had always been their main concern, even before they came to America in the mid-1960s and settled in the Midwest, where my dad went to grad school.

You know the saying parents often use, "When I was your age, I had to walk an hour uphill in the snow to get to school"? My mother walked an hour every morning through the rural countryside just to get to the *bus stop* for school. The house she grew up in had no indoor plumbing; she had to shit in an outhouse, inches from where the chickens they'd eat for dinner were roaming around. But my parents, trying to shelter us, didn't tell us about these hardships until we were grown. Then I finally understood why they were so annoyed when we complained about them not buying enough Halloween candy or why they constantly bugged us to turn off the lights when we left a room.

While my dad worked toward his PhD in forensic toxicology, my mom stayed home and took care of my brother. When I was born five years later, my mother was so happy. She'd been hoping for a girl to round out the family.

"I remember the day after we brought you home from the hospital," she told me. "I took you for a walk in the stroller and an old neighbor lady saw you and thought you were so cute." I still find this hard to believe. Pictures show I was an extraordinarily fat baby with a shock of dark hair that looked like I'd stuck one of my pudgy sausage fingers into a socket. "She knitted you a little white cape. And after that I always put the cape on you whenever we went out."

So, as a baby, I was often dressed like a cross between a superhero and a tea cozy.

My mom didn't mind not having a job even though she had a bachelor's degree. Despite the women's lib movement, she had a traditional view of a woman's role, instilled in her by many previous generations: wife and mother came first. As the oldest of five children, she had helped raise her siblings. Though these family obligations continued throughout her life and weighed heavily on her, it was clear that much of her self-worth and pleasure came from caretaking. She loved being a mom. Every afternoon she'd pick me up from kindergarten and take me to the bakery for a cupcake—the kind with lard for frosting and a plastic smiley face on top—and watch with delight as I licked every morsel off the plastic. To this day I am helpless to resist cupcakes, associating them with the memory of having my mom all to myself.

But our family needed a second income to supplement my dad's salary as a toxicologist at the state medical examiner's office. As soon as I was old enough for my brother to watch me, my mom started working as a librarian at a psychiatric hospital. To her it was just a job, not a career. Her focus was still on us. She kept the house immaculately clean, grew flowers and vegetables in the yard, and cooked delicious meals every night. Sometimes she'd make Taiwanese sausages from scratch, stuffing sweet ground pork into casings and hanging them from wooden poles strung around the kitchen. She'd also make American food my brother and I liked, so we'd have pot roast with Pillsbury crescent rolls next to lion's head soup.

Holidays and special occasions were her excuse to go nuts and make a feast. Her specialty was a crispy duck that required three days of prep. Sometimes, to mix it up, she would debone a duck instead, fill it with a sticky rice stuffing, roast it, and slice it like a meatloaf. Her cooking was renowned among our friends, and we were proud of her for it. After dinner parties at other people's houses, all four of us would do a postmortem in the car and trash whatever the hostess had served. "Can you believe she didn't even marinate the chicken?" Though my mom didn't teach me to cook, I picked up a lot just from watching her and ended up being a pretty good cook myself. A few times I asked her for specific recipes, but my dishes never came out like hers, and I wondered if she had intentionally left things out to protect her trade secrets.

While my mom's personality loomed large, my dad was a quiet, steady presence. Every day when he came home from work, he would change into the same T-shirt and sweatpants, like Mister Rogers putting on his cardigan and sneakers. He helped around the house, even making the peanut butter and jelly sandwiches for my lunches. Because he liked spending extra time with me, he was often the one who stayed home when I was sick, bringing me cheeseburgers from Burger King while I lay in bed reading my Oz books. And he was the one who read to me at night, even though he wasn't as fluent in English as my mom. We joked about his frequent malapropisms, like when he called our favorite clothing store "Banana Republican." In the evenings he'd sit at the dinner table, studying his old chemistry textbooks for work, his lips moving as he sounded out the words.

Because of their spartan upbringing, my parents loved the comforts and conveniences of suburban America. We lived in a two-story

Colonial on a cul-de-sac that had a grassy island where the neighborhood kids played Running Bases in the summer and built snow forts in the winter. Our house, which had been a model home for the development, had loud seventies wallpaper and flouncy curtains. My happy place was my bedroom. I'd stare at the blue gingham wallpaper while I lay in bed, watching the pattern lift off the wall like a Magic Eye poster. I'd spend hours tucked away in the window seat, surrounded by stuffed animals, reading and gazing out at the field beyond our backyard.

My parents, though raised Buddhist, were not religious. One Easter my mom suggested we go to church. "Why?" my dad asked, and that was that. Our family spent most of our leisure time at shopping malls, supermarkets, and fast-food restaurants. On special occasions we'd go to Ponderosa for cheap steaks and the all-you-can-eat salad bar.

Even though in some ways we were a typical American family, I was hyperaware of how we were different from my white friends. Like the two cuisines at dinner, there were two conversations at our table: the one my brother and I had in English, and the one my parents had in their Taiwanese Hakka dialect. They didn't ask us what we learned in school or what we did with our friends. Though our basic health and safety were important to them, they took no interest in our inner lives; they assumed that as children we didn't have any. One reason I loved *The Brady Bunch* was that the kids confided in their parents about their intimate thoughts and feelings, and though the parents sometimes offered stern admonitions, they always treated the kids as fully realized people. Even more foreign to me was the way the Bradys enjoyed spending time together, unlike our family, which struggled just to find common ground.

One thing that helped bridge the cultural and generational gap in our family was, in fact, television. On Saturday nights we'd all pile up on the couch and watch *The Muppet Show*, followed by *The Love Boat* and *Fantasy Island*. We would mimic Tattoo's catchphrase, "Da plane! Da plane!" I'd usually fall asleep halfway through the show, just when it was getting creepy. My fondest childhood memory is drifting off to sleep with my head in my mom's lap, to the dulcet voice of Ricardo Montalbán. I'm sure that deep in my subconscious there's a link between primetime TV and a sense of love and security—even now, after working in TV brought me exactly the opposite.

When I was very little, I drew a picture of Mickey Mouse and showed it to my parents.

"You drew this?" my mother asked.

I nodded, chewing the end of my marker. I had captured that iconic mouse exactly—his big round ears, white gloves, bulbous yellow shoes. The look on my mom's face was a mixture of pride and surprise. If my parents had been different people, they would've begun enrolling me in art programs, finding me teachers and mentors. But to them, being able to draw was a quirk, one that I'd probably inherited from my maternal grandmother, who would dash off sketches of her chickens on scraps of paper. It was like being tall—you were lucky to have it, but there was nothing to be done about it.

The first time you get attention for having talent is intoxicating. But here was the problem: I had drawn Mickey Mouse from copying the character on my lunchbox. I couldn't draw from memory or imagination like my favorite artist, public television's Bob Ross, who could casually conjure a landscape of "happy little trees" that existed only in his mind's eye. I had to have a reference. Though many artists work this way, to me it seemed like a crucial limitation, proof that I wasn't a real artist. And thus began my lifelong dance with imposter syndrome, the feeling that no matter how much talent I appeared to have, I was a fraud.

When I was in third grade, my elementary school launched a creative writing program. We wrote for an hour every afternoon, and I loved it. I was a voracious reader and found it easy to write my own stories. Like my knack for drawing, it runs in the family; my mother had once been a very good writer and would write term papers for her friends to earn extra money. My teacher, Mrs. Aschauer, pear-shaped and prematurely gray, would tell us to take out our notebooks as she scribbled the day's writing prompt on the chalkboard. I never used the prompts because I was bursting with so many ideas of my own—like one about a beloved pig, inspired by *Charlotte's Web*, who eats so much that he tragically explodes.

Supportive and encouraging, Mrs. Aschauer was the perfect mentor to shepherd my fledgling creativity. She was a progressive educator who never talked down to us. Once, when I was working on a story, I went up to her to ask for help, cradling my spiral notebook with its tattered Holly Hobbie cover.

"How do you spell *hell*?"

Mrs. Aschauer hesitated, her eyebrows raised.

I went on, oblivious. "You know, the opposite of heaven?"

She must've realized that I had no idea I'd just said a "bad" word, and so she spelled it for me without any further incident—no doubt saving me many hours of therapy. I have never forgotten this kindness or the lavish praise she heaped upon my writing.

When I drew that picture of Mickey Mouse, my parents could see with their own eyes that I had artistic talent. But until Mrs. Aschauer told them I was a good writer, they had no idea because I wrote in their second language. It was a struggle for them just to understand English, let alone judge its artistic merit on the written page. This wasn't so much an issue with "The Pig Who Exploded," but as I grew older and my writing grew more complex, they had to rely on external sources like teachers, grades, or job status to vouch for my talent. Someone else had to tell my parents I was good, because they had no way of collecting this empirical evidence.

Everyone tries to prove themselves to their parents. I always had to do it through a third party. It's no wonder I became desperate to get approval from anyone in my life who had even a modicum of authority.

In 1983, my dad found a better-paying job in New Jersey and we moved to East Hanover, about an hour west of New York City. I didn't want to leave Downers Grove, where I was happy and outgoing. I had a close-knit group of friends, competed in sports, sang in choir, and performed skits in talent shows. But my parents didn't ask me how I felt about moving. Since Harry had only one year of high school left, they let him stay behind and live with his best friend, so I essentially lost my brother in addition to my friends and my childhood home.

Soon after the move, I got my first period. My mom was back in Downers Grove, tying up loose ends at the old house. I had been looking forward to this female milestone ever since reading *Are You There God? It's Me, Margaret* by Judy Blume and stumbling on a TV special about menstruation hosted by Marlo Thomas. I was so fascinated by this program that I grabbed a piece of paper and copied the diagram of an ovum making its way through a fallopian tube toward the uterus. The next day I heard my parents conversing in hushed tones.

"What are you talking about?" I asked.

"Nothing," my mom said with a nervous laugh. "Just . . . what you're learning in school."

She had found the diagram in my room. But instead of giving me "the talk," she remained tight-lipped, assuming that my school had it covered, much to her relief. She would have rather gouged out her own eyes than talk about sex. I wanted to explain that I'd learned about periods on my own, a self-directed education gleaned from Judy Blume and Marlo Thomas. But it was clear from my mom's discomfort that the subject was closed.

The day I found blood in my underwear, I snuck some pads from under her bathroom sink and hid my secret from my dad while he unpacked our things and got settled at his new job. Not wanting to add to my parents' burden, I had always kept quiet and handled things by myself.

A couple of weeks later, I started seventh grade. I walked into my new school wearing the preppy clothes favored in the Midwest: Izod polo, plaid skirt, and knee socks. My straight hair was cut in a childish bob with bangs. The New Jersey girls had permed, teased coifs shellacked with Aqua Net and wore off-the-shoulder tops, tight pants, and pumps. Pumps! My first attempt to emulate them resulted in a poodle perm that I had no clue how to blow out into the feathered style I coveted. I suddenly hated how gawky and uncool I looked. The only kids who would talk to me were other misfits.

I started getting crippling migraines. After school I'd lie on the couch with the curtains drawn, burrowing under a blanket until dinner. My stomach hurt all the time and my legs would twitch with muscle cramps. I became a hypochondriac, convinced that I had appendicitis, leukemia, or a brain tumor—but I mentioned these fears to my parents only when my now-constant anxiety ballooned out of control, and they didn't seem to take it seriously. These symptoms were no doubt *caused* by my anxiety, along with the hormonal roller coaster of puberty. It's no exaggeration to say that moving at such a formative time upended my life. It was the instant the rug was pulled out from under me with a brutal yank.

I turned to writing as a salve for my loneliness, filling notebook after notebook with stories about my future marriage to Boy George, the lead singer of Culture Club. They were huge at the time for catchy hits like "Do You Really Want to Hurt Me" and "Karma Chameleon." I was obsessed with the androgynous pop star, even though I knew he was gay and in love with his drummer—building a capacity for denial that would foreshadow both my career and my love life. My stories were variations on soap opera clichés: affairs, babies out of wedlock, the sort of stuff I'd picked up from *Dallas* and *Dynasty*. But the recurring theme was George being on tour for months on end and me being lonely without him, feeling I had no right to demand his attention when the whole world wanted a piece of him. That's what I thought love was: longing.

"I don't know how I got that idea," I told my therapist decades later. "My parents weren't divorced. They had a stable marriage; my dad was home every night."

"The stories you wrote weren't necessarily about romantic love," she said. "You had just lost all your friends and your support system, and you felt like you couldn't talk to your parents because they had more important things to deal with. That's the longing. You were clearly working something out."

The Boy George fan fiction trickled off when I got to high school and started coming out of my shell again. I made more friends, learned to use a blow-dryer, and got involved in activities like the high school newspaper. The editor in chief was my best friend, Melissa, a curly-haired girl who was in all my advanced placement classes. She gave me free rein to write whatever I wanted, like a food review detailing the results of our taste-testing the five most popular pizzas in town, comparing them in categories like "cheese adhesiveness." I once wrote an opinion piece about the double standard when it came to sex: girls were judged for being either sluts or virgins, while guys were considered healthy and normal for trying to put their dicks into everything that moved. My article stirred up a lot of conversations, not just among students, but also with faculty and parents. I liked having that kind of effect on people.

The place where I really blossomed was the theater. When I was in the chorus of *Anything Goes* my freshman year, I made up for my lack of experience with unbridled energy, earning me the nickname "The Human Sparkplug." The next year my drama teacher cast me and his daughter as the leads in the musical *Wonderful Town*, playing sisters even though she was white. I had heard Asian kids from other schools never got cast unless they were doing *South Pacific*. I also starred in *Bye Bye Birdie* and the controversial *Lie, Cheat, and Genuflect*, a farce in which a criminal impersonates a nun. I started to think about the creative process behind the plays I acted in—how the stories and characters were constructed; how to create a beginning, middle, and end—and this curiosity extended to the TV shows I watched, especially my favorite one: *thirtysomething*.

If you were around during that golden age of late-eighties TV, you might remember this show as a bunch of well-educated, white baby boomers talking endlessly about their relationships and the struggle to stay true to their hippie ideals while entrenched in their yuppie lifestyles. In the first episode I ever saw, Michael and Hope Steadman, a married couple with a new baby, attempt to have a date night— not a remarkable premise. But interrupting the narrative were these dreamy interstitial scenes on a darkened soundstage, where Michael Feinstein sings and plays "But Not for Me" on a grand piano complete with candelabra. What the . . . ? It boggled my mind that a mainstream TV show about suburban domestic life would have the balls to do something so bizarre. I was hooked.

Thirtysomething was the first show that got me to think about writing for television. But I still had no idea that someone like me could work in show business—I assumed that TV writers were all white middle-aged men. And whenever I dreamed about what I might want to do for a living, it was constrained by my parents' expectations. My dad was a toxicologist, and my mother was now a consumer protection investigator. No one in our family did anything creative as a career. Making art was a luxury, not something to build your life around. My parents harbored the stereotypical and, in our case, irrational hope that my brother and I would become doctors, even though neither of us had an affinity for science.

All through high school, Harry had excelled in the language arts and was involved in plays, broadcasting, and forensics, a competitive public speaking team. He was the guy who did the morning announcements over the loudspeaker. But one year for his birthday, my parents gave him a book titled *Getting into Medical School.*

"I don't want to be a doctor!" he exploded over dinner that night.

"It's just in case," my mom said, as if she'd handed him an umbrella on a sunny day. "You never know. You might change your mind. . . ."

"That's never gonna happen! You don't even know me!"

He threw down his fork, shoved himself away from the table, and stormed out the back door, slamming it behind him. Stunned, I turned to peek out the window and saw him standing in the snow with his back to us, his arms folded across his chest and his breath coming out in white puffs. It must've been thirty degrees out there. A frenzied conversation raged between my parents in Taiwanese before my mom opened the door and begged Harry to come back inside. But he stood his ground for an impressively long time, long enough to make his point. He never read the book, and he went on to major in communications and work for a public radio station, various tech start-ups, and eventually IMDb.

Many years later, I emailed Harry to ask if he remembered that book. He replied, "It remains the worst gift I have ever received, including random crap at bad office parties." But even though the gesture had caused him much pain, in retrospect he understood where it was coming from. "What they were really giving me was all their immigrant hopes and dreams for a comfortable, respectable life in America. At that time in their own lives, they had such a limited scope of what was possible for an Asian man in America, that being a doctor was the best they could imagine for me."

When I watched this incident play out, I felt both grateful that I had an older sibling to "break in" my parents and wary of causing them the same distress. The typical baby in the family, I was all about keeping the peace and would often go to great lengths to not be a squeaky wheel. As my parents agonized over my brother freezing in the snow, the gears began to turn in my head: *How can I do what I love without disappointing them?*

Being an artist was my dream. I was still drawing, and now also painting and sculpting. In my senior year, I did an independent study project for which I made portraits in the styles of Andrew Wyeth, Van Gogh, and Warhol. But it was one thing to reject med school and entirely another to go to art school. Perhaps more important, I still felt like a fraud. Still copied other artists instead of inventing my own style. If I was going to stray so far from how my parents saw my future, I had to be fucking great. And I was afraid I never would be.

Much later, after I became a TV writer, people would assume my parents were horrified. And in a way they were. But to my mind, even writing for TV was a compromise I made for their benefit, as was my initial plan to go into advertising, because these jobs were potentially legitimate and paid well. It could've been so much worse. I could've been an artist.

In 1989, I graduated from high school and enrolled at Cornell University. Like my brother, I decided to major in communications. During my freshman year, while my friend Melissa and I were both home for winter break, we took the train into New York—or, as we Jersey folk call it, "the city"—to go ice-skating under the Christmas tree at Rockefeller Center, a giant spruce swathed in twinkling lights. Inside the building was NBC Studios and the famous *Today* show window overlooking the festive scene. Despite being bundled up in our heaviest winter coats, we were freezing our asses off and decided on the spur of the moment to ditch the tree and go to a taping of *Late Night with David Letterman* instead.

Decades before he grew a Santa Claus beard and started interviewing people like Barack Obama on Netflix, David Letterman was a young, irreverent comedian who arguably defined the late-night talk show genre populated today by hosts like Stephen Colbert and Jimmy Kimmel. In 1982, Letterman broke the mold set by the legendary Johnny Carson and launched *Late Night*, a show that felt way more edgy and underground than *The Tonight Show*. I became a die-hard fan from the moment I saw a turtle stand up on its hind legs before falling backward onto its shell in a "Stupid Pet Tricks" segment. I loved Letterman's quirky comedy, whether he was lowering himself into a water tank while wearing a suit covered in Alka-Seltzer tablets or just throwing pencils at the ceiling tiles.

Melissa was also a fan, and the two of us talked about "Dave" as if he were a pal. We didn't know how to get tickets to his show but figured it wouldn't hurt to ask. We pushed our way through the crowd of tourists in the gleaming black marble lobby of 30 Rockefeller Plaza and approached the information desk, manned by an NBC page. He was a heavyset guy in his early twenties with expressive puppy eyes and thick brown hair. Pinned to his navy-blue blazer was a name tag that read CARL H.

"Excuse me," I said. "We were wondering if we could get tickets to the *Letterman* show."

Carl H. stared at me, incredulous. "For tonight?"

The taping started in less than an hour, and most of the audience had requested tickets months in advance. The rest were standbys who had shown up at the crack of dawn and waited in line all day. We had no chance and now felt embarrassed just for asking. Though Carl probably delivered this bad news a dozen times a day, he seemed playful about it. He was joking around, maybe even flirting.

While we were chatting, people kept interrupting us to ask him questions. One was a teenage girl with an enormous button of rock star Jon Bon Jovi pinned to her coat. The button was no smaller than four inches in diameter. In the middle of answering her, Carl paused and said, deadpan, "You should get a bigger button." That cracked me up. Not so much the joke, but the masterful way he delivered it. Bob Newhart couldn't have done it better.

Melissa and I asked Carl a lot of questions about his job. The life of a page wasn't very glamorous, but the idea of working in television in any capacity fascinated me. This was the moment I realized that someone like me could break into the world of entertainment. Carl H. was just a regular guy from Queens with no showbiz connections, and here he was wearing the NBC peacock on his lapel and acting as a gatekeeper for Dave.

I knew *Late Night* employed college interns; Dave sometimes referred to them on the show. I asked Carl how to apply for such an internship.

"Just write a letter to the producer and tell him you want to be an intern."

"That's it?"

"Yeah. They'll bring you in for an interview."

Could it really be that simple? I decided right then to apply for a summer internship at *Late Night*. All I had to do was write a letter! The worst thing that could happen was I'd never hear back.

Since we weren't getting into *Letterman* that night, Melissa and I settled for an NBC Studios tour instead, a much less exciting proposition. We thanked Carl for his help and he scribbled his phone number on a scrap of paper—you know, in case I wanted to ask him more questions. Melissa and I got our tour tickets and went to stand in line until it started. Fifteen minutes later, I spotted Carl striding toward us.

"Oh my God." I nudged Melissa. "Carl H."

He motioned for us to step away from our place in line. People stared at us as if we were VIPs.

"I got you *Letterman* tickets," he said, looking proud of himself.

Now I knew for sure he was flirting. Using his teeny bit of power to impress a girl was a cheesy move. But it worked.

Melissa and I had a blast at the show. It was the first and *last* time I would sit in the *Letterman* audience.

A few weeks after I sent a letter to *Late Night*'s executive producer, Robert Morton—known as "Morty"—his assistant, Collette, called me to set up a job interview for a summer internship. Throughout the call, my heart thumped like crazy. It felt so incongruous to be sitting on a bunk bed in my little dorm room in Ithaca, talking to someone who worked for the executive producer of a big TV show in New York City.

My interview was scheduled for spring break. On a beautiful day in March, I went back to Rockefeller Center, this time bypassing the tourists and taking the employee elevator upstairs. The *Late Night* offices were on the fourteenth floor (actually the thirteenth, but labeled the fourteenth for superstitious reasons, as is the case in most tall buildings). I was more nervous than I'd ever been, but I tried to appear calm as I approached the receptionist. She invited me to sit on the couch across from her desk until Collette arrived.

I pretended to read a magazine while I watched staffers breeze in to pick up their mail and pink phone message slips from a wall of cubbyholes. Most of these people seemed to be in their early- to mid-twenties, white, and hip. What struck me most was how nonchalant they were, like they were just there to hang out. The guys wore T-shirts and jeans. The women wore cute, trendy outfits, none of which required pantyhose. In those days I worked hard to be stylish, spending over an hour every morning putting together my look, which involved a lot of black eyeliner and a hairspray called Stiff Stuff. I was still getting perms, and now my hair was teased and highlighted with reddish streaks. Plus, in high school, I had switched my glasses for aqua-tinted contact lenses that look really weird on an Asian person. Compared to the effortless chic of the *Letterman* people, I felt unfashionable and self-conscious.

Still, everyone treated me like I belonged there, smiling and saying "hey" without bothering to introduce themselves, as if we'd known each other for ages. This instant camaraderie was one of the first things that drew me into show business, and it would soon come to seem totally normal.

When Morty came in to get his messages, I knew who he was because he appeared on the show every now and then. He stopped and looked at me with a bemused stare.

"You've got blue eyes."

"They're contacts," I explained, like it wasn't obvious.

He strolled away toward his office, grinning, and I felt a tiny bit less nervous.

My job interview lasted all afternoon. I was shuttled between departments, hanging out in people's offices as they answered phone calls or ran around delivering videotapes. The only part that felt like a real interview was when Collette asked me where I was from and what I was studying in college. Even though the internship was unpaid, I wanted it badly. But I couldn't imagine she'd hire someone with my plebeian work experience: summer jobs at an ice cream parlor and a kids' day camp. Eager to convince Collette I was capable, I told her, "I work well under pressure. I love stress."

"You love stress?" she asked, eyebrows raised. "You *must* be from New Jersey."

After my tour of the office, she asked me which department I felt most drawn to. The obvious answer would've been the writers. But interning for them would've meant fetching their coffee while they brooded over their typewriters. I wanted to actually work.

The research department was where interns saw the most action. Research interns did the legwork of digging up articles, books, TV and movie appearances, and other materials about the show's guests, so that the researchers could come up with interview questions for Dave. The two researchers—a ruddy-faced bro named Daniel Kellison and a tall, serious woman named Mary Connelly—shared a sunny corner office cluttered with videotapes and toys. When I met Daniel, he was sporting a BEER NUTS T-shirt and attempting to draw

Garfield the Cat on an Etch A Sketch. I thought he would make an excellent boss.

A few days later, Collette called to tell me I'd gotten the research position. I managed to enjoy the good news for about an hour before fear started settling in. I was going to have a real job—a job in television! Since this was years before shows like *The Larry Sanders Show* and *30 Rock* existed, I didn't even have a fictionalized version to base my expectations on. I had no idea what I was getting into.

After finishing my freshman year in June 1990, I headed back to my parents' house in New Jersey and started commuting to my internship. I was one of about a dozen college interns, and there was no official training process. Part of being a good intern was being able to intuit what was expected of us—not only how to do the work, but how to behave in the *Letterman* culture. Personality was as important as productivity, possibly more so. If you were competent but everyone found you annoying, you were in trouble.

I worked closely with the other research intern, the two of us stationed at a narrow table in a windowless hallway next to the Xerox machines. Whenever someone needed a box of staples, they'd have to reach over us to rummage through the supply cabinets. We had to do all our business in public: make phone calls, read articles, type memos. We ate our lunches amid a constant parade of coworkers remarking, "Mmm, that sandwich looks good," or, "Jesus, how can you work after eating that?"—something we'd hear a lot on Wednesdays when the commissary special was fried chicken.

Back in those pre-internet days, we did most of our research on an ancient artifact called a microfiche machine. You'd go to the NBC library, sit at a console that looked like a joyless arcade game, and use big knobs to scroll through dim photos of old newspaper stories. My job also involved reading a lot of magazines like *People* and *Us Weekly*, which, lucky for me, was something I already did for fun.

When a guest was booked, I'd comb through all these materials and put the best ones in a packet for the researchers. They would write possible interview questions for Dave. After the segment producer "pre-interviewed" the guest, a script was created. When Daniel saw how well curated my packets were, he started encouraging me to write my own Dave questions, and occasionally they'd appear in the script and it would make my day. That was the best thing about my job: knowing I'd had a tangible hand in the making of the show.

Most of the interns were gofers, running errands for their bosses. I ended up doing some grunt work too, as there was plenty to go around. When Morty's intern was busy, I was charged with picking up his breakfast, a salt bagel from Zabar's and an unsweetened iced tea. Whenever I delivered it to his office, Morty would comment on my hair or something I was wearing.

"What's that?" he asked one day, pointing to the charm on my necklace.

"It's an ankh." At that age I was partial to the pseudo-religious jewelry that street vendors sold off dirty blankets on the sidewalk. "It's a symbol for eternal life."

Morty nodded. "It's sex. It's about sex."

"What? No—it's not," I stammered. "It's, um, Egyptian."

Morty just grinned and bit into his bagel.

Ever since #MeToo and the fall of Harvey Weinstein, there has been a lot of attention on sexual misconduct in the entertainment industry. It's way past due, because that shit happens *constantly*. In freewheeling showbiz culture, lines are often blurry. During my internship, I witnessed and was sometimes the recipient of looks and remarks that, in retrospect, were on the edge of inappropriate. Like when one of the segment producers, a distinguished fellow with salt-and-pepper hair, asked me what perfume I was wearing.

"It's called Knowing," I said.

"Aren't you a little young for that?" he replied with a wink, and then cut in front of me at the Xerox machine.

But I didn't think anything of that behavior back then. I considered Morty's comments to be harmless flirting and even felt flattered by the attention. It's not like he ever masturbated into a potted plant—not in front of me, anyway.

Now, I know what you're thinking: *What about Dave?*

I was starstruck the first time I met David Letterman while I was waiting to take an elevator downstairs. Dave, who was very private, usually spent most of the day sequestered in his office until show-time, at which point he'd make a beeline down to the studio, hoping not to run into anyone on the way. And now here at the elevator bank was a flummoxed intern he'd have to acknowledge.

The countless times I'd seen him on TV didn't prepare me for his charismatic presence. Most celebrities turn out to be much smaller than they look onscreen, with disproportionately large heads atop diminutive bodies. But Dave was well over six feet, with broad shoulders and a nicely proportioned head. Even if he hadn't been famous, he would've commanded attention. Dressed in a double-breasted suit, he was freshly showered and trailed a sillage of what I would later learn was his favorite cologne, a drugstore brand that smelled like Irish Spring soap. My heart was racing while we waited for the elevators. Thank goodness Dave always took the express alone. Riding in the same elevator with him would've sent me over the edge.

He smiled at me, exposing the gap between his front teeth, and said hello. I said hello back and blurted, "You smell nice." And then, to be more specific, I added, "You smell soapy."

Dave replied, "That was my nickname in college . . . Soapy."

Then his elevator arrived and he was gone. I proceeded to run my errands, floating through the streets in a daze, wondering how I'd gotten so lucky.

Sometimes Dave's personal assistant would summon me to run an errand for Dave. I approached these mindless tasks with nervous anticipation. Once, she sent me to a sporting goods store to buy him a pair of Nikes. I asked him what size he wore.

"Ten and a half, and don't let anyone tell you different."

I giggled, though I didn't quite get the joke. As the assistant handed me a wad of bills from her petty-cash drawer, Dave added, "Oh, and pick up a pair for yourself."

"Really?"

But no, that was another joke. I could tell because his assistant guffawed.

Even though she was always nice to me, I was scared of her. She was high-strung and loud, and she could turn mean on people if they pissed her off. Her fierce devotion to Dave and his loyalty to her tended to raise eyebrows. Had they ever dated? Slept together? To this day I don't know.

By this time Dave had split up with his former head writer Merrill Markoe and was quietly dating a former segment producer named Regina Lasko. They would end up marrying more than a decade later after having a kid together. I'd heard rumors about him and interns, and in 2009, after he was threatened with blackmail, he would admit to having had sex with women who'd worked for him on the show. But even though I worshipped Dave, I never thought of him in a sexual way. Besides, the few times he paid me any attention, he was nothing but polite and professional. And jokey.

One of the staffers who'd been at *Late Night* the longest was a production manager named Peg, who was in charge of the show's budget. She was fifty, divorced, no kids. Her chestnut hair was cut in a pageboy, and she wore granny glasses that she'd peer over while delivering persnickety remarks like, "Someone is leaving coffee stains in the kitchen sink." Obsessively neat, she took great pleasure in chastising other staffers for their slovenly ways. But despite her primness, she would often erupt into profanity, railing against "fucking" this and "fucking" that. One of the staffers described her as "Mary Poppins with Tourette's."

Peg had worked at *Late Night* since its very beginning, after doing the same job at *Saturday Night Live*. She loved telling us youngsters about the glory days of *SNL*. I was in awe of anyone who'd rubbed elbows with comic geniuses from that era, like Bill Murray, Steve Martin, and John Belushi, even though Peg rarely had anything positive to say about them. According to her, "Chevy Chase is not a nice man." He was in the habit of throwing wild parties in his office (read: cocaine) on the show's tab. Peg sent him a memo to make him stop. He taped it to his door for everyone to goof on, and the parties continued, unabated.

I soon learned that, though she seemed harmless at first, Peg had a dark side. She came in at six a.m. so she could snoop through everyone's offices before they arrived. I tried to stay out of her way as much as possible, but unwittingly caught her attention. The show's research materials were stored in overstuffed file cabinets, and after weeks of struggling with this mess, I took it upon myself to reorganize it. Peg saw me and stopped in her tracks.

"Finally, someone who gives a shit," she said with a glint in her eye. "Patty, you and I are birds of a feather."

I was grateful for the praise. I didn't know it was the seed of a relationship that would make my life miserable for years to come.

Between the long hours and the commute, I had very little free time that summer. On weekdays I had to wake up at the crack of dawn to shower, get dressed, and hitch a ride with my parents on their way to work. They'd drop me off at the bus station in Parsippany, where the line of commuters was so long that I'd often have to take a jitney cab instead—just a random dude driving a van in exchange for cash. After work I'd head straight to Port Authority and take the bus back to Jersey, then scarf down some leftovers and collapse into bed.

On weekends I occasionally went down the shore with old friends who were home for the summer. Once, I went to a party on Long Island with Collette's intern and drank myself sick on vodka tonics. But my job was so all-consuming that I didn't have the energy to date and rarely thought about sex. The few times I tried to masturbate, fantasies about college hookups would get interrupted by the thought of running into Morty at the mailboxes— or some other dry, work-related scenario—and I'd give up on the whole endeavor.

Despite my grueling schedule and lack of a personal life, I adored the shape of my days. New York was like a power source supplying me with boundless energy; the minute my feet hit the grimy pavement, I felt alive. The city was seedier back then—not like *Taxi Driver*, but more dangerous than it is now. Walking east on 42nd Street each morning, I'd hurry past the porno shops and peep shows, buzzing with low-level terror whenever a derelict or construction worker catcalled at me—but feeling like a definite part of the city's fabric.

After my internship, I had a new sense of purpose: I wanted to work in entertainment. I began to take filmmaking classes at Cornell and did a second internship at *Letterman*, again in the research department. For the next couple of years, I kept in touch with my colleagues, hoping to be hired for a full-time position when I graduated. The timing was perfect. On May 22, 1992, Johnny Carson retired from *The Tonight Show*. Even though Letterman was the obvious choice to replace him, the network passed the torch to the less edgy Jay Leno instead. Dave said "fuck you" to NBC and defected to CBS. His new show would be called *Late Show* instead of *Late Night*, and it would air at eleven-thirty p.m., the same time slot as Leno.

Luckily for me, the move to CBS created a bunch of new job openings. In the spring of 1993, just as I was about to graduate, I got a call from Peg.

"Would you like to be my assistant?"

She warned me the job didn't pay much, only five hundred a week before taxes. That sounded like a fortune to a broke college student, but the truth is I didn't care how much it paid—of course I wanted it! Assistant to a production manager wasn't *exactly* my dream job, but it was the show I'd loved since I was a kid, and I figured that I could later move to a different department, something more creative. I accepted on the spot.

In June, I went looking for a place to live in Manhattan and found a studio in a six-story walk-up on Minetta Street, the most picturesque spot in Greenwich Village. The street runs diagonally from the corner of Bleecker and Sixth Avenue and ends next to the historic Café Wha?, where Bob Dylan got his start. The neighborhood was perfect for a twenty-one-year-old: lots of cheap ethnic restaurants, head shops, boutiques selling bohemian jewelry, and an independent video rental store that stocked virtually every movie ever made.

In fact, I loved the location of my apartment so much that I overlooked its size: a mere 100 square feet, not including the bathroom, which was the only part of the place that seemed made for an adult human. The kitchenette had a stovetop with two burners, a mini-fridge, and a sink not much bigger than what you'd see in an airplane lavatory. There was a fireplace, but it was big enough for only one or two logs. I would use it quite a few times before finding out that the chimney had been sealed off for years, which explained all the smoke.

My mom came over to help me clean before I moved in. First, we went to lunch at a Chinese restaurant on Bleecker. She ordered a ridiculous amount of food, since we were celebrating the fact that I had graduated and secured a full-time office job.

"Now all you need is to find a husband," she said, unwrapping her chopsticks.

There it was. I had checked off one box and she was moving to the next. Given her own life trajectory, it made sense she was already thinking about my marriage prospects. She'd been married and was having her first kid at twenty-five. My brother had married his college sweetheart. I'd had a couple of boyfriends in high school, but since then, only random hookups and two-week relationships with guys who didn't want to be in a relationship. Finding a husband, unlike finding a job, was not something I had control over and not something that was a priority for me at the time. It hurt when my mom glossed over my good news and zeroed right in on what she perceived was lacking.

After lunch we bought buckets, sponges, and disinfectant and headed to my apartment. My mom stepped inside as if entering a

Superfund site. Clearly, no one had cleaned in years. While we were scrubbing the place down, she noticed a small cluster of beige bulbs sticking out from the edge of the filthy, stained carpet.

"What *is* that?" She poked it with her finger and recoiled in disgust. "Mushrooms!"

When she got home, she took a hot shower and told my dad I was living in a hovel. They implored me to live with them instead, but I knew from my internship days that the commute would've killed any chance of having a social life. Tiny and overpriced as it was, I adored my new digs. I gave it a fresh coat of paint, hung up a *Goodfellas* poster, and got a sofa bed that pulled out into a twin-size mattress made entirely of foam. Since there was no oven or microwave, I bought a toaster oven in which I'd cook ambitious meals like turkey tetrazzini and Cornish game hens.

A few days before I started my job, I was on my way to the grocery store when I passed a grizzled homeless man perched on a milk crate, holding a cardboard sign that said PALM READINGS. He asked if I wanted to hear my fortune. I gave the guy a dollar and he studied my hand.

"You got a shit job." He shook his head in a way that implied, "I'm so glad I'm not in your shoes, even though I could really use some shoes."

"Oh, really," I said, skeptical. I was going to be working for Dave Letterman, for God's sake. My new job was fucking cool!

"Yeah, a real shit job," he insisted. "A corporate job."

Despite my youthful face, wrinkled tank top, and cutoff shorts, the homeless fortune teller had sussed out that I worked in an office, for a corporation—albeit one that produced entertainment. Within a few weeks, his prophecy had proved true.

2

Cell Block Eight

Now that *Letterman* was on CBS, we had moved from Rockefeller Center to the Ed Sullivan Theater on 53rd and Broadway. Far from its 1960s heyday, the theater had fallen into disrepair and was undergoing major renovations. Our neighbors included a tacky souvenir shop and a fast-food chicken restaurant that pumped the smell of rancid grease into our offices. The Bangladeshi owners of the souvenir shop would become regulars in our comedy bits, and the chicken place was later replaced by a deli whose owner would also make frequent cameos.

The staff had expanded quite a bit after leaving NBC, and our offices were now spread out over four floors, several stories above the theater itself. I missed the intimacy of everyone working in the same space. My department was a few floors below the others, and even though it was a short elevator ride away, the symbolic distance was huge.

But it was nice to have my own office after all that time squatting in the hallway. I had a big wooden desk and matching file cabinets that I learned to call "credenzas." My picture window had a clear view of Hell's Kitchen. Best of all, everyone had a television set in their office to watch the studio feed, and for most of the day I kept mine tuned to MTV. My parents didn't get cable until well after I'd left home—I was making up for lost time. Radiohead's "Creep" was in heavy rotation that summer, and the sight of Thom Yorke's consumptive face made my paperwork a little more tolerable.

When it came to my responsibilities, I was essentially an accountant. I processed invoices, business expense forms, actors' contracts, and paychecks. I was the person who had to call Deer Park to complain that they'd overcharged us by two cases of bottled water on last month's bill. Organized and efficient, I did my job well. But the writer in me had no interest in these mundane, repetitive tasks. By the time I learned the ropes, I was already bored.

Though Peg didn't make me run her errands or even answer her phone, she did make me do her dirty work. The queen of passive aggression, she always had a beef with another staffer over some picayune issue. But instead of confronting the person face-to-face, she'd leave them a handwritten note. More often she'd write *me* a note, instructing me to call the staffer and deliver her inane message. Everyone knew Peg was behind it, but that didn't keep them from shooting the messenger.

Peg micromanaged me all day long. She eavesdropped while I made the dreaded phone calls, either yelling her commentary from her office next door or, worse, sidling over to peek in my doorway and doing it in a stage whisper. She seemed overly curious about all my interactions, professional and personal. Once, when I was twelve, I was writing to a friend back in Downers Grove, and my mother stood behind me and read the letter over my shoulder. It was like reading your daughter's diary *right in front of her*. I just sat there and kept writing as if it didn't bother me, even though I felt violated.

It was uncanny how I ended up with a boss who disrespected my boundaries in the same way. I felt like a prisoner under the surveillance of a deranged guard.

Thank God for Paula, the other accountant who worked under Peg. She was a quiet girl from Connecticut who killed me with her dry sense of humor. Our offices flanked Peg's at the end of the eighth-floor hallway, and we dubbed our little enclave "Cell Block Eight." After Peg left for the day, we'd convene in my office, close the door, and vent for a good thirty minutes, reviewing all the maddening things Peg had done and the asinine notes she had given us. We called them "P-Notes" because she always signed them with her first initial—kind of dumb, since all three of us had names that began with *P*.

Many of her notes were complaints about money being overspent by staff members. When the show was nominated for several Emmy Awards, the whole staff was invited to Los Angeles to attend the ceremony, and Peg bristled when one of the stage managers booked himself a stretch limo. She wrote a P-Note ordering me to downgrade his car to something "more appropriate." The note ended with a sarcastic, "Stage manager in a stretch!"

Paula and I started chronicling our P-Notes in a scrapbook we called *The P-Book*. We pasted each note in a spiral notebook, underlining the most egregious parts and scribbling our commentary in the margins, followed by an army of exclamation points. Soon we outgrew the spiral notebooks and graduated to jumbo three-ring binders. By the end of my four years at *Late Show*, we had amassed *seven volumes* of P-Books. You might think that's unhinged, but trust me, those books were the only things keeping us sane.

I had no aspirations to write comedy for Dave or anyone else, since I didn't think of myself as being funny. But I still thought of myself as a writer. That's why, of all the *Letterman* staffers, the writers were the ones I looked up to the most—and found the most attractive. Most of them were young guys fresh out of college, cute Ivy League nerds in baseball caps. There were a few exceptions, a handful of older guys who had tenure. The younger ones were on probation, hired for thirteen-week cycles. In four years, there was only one female writer on staff. You will no doubt be shocked to learn that the world of late-night TV was overwhelmingly male.

It was also small and incestuous. New York didn't have hundreds of TV shows in production like Los Angeles. Everyone knew one another, especially at *Letterman* and *Saturday Night Live*, sister shows that used to be produced in the same building. That's how Carl H., the former NBC page, came back into my orbit.

In December 1993, *Letterman* had a Christmas party at Wollman Rink in Central Park. I was sitting rinkside, lacing up my ice skates, when I glanced up and saw Carl among the guests. Now twenty-seven, he was still on the heavy side, and he'd grown a thick beard and shoulder-length hair that made him look somewhat biblical. When he spotted me, his face lit up like the Christmas tree behind him, and I knew it was *on*. In a way, the advice he'd given me in the NBC lobby four years earlier had led us to this moment. We spent the next few hours catching up over mugs of hot cider and skating side by side, and when the party wound down, we took a cab to my office and kept talking late into the night.

When he was a page, he had told me that his dream was to write for *Saturday Night Live*. Since then, his dream had come true—after he'd worked relentlessly to make it happen.

"I can't tell you how many nights I stayed after work, writing jokes and coming up with sketches." They were *sketches*, not *skits*, he told me. *Skits* was dismissive, like calling a woman a *girl*. "Sometimes I'd even sleep in the pages' locker room so I could go in early and pitch ideas before work."

"Wow. Did they use any?"

"Most of those guys wouldn't even give me the time of day."

I couldn't imagine holding strong in the face of that much constant rejection. Unlike many *SNL* writers, Carl didn't go to Harvard and write for the *Lampoon*. He didn't know anyone in the business. But he had always believed in himself even though his family, like mine, had pushed him to take a safer path.

"My dad was a mailman. He wanted me to go to law school."

I thought about the med school book and my brother standing in the snow. "Did you have any interest in being a lawyer?"

"God, no. I used to act and sing in my school plays." Another thing we had in common. "When I went to college, I didn't know what I wanted to do. And then my dad got sick. . . ."

"I'm sorry."

"No, it's okay. He's fine now. He's a tough guy. But when he was diagnosed, I wrote this play about it. It was called *Family Tumors*." We both laughed. "I know, it's a dumb title. But that's how I got into writing . . . and then I decided to try stand-up. I worked a few crappy clubs in Queens and realized I was better at writing jokes than telling them."

I'd met few people who had done stand-up. To me, that was the most balls-out form of self-expression, the creative equivalent of skydiving. If Carl was trying to impress me, like he did by getting me *Letterman* tickets years ago, mission accomplished. His audacity and ambition were inspiring. I was in awe of him.

But it was clear that our interest in each other wasn't solely professional, and soon we were sharing our relationship history. I told him I'd recently dated one of the *Letterman* writers, who dumped me after two weeks, and then I saw him holding hands with a blond intern in the hallway outside my office.

"I just broke up with somebody, too," said Carl. "We met when we were both pages."

"How long were you together?"

"Two years." When he saw my reaction, he added, "We should've just been friends. We had no romantic chemistry. I think that's why I stayed in it for so long. I needed to focus all my energy on my career."

Talk about a red flag. But I was so taken by Carl's charm, humor, and honesty that I blithely ignored the flashing danger sign right in front of me. If you listen closely, people will tell you in the first five minutes exactly why you should stay away from them. Most of us don't listen. Or we don't want to.

Carl wasn't ready to start dating again, so we agreed to just be friends. Two dates later, while dropping me off at my place, he held the taxi door open for me and kissed me on the lips. His Brawny Man beard felt strange against my face, which up to now had known only clean-shaven boys. But I knew chemistry when I felt it.

We fell in love fast. We had a deep connection *and* an enormous amount of fun together. In the early days of our courtship, Carl would sometimes sneak away from work late at night and come over, sprinting up the four flights of stairs to my apartment, where I'd greet him at the door wearing nothing but a black velvet choker. On one such occasion, we made love on my squishy sofa bed a record number of times—I counted six orgasms in an hour. For years, "six orgasms" would be our code for his prodigious ability to pleasure me.

But from the start, we agreed our careers were top priority. I never wanted to stand in the way of Carl's success and vice versa. We were both ambitious and worked in a business that required total dedication. The problem was that *his* dedication bordered on obses-sion. My hours were long, but his were insane. Every Tuesday the *SNL* writers would pull an all-nighter, preparing sketches for the next day's table read. Carl wouldn't even go home, instead crashing for a few hours on a saggy couch in his office.

During the weeks when *SNL* was in production, we hardly saw each other. The days of his sneaking off to rendezvous with me were over quickly, and our relationship began to consist largely of hasty phone calls squeezed in at work. On Tuesdays he was particularly irritable, gearing up for the all-nighter, and we'd get into stupid argu-ments over nothing. He was even busier on the weekends, so I'd go out with my friends instead, who referred to Carl as "Snuffleupagus" because they never saw him and started wondering if he might just be an "imaginary friend."

Occasionally I'd attend the *SNL* taping on Saturday night, but Carl would be too busy to hang out with me, which was also why I didn't like going to the after-parties, usually held at a bar or restau-rant. But Carl never failed to attend, so that he could schmooze with his coworkers and boss, the famously aloof Lorne Michaels. It wasn't until the last partygoer had either left or passed out that Carl would come over to my place and crash until late Sunday afternoon.

On Sunday evenings we'd go to dinner and a movie. But even then, Carl would be trying to come up with sketch ideas for next week's show, treating everything as potential material. At first, I was flattered that he let me in on his creative process and valued my opinion. But these conversations soon became tedious. Like many of the comedy writers I've known, Carl was brilliant but insecure, and it wasn't long before I was sick of hearing him ask, "Is this funny?" Those three words will probably be etched on his tombstone. In fact, he was so brainwashed by comedy writers' rooms that, to him, the word *funny* was synonymous with *good*. I'd ask, "How's your steak?" and without thinking he'd reply, "Funny."

Thankfully, both *SNL* and *Late Show* had many dark weeks—that is, weeks when we weren't producing new episodes and the studio was "dark." These were usually vacation weeks for Carl and me. When our dark weeks coincided, life was sweet. We would escape the stresses of our jobs and rediscover each other, often going on romantic trips out of town. Once, we rented a car and drove upstate to a twee bed-and-breakfast, where we spent the whole weekend in the Jacuzzi, eating homemade chocolate chip cookies that the proprietor left in a basket on our doorstep. Another time we went to a campground in Rhinebeck and stayed in a log cabin next to a babbling brook. We relaxed in Adirondack chairs, reading, and then cuddled by the campfire at night, sharing a joint and singing songs from *Grease*.

Sometimes we went to more luxurious locales, like a Hamptons spa or a Bahamian resort. I had never imagined living so large, especially since I was barely earning enough to pay my rent. But Carl was making a decent salary, and even though he was cheap about a lot of things—like allowing himself to take a cab only between the hours of three and five a.m., when he was afraid of getting mugged on the subway—he was willing to splurge on expensive hotels and restaurants when we were together. I'd get excited about planning our excursions, even just picking out a place for dinner.

"Hey, honey, listen to this," I'd say and then read from the Zagat guide, the precursor to Yelp. "'The granddaddy of all NYC steakhouses, this Midtown temple to meat remains rock solid, with succulent Flintstones-size slabs of beef; it's not for the weak of wallet, but you won't regret splurging'!"

Carl would roll his eyes, but then we'd head over to that Midtown meat temple and have a great time, gorging ourselves on so much steak, chocolate mousse, and red wine that we'd pass out on the cab ride home. I'll admit that I liked going to classy places and eating good food. Even when Carl complained about the exorbitant bill, he never asked me to pay or split it. We fell easily into traditional gender roles.

We'd been dating for at least six months when he met my parents. The night before, I was a nervous wreck. I'd dated guys who weren't Asian, but Carl was my first serious boyfriend, and I knew my mom would be vetting him for husband potential. What if they rejected him for being white or Jewish? But when they met, he was polite and charming, showcasing his accomplishments in a humble way, even making them laugh.

After, my mom told me she liked Carl. "It's good that he's a little older than you. He can take care of you."

"I can take care of myself."

But the truth was that I had internalized a whole society's worth of messages telling me I'd be taken care of by a man. How much did this affect my willingness to stay in a relationship that started out rocky and would only get worse? Probably more than I could ever know.

Right before one of our dark weeks, Adam Sandler invited Carl to join him on his stand-up comedy tour. At that time, Sandler was known for his *SNL* characters like Opera Man and original tunes like "The Chanukah Song." Not yet a movie star, he was still doing stand-up at colleges, albeit with packed audiences. He wanted Carl to keep him company and help him tweak jokes.

I'd hardly seen Carl at all lately, and the only thing keeping me going was the prospect of our week off. As usual, he'd been dragging his heels about making plans, and we had decided to visit Howe

Caverns—a set of caves in Schoharie County, New York—pretty much because it was too late to make reservations elsewhere. I was looking forward to this lame attraction like a trip to Europe, simply because I'd have Carl all to myself. When he decided to go away with Sandler instead, I broke down in tears.

"But what about Howe Caverns?"

He sighed. "You really think I should pass up touring with Adam Sandler so we can go look at a bunch of caves?"

Of course I didn't. His career came first. I would face this situation again and again: competing with Carl's work for his attention and feeling guilty about it. Because when I complained, I felt like the needy girlfriend I never wanted to be.

Our relationship was a constant struggle. Carl loved me, but it always seemed that he loved me *in spite of.* In spite of his devotion to work, his fear of commitment, and his belief that marriage would mean the death of his dreams. Carl's father had abandoned his aspirations of opening a furniture business and toiled away in a blue-collar job to support the family. Carl used this as a cautionary tale to justify his own repudiation of marriage.

Not that I was anywhere near ready to get married. But I wanted to in the future, and I assumed Carl would get there one day. Both of us thought we were fated to be together, from the day I first met him while trying to get tickets to *Letterman,* to our unlikely reunion four years later. But no matter how much he loved me, it felt like he was always pushing me away.

And with that dynamic, we fell into a pattern: Carl would get obsessed with work and I'd feel neglected. To avoid missing him, I'd pretend he didn't exist, erasing him from my memory like they do in *Eternal Sunshine of the Spotless Mind.* I'd start spending more time with my friends, going to parties and cavorting until all hours of the night, Carl called this "Independent Patty." The rise of Independent Patty would send him into a panic, and he'd pour himself into winning me back. He'd grant me his undivided attention, shower me with affection, and—the trick that never failed—he would make me laugh. Oftentimes making me the butt of his jokes. He once wrote a sketch where a long-suffering Adam Sandler is losing his mind because his wife, played by Chris Farley in drag, keeps reading aloud from the Zagat guide and giggling with excitement. At last, Sandler pulls out a gun and shoots himself. The Chris Farley character was based on me.

When Carl and I hit our first serious rough patch, he whisked me off on a fabulous vacation to Disney World. He booked a room at the Wilderness Lodge, a Disney resort with a woodsy theme. Aaron Copland–esque music played everywhere on the property, making a visit to the sundries shop feel like an expedition. On that trip, Carl did everything I wanted to do: ride the teacups, sing along with the hitchhiking ghosts at the Haunted Mansion, groan at the corny Jungle Cruise jokes. Because I was a huge *Star Wars* fan, he let me drag him on Star Tours several times—a ride that's designed to be like a commercial space shuttle flight to the forest moon of Endor. To make me laugh, he approached a Chewbacca near the entrance and said in his trademark deadpan, "Excuse me, sir. Does this shuttle go to Endor?"

Most important, he didn't do a lick of work the entire trip.

When we made love, it was the first time in weeks, maybe even months. That was how distant we had become. As we lay in a post-coital embrace, Carl buried his face in my neck and let out a satisfied sigh. "You know why I brought you here, don't you?"

"So you could chop me up into little pieces and bury them on Tom Sawyer Island?"

"No, but that's a good idea." He pulled me closer. "I knew this was it. I knew if I didn't do something—something big—you were going to leave me."

He was right, and his plan worked. But after we got home, we fell back into the same old dysfunctional routine. Crisis now averted, we had a brief honeymoon period before he went back to his old ways and became obsessed with work again. And I went back to scrubbing him from my memory.

Working for Peg was getting on my last nerve. She had carried over her unusual habits from NBC, still coming in at dawn and slipping P-Notes into inboxes. Still snooping through people's offices, looking for incriminating evidence. She even searched the restrooms and became hysterical if she spotted an unflushed turd in one of the toilets, analyzing it like a forensic criminologist to determine its owner.

I tried not to let her outrageous behavior get to me, but it took all my energy just to remain civil with her. I stubbornly refused to listen to her gossip or validate her neuroses and her ridiculous way of doing things. Perhaps because I was so unwilling to share any details of my personal life with her, she seemed even nosier with me than she was with anyone else. Paranoid, I locked all my desk drawers and file cabinets every night before I went home. There was nothing to hide—except the P-Books, of course.

The stress of her constant scrutiny started to take a toll on my immune system. I began getting canker sores and head colds all the time. My declaration to Collette that "I love stress" was becoming less true with each passing day. Before long I was, as the Loverboy song goes, working for the weekend. I was living the cliché, white-knuckling my way through the week until T.G.I.F. And no matter how much fun I had on the weekend, by Sunday night I would be sick with anxiety. Paula and I called it "the dreads."

The worst part was working on a show I loved so much, in a capacity that was so far from what I wanted to do. The writer in me was wasting away—and dying of shame. Whenever I met someone new, I feared the moment they'd ask what I did for a living.

"I work for the *Letterman* show."

"Oh my God, seriously? That's so cool! What do you do there?"

"I'm an assistant to a production manager."

"What is that, exactly?"

And pretty soon the excitement would drain from the person's face.

When a researcher position opened up in the spring of 1994, I jumped to apply. Though not entirely creative, research was a big step away from the drudgery of accounting. It was the first glimmer of hope I'd had since working for Peg. But I knew the competition would be tough. I wasn't the only applicant who used to be a research intern, and the others were now doing things that seemed more relevant to the position. I was afraid that no one would see me as anything other than Peg's lackey from accounting.

Each of us had to compete for the job by compiling a mock research packet on the actress Raquel Welch. I watched her past interviews, studied magazine articles and books about her, and even dug through the dusty stacks at the indie video store to find a tape of *Mother, Jugs & Speed,* a lame 1970s comedy in which she costarred with Bill Cosby and Harvey Keitel. (She, of course, played the character named Jugs.) I spent every spare moment working on my packet, as if cramming for a final exam.

The day after we handed them in, Mary, the former researcher who was now a producer, called us into her office to deliver the verdict. Our relationship had never been more than professionally cordial, but I hoped she knew how much I wanted this job and how hard I'd work if I got it.

"Everyone's packet was great," she said, "but there was one person who stood out above and beyond the rest."

That person turned out to be a guy who worked in the tickets department. He deserved the position and would go on to have a long career at *Late Show*, but I was devastated. Though Mary's rejection spiel wasn't unkind, all I could see in that moment was a hopeless future, the rest of my days spent stamping invoices and stuffing checks into envelopes while Peg held me captive under her probing stare.

As I left Mary's office, I struggled to keep it together. Waiting for the elevator, I could feel the tears coming on and knew I needed to get back to the eighth floor, stat, so I could lock myself in my office and bawl. Just my luck—when the doors slid open, the elevator was packed with chatty staffers, including Morty's new assistant, who had replaced Collette a few years back. This new assistant was an incorrigible gossip who was always up in everyone's business. So I'm sure that when she saw my face crumpled up like a raisin, she knew exactly what had happened.

"How'd it go?" she asked, feigning excitement.

I burst into tears. Right there in front of the office yenta.

It wasn't long before I realized that waiting for another opening at *Late Show* was futile, especially since there were no positions I truly wanted. The only way I'd ever have a more fulfilling job was to take matters into my own hands. Carl understood my disgruntlement because he'd once been in the same boat. "You need to do something creative," he often said. "This is not who you are."

A big part of my decision to pursue TV writing was my love for and familiarity with the medium. The countless TV shows I'd consumed

growing up had become part of my DNA. Another part of my decision was practical. I knew it was possible to earn a living as a TV
writer, as I was surrounded by people doing just that. I wasn't fantasizing about getting rich, living in Beverly Hills, or hanging out
with celebrities. I just wanted some financial security, the assurance
of a middle-class lifestyle like the one I'd been given by my parents,
without the drudgery of their nine-to-five jobs.

But the biggest draw was validation. It never occurred to me I
could be creative *outside* of my job. Paula, for instance, painted in
her free time. I'd given up on art back in college, choosing to pursue
more "productive" activities like studying. I also could've written on
the weekends. But I wasn't interested in being a hobbyist. I couldn't
justify any creative effort unless it wielded a salary and a job title. I
needed an external source to acknowledge my talent, because otherwise how would my parents know if I had any? How would I?

I didn't really know what a TV writing job would be like. I didn't
have access to the writers' room at *Letterman*. Through Carl, I
knew what writing for *SNL* was like, but I assumed that both these
shows were different from the ones I wanted to write, dramas like
thirtysomething. Sure, I could've done more research or asked
someone with experience so I could make an informed decision.
But even if they'd warned me about the pitfalls, I may not have
listened to them. Aspiring writers often ask me for advice, and I've
noticed that they never listen to things they don't want to hear.

Seeing Carl go from peon to writer gave me the courage to take
my next step: writing a spec—short for "speculative," a sample script
of an existing show. That was what you needed in order to land an
agent and get on a show as a regular writer. I would've written a
thirtysomething spec if it were still on the air, but instead I went with
the next best thing: *My So-Called Life*. Produced by the team that

made *thirtysomething*, this ultimately short-lived show was about a high school misfit played by a young Claire Danes, whose love interest was the super-hot Jared Leto. The show was funny, deep, moving, and real. And since I had only recently grown out of my teens, I could relate to its adolescent angst.

My spec was about Jared Leto's character (who, like the real Leto, was a musician) playing guitar in a promising local band but self-sabotaging because he's afraid of success. I wrote it on a Power-Book 150, by then already a dinosaur of Apple laptops, a gray plastic behemoth reminiscent of a Sherman tank. I didn't know I needed screenwriting software, so I used a word-processing application and approximated the script format using tabs. Carl procured one of the show's scripts from his agent so I could study the structure, but other than that, I had no idea what I was doing. I was going mostly on instinct.

During my freshman year of high school, my English teacher made us write a scene in the voice of Holden Caulfield, the teenage protagonist in *The Catcher in the Rye*. I wrote one where Holden meets the country-western singer Dolly Parton. He keeps referring to her as "old Dolly," and even though she's a "phony," he can't help but think about "giving her the time" (Holden slang for sex). It was the most fun I'd ever had doing a homework assignment. Taking on the voice of a character came easily to me, and this skill would become the foundation of my television writing career.

But working on my spec was way harder than writing that Holden Caulfield scene. The happy-go-lucky, inspired moments when I was truly lost in my work were few and far between, overshadowed by the fear of doing it wrong. I was usually too tired and demoralized to write after work, so I wrote on weekends and vacations when I could manage to scrape up the motivation. In my mind, my whole career was riding on this spec. It had to be brilliant. Trying to meet that standard was about as much fun as scrolling through microfiche.

One of the reasons it was hard to get motivated was that, even though I hated my job, I loved my coworkers and the perks we enjoyed. Though many of us were living hand to mouth, we were showered with extravagant gifts from Dave on celebratory occasions. When the show premiered, everyone got a bottle of Dom Pérignon. I hoarded mine like a precious artifact, refusing to open it until years after it had gone bad. Every Christmas we would get a new varsity jacket, blue with yellow sleeves, the back emblazoned with the show's logo. I wore them proudly, even though they were always too big on me.

For that trip to the Emmys, the show chartered a plane to fly us all out to L.A. We assistants didn't mind being stuck in coach while Dave and the upper echelon were in first class—we were having a blast. While everyone got tanked on miniature bottles of booze, the pilot periodically got on the loudspeaker to give us updates on our altitude. Soon his announcements started to sound a little jokey, as if the writers were feeding him lines. When the show's film coordinator—a dorky, bug-eyed guy named Shecky—was parading up and down the aisles, blathering loudly, the pilot said, "Just wanted to let y'all know that Shecky is shitfaced. I repeat: Shecky is shitfaced."

We were put up at the Loews Santa Monica, and Dave had a suite at Shutters on the Beach, an even nicer hotel a few blocks away. Dave didn't socialize with the staff, even on trips. An event known as the "Johnny Carson dinner" was held at a Wolfgang Puck restaurant in Malibu, where the godfather of late-night TV was supposed to drop in on us. Our staff took up the entire patio; Dave was tucked away at

the table farthest from any access. Again, everyone got hammered—
well, everyone at the "kids' table," anyway—and if Johnny Carson
ever showed up, I was having too good a time to notice.

There was no better place for someone in their early twenties to
work. Two of the assistants shared an apartment a few blocks from
the office, and it became our unofficial clubhouse, where we'd take
bong hits and gossip about work minutiae and cute boys. They threw
parties constantly, very few of which were attended by Carl. They
had one where you were supposed to write your best pickup line on a
piece of paper and tape it to your chest. Mine was "Is that a mirror in
your pocket? 'Cause I can see myself in your pants." I'm pretty sure
I'd heard that somewhere and didn't make it up. One of the writers,
a preppy Stanford grad, had one that read "Do you like apples? How
about I shove one up your ass? How do you like THEM apples?"

The office camaraderie was the only relief from the tedium of
my work. When the O.J. Simpson murder trial began in 1995, we
all became glued to the Court TV coverage. Now, instead of music
videos, I watched Johnny Cochran hold up a leather glove crusted
with dried blood, intoning, "If it doesn't fit, you must acquit." My
coworkers and I would discuss the day's trial developments while we
ate our brown bag lunches in the conference room. On the day the
jury deliberations began, I organized an office pool where we took
bets on the verdict—on the down-low, of course, since it was in such
terrible taste. Only three people predicted O.J. would go free, and not
because he was innocent. I was one of them.

Given all the distractions, it's no wonder it took me months to
write my spec. When I finally completed it, Carl was the first person
I showed it to. I didn't trust myself and wanted a professional's
opinion. To my relief, he loved it. *Impressed* was the word he kept
using. I suppose I could've taken offense at how surprised he was, but

my self-confidence was so shaky that I lapped up the praise. He gave me a few suggestions, but the most important thing was that I now believed it was viable: I wasn't investing in a pipe dream.

With renewed enthusiasm, I revised my spec and started working on a new one. The rule of thumb was you needed at least two to get an agent. I decided to write a *Party of Five* spec, as this drama about a bunch of orphaned siblings who inherit the family restaurant (rebooted in 2020 with a more diverse cast) was one of my guilty pleasures.

Meanwhile, I strove to be more efficient in my job so I'd have more time to write. I was always streamlining tasks, creating better systems for processing invoices and contracts. But the more productive I became, the more work piled up on me. Peg gave me a raise and a title change to boot: production finance coordinator. I was grateful for these rewards, but they also made me feel more trapped. Though not quite "golden handcuffs," the higher salary made it harder to fathom starting over.

At work, no one but Paula knew I was writing scripts, and I swore her to secrecy. The rumor mill at *Late Show* was out of control. I didn't want everyone knowing what I was up to, especially Peg, who would surely flip out over me plotting my escape. But mostly, I wanted to avoid feeling humiliated if I couldn't accomplish what I had set out to do. They say if you want to achieve a goal, make it public. Conversely, if you don't want to look like an idiot when you fail, keep your mouth shut.

In the spring of 1996, Carl got an offer to write for *Seinfeld*, which was produced in Los Angeles. *Seinfeld* was the most popular sitcom on TV and every comedy writer's dream job. The offer seemed like a no-brainer to me, but Carl drove himself and everyone else crazy with his dithering.

Quitting *SNL* was like leaving a close-knit family, and tearing himself away from the patriarch wasn't easy. But, hey, if you're going to leave Lorne Michaels's nest, flying to the left coast to roost with Jerry Seinfeld is a pretty badass way to do it. So Carl gave his notice, and we agreed to try the long-distance thing until I was ready to move to L.A., too.

Neither of us saw ourselves living there for the long haul. We were both East Coast people at heart. But there was only so far you could go in TV if you weren't willing to go to Hollywood. We resigned ourselves to it, with the intention of moving back one day.

After Carl left, I unofficially took over his lease and moved into his apartment on the Upper East Side. Though the rent was the same, his place was twice the size of my cubbyhole on Minetta Street. The apartment was a one-bedroom at the top of four flights of creaky stairs. The building was on 60th Street between Park and Lexington, sandwiched between a Chinese restaurant with greasy windows and a gay bar called Pegasus, where, to my chagrin, they hosted a boisterous cabaret karaoke at two in the morning. Carl left most of his furniture behind, but the only pieces I kept were his queen-size mattress and a midcentury Steelcase tanker desk with tan drawers and a woodgrain top. It looked like something a buxom secretary had perched upon with her legs crossed while her boss tried to look up her skirt.

I spent the next few months sitting at that desk, writing my *Party of Five* spec. It didn't go much faster than the first spec because my social life was so busy. I was so accustomed to doing things without Carl that I adapted easily to his absence. I hung out often with his best friend and former college roommate, Ezra, who was pursuing a PhD in psychology. Ezra's girlfriend had to travel a lot for work, so he was orphaned like me. We'd get together on Thursday nights to smoke pot, eat pizza and fried clams, and watch *ER*—a poor choice, as the show's frenetic opening music would instantly harsh our mellow.

On Friday and Saturday nights, I'd go barhopping with coworkers or to parties that didn't even start until midnight. There was alcohol, weed, leather pants, hot guys. The mid-nineties were a good time to be twenty-four. It was easy to forget that I had a boyfriend and that I was supposed to be writing.

Nevertheless, I finished my *Party of Five* spec in the fall and sent both of my scripts to Carl's agent, Ted, at Creative Artists Agency (CAA), one of the most powerful talent agencies in Hollywood. I'm sure Ted read them only because Carl was an important client to him. I knew how fortunate I was to have this connection—it was nearly impossible for unknown writers to get their scripts read by an agent. If you didn't have someone vouch for you, you'd end up in the slush pile, no matter how good you were.

Ted arranged to meet me while I was visiting Carl in L.A. I drove my rental car to Beverly Hills, left it with a valet, and walked into the cavernous lobby of CAA with its enormous Lichtensteins decorating the walls. I'd never felt so intimidated in my life. But Ted was friendly and easygoing. After some small talk, he told me that, although my specs were well written, he had decided not to represent me at this time. He didn't explain why. The lack of feedback could be just as crushing as harsh criticism.

"But keep sending me your stuff," he added.

I hung on to that crumb with every bit of hope I could muster. Even though it probably meant nothing to Ted—like guys who say "I'll call you" at the end of every date, good or bad—I chose to see it as encouragement. I had to, or I would've given up.

Carl came back to New York for Christmas, along with the other *Seinfeld* writers, most of whom were East Coast transplants. A flurry of posh parties ensued. At one of these, in a banquet room at the Four Seasons Hotel, I met an agent who represented some of the

Seinfeld staff. Her name was Sue Naegle and she worked for United Talent Agency (UTA), another top-tier agency. Sue was in her mid-twenties, with straight blond hair and a strong nose. She was funny and down-to-earth, and we hit it off right away. When we found out we were both from New Jersey, we bonded over our memories of the Rockaway mall.

Meeting Sue was the opportunity I'd been waiting for. Even though I felt self-conscious and cheesy about networking, I knew I had to get over it. Trying my best to not seem pushy, I told Sue that I had written two TV specs.

"Send them to me," she said without hesitation. "I'd love to read them."

With hopes soaring, I mailed her my specs after she returned to L.A. Before long, she called me at my office while I was Scotch-taping receipts to an expense report. My pulse quickened when I saw the 310 area code on my caller ID. I raced to shut my office door and forced myself to take a few deep breaths before picking up the handset. My whole future was riding on this phone call.

Sue liked my specs. *Holy shit, she liked my specs!*

"But," she qualified, "both of them are soft. There aren't a lot of soft relationship dramas on the air these days. You need to write something harder-edged."

This was bad news. I didn't know how to write shows about cops, lawyers, doctors, or gangsters, despite watching a lot of them. I couldn't imagine writing any hard-edged drama, except for one that I absolutely loved: *The X-Files*. I was a huge fan of this cult-hit sci-fi series about a pair of FBI agents who investigate paranormal cases—and not just because the costar David Duchovny was catnip for geeky women like me. Thanks to my older brother, I had grown up on sci-fi—*Star Wars, Blade Runner, The Twilight Zone.*

So, with much trepidation and determination, I embarked on writing an *X-Files* spec, poring over the compendiums I found at the bookstore and deconstructing a few episodes until I understood their format. Then I worked my butt off for the next three months, writing a story that was a huge departure for me. It was about a serial killer who targets artists and literally sucks the talent out of them. My spec did not come out brilliant; it wasn't even half as good as their mediocre episodes. Writing a genre show is *hard*. When Sue called to tell me that she loved my script, I could hardly believe I'd pulled it off.

She arranged to meet with me in mid-May while in New York for the upfronts, an annual event where networks announce their fall schedules to advertisers and the media. Trembling with excitement, I scribbled "meeting w/Sue" in my datebook, already forgetting about "Keep Sending Me Your Stuff" Ted at CAA. Sue was the one for me—I was sure of it.

The morning of my meeting, I told Peg I had a doctor's appointment and would be coming in late. Sue invited me to have breakfast in her room at the St. Regis, a ritzy hotel in the heart of the Fifth Avenue shopping district. The hotel's ostentatious decor, with its massive crystal chandeliers and gilded everything, didn't strike me as gaudy: it was befitting of the fairy tale I was walking into.

Sue answered the door wearing a white designer pantsuit, glasses with chunky black frames, and disposable hotel slippers. I was glad I'd recently ditched the blue contacts and gotten a pair of nerdy-chic glasses myself. They were the cornerstone of my "writerly look."

As we nibbled on croissants and drank coffee from a silver pot, Sue told me about the new shows that were launching in the fall. Unfortunately, she wasn't putting me up for any of them. She explained that TV hiring season ran from March until mid-May, at which point the networks announced their fall lineups, and shows finalized their writing staffs. (This was before the streaming era, when shows would be in production all year round.) In other words, I had just missed the boat. I was disappointed that I'd have to wait at least another year before I could get hired as a writer. But a lot had to happen in the meantime.

"If you're serious about writing for TV," she said, "you have to move to L.A."

Here it was: the dreaded move west. The thought of uprooting my life and starting over in a new city had always been daunting. But now I had to face it because shit just got real: I had an agent. Sue never said the words "I'd like to rep you" or made me sign any contracts. But the understanding was that, if I proved to be serious, UTA would take me under its wing.

I was euphoric—and terrified. Was I ready for this?

Over the next month I planned my course of action, keeping the whole thing under wraps. During the last week of June, with my nerves ready to snap, I scheduled a meeting with Peg and the head of human resources. As soon as the three of us sat down, I told them I was giving my notice.

"I've always wanted to do something creative, and for the last couple of years I've been writing TV spec scripts." I was amazed at how such a tumultuous journey could be boiled down to a single sentence. And then the kicker: "I got an agent and I'm moving to L.A."

I was dreading Peg's response. The last thing I wanted was a big emotional scene with her. This was the woman I'd been trying to avoid as much as possible for the last four years—the boss who, by this point, probably resented me as much as I resented her. Bracing myself, I turned to her and was shocked that, behind her granny glasses, her eyes glistened with tears.

In all the times I'd imagined this scenario, I pictured Peg being mad at me, hating me for keeping this secret from her and now abandoning her. But she couldn't have been more gracious.

"Thank you for working so hard all these years. I don't know what I would've done without you." She blew her nose into a tissue. "I'm so proud of you, Patty. You're going to do great things."

My reaction shocked me even more: I felt my own tears threatening to spill. This was not the woman who spied on me and tortured me with P-Notes, but the genuine, good-hearted woman underneath all that neurosis. And though I couldn't say that I would miss her or the job, I cried because I was leaving my home.

The news of my quitting spread like wildfire. All day my phone rang off the hook with congratulatory calls. My closest friends were wildly happy for me, and even coworkers I didn't know very well crawled out of the woodwork to confess their own creative ambitions and to tell me that I was inspiring them, doing what they always wanted to do. And to think that all this time, I felt like I was the only one dying a slow death.

That Friday was the best day of my life. I called it my "*Shawshank Redemption* moment"—like in that movie where Tim Robbins breaks out of prison by digging a tunnel with a rock hammer through his cell wall behind a poster of Raquel Welch. I had been a prisoner in Cell Block Eight for four years, steadily chipping away at that wall until I could bust out.

3

Green

Even though it was Sue Naegle who brought me in as a UTA client, she wasn't my principal agent, the one I would deal with on a day-to-day basis. That agent turned out to be a guy named Larry Salz. Sue vouched for him in glowing terms, calling him "one of the rare agents who is truly passionate about his clients' work."

Shortly after I arrived in Los Angeles in the summer of 1997, Larry and I had an introductory breakfast meeting at Hugo's, a health food café in West Hollywood where everything was served with a side of quinoa. When I walked in, I could tell right away who the agent was, because he was the only person in a dress shirt and tie. (I soon found out almost everyone in L.A. looks like they're unemployed.) I joined Larry at his table near the window and we shook hands. He was about my age, toothy and slight. A lifelong breakfast enthusiast, I was never one to pass up an omelet, but I was too nervous that morning to order anything but a cup of coffee and a blueberry muffin.

"That's all you're going to have?"

Larry told me that most writers would order a gigantic meal when they knew it was on the agency's dime. One client would even order an extra entrée and take it home in a doggy bag! I couldn't imagine being so audacious, at least not until I'd gotten a gig and earned Larry a commission.

He sounded optimistic about my prospects, echoing Sue's enthusiasm for my material. But I left our meeting feeling unsure. Now that I was no longer in the *Letterman* bubble, my lack of experience stood out in sharp relief. The truth was, I didn't know how this business worked and was relying solely on my relationship with UTA.

But I had made it to Hollywood and I was following my dream. That was no small thing, especially after my parents had given me a vote of no confidence. Not long after my meeting with Sue, I had gone home to tell them I was quitting my job and moving to L.A. While living in New York, I often went home on the weekends to eat my mom's cooking and peruse sales at the mall with her. This time, on my way to Port Authority, I stopped at a bodega and bought a bouquet of flowers, hoping to soften the blow.

My parents were as surprised as Peg by my news.

"What's a 'spec script'?" my mom asked.

I had to explain everything, something I'd had to do with them my whole life. Because of the cultural gap, we didn't have a shorthand. When I told them I got an agent, they didn't light up, impressed, the way other people did. I had to say, "You know, it's really hard to get an agent. They don't take just anybody."

Still, they were skeptical and worried. Especially since I didn't have a job lined up.

"There's an old Chinese saying," my dad said, pausing for effect. "Never jump off a horse until there's another horse waiting."

"Don't worry, Dad. I'll find a job. I just need to get out there first."

The crease between my mom's eyebrows appeared, the one that always made my stomach sink because it meant she was unhappy.

"It's three thousand miles away," she said quietly.

"I know."

My plan was to get a job first, then an apartment, and, finally, a car. I was going to stay with Carl until I got settled. But once I got there, I did everything ass backward.

I bought a car right away because living in L.A. without one was nearly impossible. It was a used late-eighties Camry, a boxy silver sedan with tinted windows, and I had to borrow eight thousand dollars from Carl to pay for it. My parents, despite their reservations, had already lent me ten grand for moving expenses, with the hope that I'd land on my feet. As someone who had always paid the full balance on my credit card each month, I was very uncomfortable with all this debt, though grateful for the good fortune of being given these loans.

I tried to make myself at home in Carl's apartment, a high-rise condo at the base of the Hollywood Hills. This spacious rental had white walls, white wall-to-wall carpet, and a narrow concrete balcony that overlooked dozens of other apartment buildings, their rooftop pools shimmering in the ever-present sunshine. Unlike his New York apartment, it was weirdly quiet and had no character. I found myself missing the sound of gay men belting "Memory" from *Cats* in the middle of the night.

Before I moved to L.A., Carl and I had decided we weren't ready to live together. This fact was now glaringly apparent. Now thirty-one years old, he still stayed up late (a habit from his *SNL* days) and was grumpy as hell in the morning. Worse, he lived as if he were about to up and leave at any moment. His things were haphazardly crammed into IKEA bookshelves and secondhand furniture. There were mismatched beach towels in the bathroom and threadbare blankets on the bed. He didn't decorate, not even by hanging a few pictures—he said he didn't want to leave nail holes. But to me these were signs of a fear of commitment. If Carl couldn't commit to buying a towel, how would he ever commit to our relationship?

Admittedly, I was having some commitment issues of my own. My year apart from Carl had strengthened "Independent Patty," and now I missed that freedom and autonomy. Yet I knew how dependent on him I really was, and it bothered me. Would I have been able to move to L.A. without him making it easier for me, like he did with my internship, my spec scripts, and my agent? Even though he was at work most of the day, I felt smothered and antsy, mostly because I didn't have my own job, friends, or home. In short, I needed my own life.

After a lengthy search, I found a cute one-bedroom in Beachwood Canyon, a funky neighborhood just north of the Capitol Records building. Driving up the gently curving street, I caught sight of the iconic Hollywood sign, its white block letters nestled into the chaparral-covered hill, and my jaw dropped. The apartment was huge by New York standards. The living room had hardwood floors, dentil moldings, and a picture window that let in plenty of sunshine and overlooked a walkway lined with bougainvillea. The kitchen had black-and-white checkerboard floor tiles and an antique O'Keefe & Merritt stove with an oven big enough for more than a single Cornish game hen.

Beachwood reminded me of New York because you could walk to places. A short stroll down the hill led to a stretch of restaurants and boutiques on Franklin Avenue, across from a mysterious sprawling fortress with elaborate landscaping and impenetrable gates. I later found out it was the Church of Scientology Celebrity Centre, the mothership for Tom Cruise and John Travolta—not that I would ever see any A list Scientologists around, just the anonymous Sea Org drones who did their chores and errands. Like them, I would soon be a peon serving the upper echelons of Hollywood.

The first time I walked into my neighborhood grocery store, I was downright giddy. This was a far cry from the cramped, dusty Gristedes on First Avenue where I used to shop. I pushed my cart slowly through the produce section, admiring the massive piles of plump peaches, shiny avocados, and deep-green kale. I'd never even *seen* kale before! After loading up my cart, I glided up to one of the registers.

"This is the most amazing supermarket I've ever seen," I told the cashier.

She assumed I was being sarcastic. "Yeah, it's expensive, I know."

I didn't understand what she was talking about. In New York, I was used to paying two dollars for a mealy apple. Here, I was unemployed, but at least I could get decent fruit.

As soon as I had my own place, things got better with Carl. We settled into a comfortable routine of going to restaurants, seeing movies, and hanging out at my apartment. Now that I had a functional kitchen, I threw myself into cooking and loved making dinner for Carl—tuna casserole, chicken marsala, spaghetti with meat sauce from a recipe by Martin Scorsese's mother. But he never helped me cook or went to the market with me. One night when we had friends over for dinner, Carl started washing the dishes. I came up behind him and gave him a bear hug, pressing my face against his back.

"Thank you, honey! You're doing such a great job!"

His friend looked at me like I was nuts. "You gonna give him a medal?"

"She's trying to encourage this behavior," Carl said wryly as he scrubbed a skillet. "It's called positive reinforcement."

Knowing that Carl was under tremendous pressure at *Seinfeld*, I tried harder than ever to accommodate his rigorous work schedule. Though they didn't have all-nighters, the writers' hours were brutal, to the point where we girlfriends were affectionately referred to as "the *Seinfeld* widows."

I turned my attention to finding a job. The first thing I learned about Hollywood was that it's all about meetings. I spent most of September driving all over town for meetings that Larry set up for me. This was before GPS, so I'd often get lost and end up pulling over somewhere I shouldn't, then frantically flipping through a thick spiral-bound set of maps called the Thomas Guide, which everyone in L.A. had (and now no one does). Then I'd show up late, damp with flop sweat, and try to be charming for the development executives at various networks, studios, and production companies.

These were called "general" meetings because they weren't for specific jobs. But Larry insisted they were necessary; the executives would get to know me, which would boost my chances of getting hired on a show. I used to think of meetings as a bunch of smartly dressed employees sitting around a conference table, discussing serious business. Hollywood meetings are nothing like this. They're forty-five minutes of small talk on a couch, after which everyone pretends they've accomplished something. An avid hater of small talk, I approached these meetings with the same dread I brought to pedicures and cab rides to the airport.

Meanwhile, I needed to find a day job. In October, I heard through a former colleague that the head writer of *Friends* needed an assistant. The popular sitcom about six friends in their twenties living in New York City was just about to begin its fourth season and was already a phenomenon. I went to meet the head writer, Michael Borkow, at his high-rise office on the Warner Bros. lot in Burbank. He used to be a lawyer and still looked like one. His serious personality was not what I expected; he was nothing like the sarcastic wise-asses I knew from the comedy world. But in a way, that made him easier to talk to.

I was honest with Borkow about my aspirations but made it clear I wasn't angling to write for *Friends*, or any sitcom, for that matter. He was impressed that I'd written three drama specs and had an agent. We had a good conversation and what felt like a sincere connection—but I didn't get the job. Borkow admitted he didn't want to hire me because I was too smart and ambitious to last long as an assistant, and he didn't want to have to go through this process again when I moved on to bigger things. It was the best rejection I could've imagined: the head writer of *Friends* believed I would make it! That gave my self-confidence a much-needed boost.

But I was still unemployed.

My parents were starting to worry. Ever since I'd moved, they had been calling me for updates with increasing urgency. When they called me in October, they had just returned from a cruise ship vacation with some of their friends. I wanted to assure my dad I was making progress finding a job, not working on my tan, so I briefed him on my various leads. When I told him about the *Friends* interview, he got frustrated with me.

"You can't tell them you want to be a writer."

I could feel my fist tightening around the phone. My dad knew nothing about the television business, and he was giving me advice? I would never walk into a job interview flaunting that "what I really want to do is write." But everyone knows that assistants aspire to write, direct, produce, or do anything other than be assistants. My dad was telling me to lie and act dumb, which I refused to do. But what *really* stung was that he didn't have confidence in me. It killed me that Michael Borkow—a person I hardly knew—believed in my talent more than my own parents did.

My dad passed the phone to my mom, who seconded his reproach. Then, adding insult to injury, she needled me about the money I had borrowed from them. What I needed even more than their financial support was *emotional* support, but to them these were the same thing. My face grew flushed and my pulse skyrocketed as our conversation spiraled into an argument.

"Do you know what it's like," she snapped, "when all our friends have kids who are doctors and lawyers, and we have to tell them what *you're* doing?"

I burst into hot, furious tears. My own mother was ashamed of me. She cared more about what her friends thought of me than about my well-being—and my failures had ruined her Norwegian cruise. The Taiwanese immigrant community could be brutally competitive, and my mom had always compared me to her friends' kids. Back in Downers Grove, we used to participate in an annual Taiwanese bazaar, and one year a bunch of us girls were recruited to do a folk-dance number. I remember the look of pride on my mother's face when all the other moms remarked on how I had the best-looking braids, smiled the most, and knew the dance steps better than the other girls. Well, times had changed. Those girls had gone to medical school or were now married with babies. I was no longer coming out ahead.

And we have to tell them what you're *doing?* In that moment, I hated her.

"I can't believe you're saying this to me! I can't take any more of this—I'm hanging up!"

"Don't get in your car! Don't drive anywhere!"

She was always paranoid about me driving while upset and getting into an accident. I had no intention of driving—or doing anything but curling up in a ball and sobbing my eyes out—but I didn't want to give her the satisfaction of knowing that. I slammed the phone down and resolved never to speak to her or my dad again.

For the next few weeks, I gave them the cold shoulder. My twenty-sixth birthday came and went, and I didn't return their calls. A birthday card arrived with a check enclosed. In the card, my mom didn't exactly apologize for the things she said, but I could tell she felt badly. Still, I avoided talking to her, not so much to punish her as to prevent another fight. I was too fragile to withstand another blow like that.

In the meantime, my job hunt continued. UTA kept a list of entry level positions in the industry, a sort of insider's classified ads. Larry told me a director named Dean Parisot, also a UTA client, needed an assistant. Dean had won an Academy Award for a short film starring comedian Steven Wright and had just finished shooting an independent feature called *Home Fries*, starring Drew Barrymore. He also had a development deal with Sony Television.

A development deal is an agreement where a director, writer, or producer works on a certain number of projects for a network, studio, or production company. As part of Dean's deal, he was making a pilot, a stand-alone episode of a TV show that's used to sell the show to a network. The pilot, titled *ATF*, based on the Bureau of Alcohol, Tobacco, Firearms and Explosives, was a bone-dry procedural drama that didn't interest me in the least. But Larry assured me that Dean was a nice guy and, more to the point, the job would afford plenty of time to work on my writing.

I met Dean and felt like we were a good fit. We had the same sense of humor and New York attitude. He was in his forties and had salt-and-pepper hair and an impish smile. Unlike Borkow, he had no qualms about hiring ambitious assistants; several of his had gone on to become writers, directors, and producers. A couple of days after we met, he called and said, "Let's do it." I finally called my parents back to tell them I had a job. They were relieved that I was now gainfully employed, even if not as a writer, and they made a concerted effort to ease up on me after our big blowup. They were trying.

There was very little structure to the job. Mostly I rolled calls—meaning that I connected Dean's calls to his cellphone—because he didn't come in much. His office was in Culver City, in a sparsely populated building at the Sony Annex, a lifeless studio lot. Dean didn't train me, and since his former assistant had left before I started, she couldn't show me the ropes. I did my best to figure it out and made mistakes along the way. A shit-ton of mistakes.

One time I arranged a lunch meeting for Dean at Versailles, a Cuban restaurant on Pico and La Cienega. Being new to L.A., I had no idea there was *another* Versailles at Venice and Motor, and that was where Dean's lunch date showed up while Dean was waiting for him at the other location, drinking a Coke, which he then had to pay for before racing to the other side of town. *Oops.* But Dean never yelled or reprimanded me when I messed up. I assumed he was just so laid-back he didn't care.

The only people I saw regularly were a couple of other assistants who sat in nearby cubicles, rolling calls to their bosses who never came in. After working in bustling offices where I had no privacy, I thought I'd enjoy the quiet and solitude of the Sony space. But the emptiness was creepy and added to my sense of isolation. The highlight of my day was having a cup of Bigelow tea and a lemon cookie as I stared at my gray cubicle wall.

I was friendly with the other assistants, but we didn't hang out. I missed my pals from *Letterman*—the office gossip, the inappropriate jokes, the parties where everyone did stupid shit and laughed about it on Monday. Carl brought me to a few parties in L.A., and they all sucked. No one let their hair down or had random hookups. People had to drive home, so they drank responsibly, and there were no drugs, not even pot. I didn't see a single person snorting blow off a mirrored coffee table. This was not the L.A. I'd seen in countless eighties movies!

Here, people didn't go to parties to have fun and let off steam; they went to network. "What are you working on?" was the start of every conversation. And since I had no desire to talk about my boring job or my job aspirations—both of which made me feel pathetic—I hated these L.A. parties, with their unspoken hierarchy and transactional nature. You were either a player or a wannabe. Either you wanted something from someone or they wanted something from you. I knew which category I was in. And at the end of the night, I never went home with what I *really* wanted: a massive buzz and a story to tell.

At the start of 1998, after I'd had a chance to settle into the job, Larry started pressuring me to write another spec. My first three had already been read around town and he wanted to send out new material. I decided to write one for *Buffy the Vampire Slayer*, a weird, sassy show on the now-defunct WB network about a teenage girl who kills vampires. Now a cult classic, *Buffy* was a good mix of hard plot, soft drama, and dark comedy, and it featured young characters, which was starting to become my "thing." At twenty-six, I didn't yet have the life experience to write anything *but* young characters.

Working on my new spec gave me a sense of purpose as I slogged through my depressing days at Sony. I wrote during my ample downtime, feeling only slightly guilty about being on the clock, since Dean gave me little to do. I poured myself into the script, laboring over every line. I wanted it to knock people's socks off. Engrossed in my writing, doing what I came here to do, I felt truly happy for the first time since arriving in L.A.

When filming on *ATF* began, Dean's routine changed. Instead of working from home, he would go to the set every day and direct. He didn't ask me to accompany him, so I spent most of my time in the office and barely heard from him. Every so often I had to bring him mail, scripts, or papers to sign, and I found the set boring. Unlike the live tapings I was used to, drama shoots moved at a snail's pace. A minute or two of cameras rolling would be followed by a half-hour of lighting changes. Even Dean had more downtime than he knew what to do with.

One evening when I was on set, Carl called me from work—he was getting off at a semi-decent hour. This was rare, and we hadn't seen each other in days, so I jumped at the chance to have dinner with him. When I went to find Dean, he was slouched in his director's chair, waiting for the crew to set up a shot. He looked as bored as I was.

"Hey, Dean, if you don't need me for anything, I'm gonna take off."

He paused before answering, "Okay." In that split second, I should've realized he wasn't cool with it. After all, an assistant is supposed to be at work before the boss arrives and stay until after they go home. But to me it seemed perfectly reasonable to go to dinner with my boyfriend rather than sit around twiddling my thumbs.

One day in early February, Dean was driving to the set when his feature agent called. As usual, I connected him to Dean's cell and stayed on the line, muted, so I could take notes and follow up on things they discussed, like setting up a meeting or sending a script to someone.

Dean's calls with his agent usually went like this: Dean expresses dissatisfaction with how his feature career is going. Agent talks up potential projects. Dean rejects said projects. Agent tries to hide his frustration and coddles his client. Dean complains that his life is out of control. Agent suggests solutions. Dean rejects solutions. Agent gets another call and hangs up.

This call followed the same format, except this time when Dean's agent asked if he'd read the feature scripts UTA had sent over, Dean launched straight into the "my life is out of control" part. He was simply too busy to do all that reading.

His agent had an answer for everything: "Have your assistant do it."

Right away I felt defensive. I *had* read many of those scripts— stacks and stacks of them piled up on every available surface of my desk. In those early days of the internet, people didn't email scripts; they were all hard copies. As I suffered through each of them, I realized the cliché is true: everyone in this town really does think they can write a screenplay. I had told Dean what the scripts were about and described what I liked or didn't like about them. He hadn't been interested in pursuing any of them. Surely Dean would explain this.

Instead, he let out an irritated sigh. "My assistant's not very good," he grumbled.

My stomach leapt into my throat. What did he say? I was so shocked that I got confused for a moment and wondered whether he was talking about someone else. But I was Dean's only assistant, so of course he meant me. I was crushed, humiliated—and indignant. Dean never taught me how to do my job and never told me he was dissatisfied with my work. Then he complains about me behind my back? He must not have known that it was standard practice for assistants to listen in on work calls. One of the first things I figured out when I got to Hollywood was that you should never say anything on the phone that you don't want the assistants to hear.

To make matters worse, his agent immediately took his side. "You know, there are a lot of young, smart people who would kill to be a director's assistant."

Now I really felt like throwing up—and I was pissed about how much time I'd spent finding just the right present for Dean to give this asshole for Christmas (a Patagonia ski parka, for fuck's sake)! Perhaps it was naïve to expect the agent to jump to my defense and say something like, "Patty Lin is one of our clients and I won't have you disparaging her." To him, I was a nobody. Still, it was disturbing how eager he seemed to discard me just to make his client happy. I imagined him, warm and smug in his ski jacket, pulling up the UTA job list at that very moment and adding my position to it.

But Dean didn't fire me. After the call with his agent, he carried on as if nothing had happened. For the rest of the day, I kept replaying the conversation in my mind, feeling alternately queasy and light-headed with rage. No one had ever described me as being bad at my job; it went against my whole identity as a hardworking perfectionist. When I had mono while working at *Letterman*, I came in on weekends to catch up on invoices and answer P-Notes. I was the intern who stayed late to write Dave questions. Even at the ice cream parlor, I took great care to make my soft-serve swirls look pretty. But deep down I knew Dean was right: I *was* a bad assistant. I had been preoccupied with my spec for weeks, and as far as my job was concerned, I was, for the first time in my life, phoning it in.

That night I didn't sleep. I just lay in bed, letting my mind spin, trying to figure out what to do. If I told Dean what I'd overheard, it would embarrass both of us. Nevertheless, I had to do better at this job, with or without his guidance. I didn't have the time or energy to find another day job when I needed to be working the writing angle.

Fortunately, since I was done with my spec, I could now devote myself to becoming the World's Greatest Assistant. I started going to the editing bay every day to be at Dean's side while he and the editor were cutting the pilot. I volunteered to make so many Starbucks and Jamba Juice runs that no one wanted another latte or wheatgrass shot ever again. I ran all of Dean's personal errands, even the ones he'd been too polite to ask me to do. Moment by moment, I tried to put myself in his shoes and intuit what he needed—and I always stuck around until he told me to go home.

Though we never discussed it, things improved between us. I had managed to redeem myself. But part of me was still reeling from that overheard phone call. The memory of it followed me around, making me push myself harder and harder at the expense of my own health. I ate badly and had trouble sleeping because I was in a constant state of anxiety. *Did I take care of every detail? Is there anything I haven't thought of? Was I perfect today?*

One Friday in March, I was so busy running around that I didn't break for lunch. By the time I got home that night, exhausted and ravenous, it was past ten. All I'd consumed that day was a bagel and a cup of coffee in the morning. Carl was supposed to come over for dinner after he got off work, so instead of gobbling a snack like a sensible person would, I decided to hold out and make fondue—because on top of everything else, I expected myself to whip up a Julia Child–worthy spread for my man to enjoy after *his* long day.

I kicked off my chunky heels, put the *Swingers* soundtrack on the stereo, and got to work in the kitchen. I was cutting French bread into cubes when my left foot began to cramp. Over the years I'd gotten many foot cramps, often when dehydrated; though painful, they'd usually pass within a few seconds. Wincing, I gripped the cold edge of the counter, waiting for the cramp to subside—but it got worse. My foot contorted even further, like a deformed claw, as a searing pain shot up my calf. Tears sprang to my eyes and I heard blood pounding in my ears, edging out other sounds. The room started to spin and fade to black.

The next thing I remember is waking up with my face pressed against the checkerboard floor tiles, a sticky puddle of blood under my cheek. I knew I'd been unconscious for only a minute or so because the same Big Bad Voodoo Daddy song was still playing. "*You and me and the bottle makes three tonight. . . .*" I reached up to touch my face and discovered that my bottom lip was a pulpy mess—I must have bitten down into it when I passed out.

Shocked, I peeled myself off the floor and stumbled over to the bathroom to look in the mirror. The person looking back at me had three broken front teeth. Not just chipped but sheared off, as if with an ax. I stared at my reflection, aghast. When you suddenly lose your front teeth, you realize how attached you are to them. They may not be perfect, but they're an important feature of your face. Without them I looked hideous.

My hands were trembling as I picked up the phone and called Carl's office, where the writers were just winding down for the night.

"Honey? I had an acthident," I said with a new lisp, then sobbed, "*My teef are gone!*"

Carl told me to stay put; he would take me to the emergency room. While I waited for him, I drifted from room to room in a daze, changing out of my skirt into sweatpants, then venturing back into the kitchen to kneel on the floor with a roll of paper towels and mopping up the blood. When I came across the shards of my teeth, tiny and grotesque, I collected them in a Ziploc bag to bring to the hospital. In my trauma-induced stupor, I must've thought they could be reattached, like John Wayne Bobbitt's penis.

Carl got to my place in record time and, to his credit, did not recoil at the sight of my face. As he drove me to Cedars-Sinai, aggressively fighting the Friday night traffic, I sat slumped in the passenger seat of his Honda Accord with a wad of paper towels pressed to my bleeding mouth, gagging on the metallic taste. Soon the paper towels were soaked, so when we stopped at a red light, Carl took his shirt off and handed it to me. "Here, use this." He joked about how we must've looked with him driving like a maniac, shirtless, next to a girlfriend nursing a busted lip.

"It's like an episode of *Cops.*"

He had managed to make me laugh even in the direst of circumstances.

The emergency room was packed. Sitting on the hard waiting room chair, I had plenty of time to worry about whether there was something seriously wrong with my health and whether I'd be disfigured. When I was a kid, I saw a made-for-TV movie about a woman whose mouth got mangled in a car accident. She underwent seventeen reconstructive surgeries and finally *had to have tissue grafted from her labia to make a new pair of lips.* I was haunted by this story for weeks. I would stare at my eight-year-old face in the mirror, delicately applying strawberry ChapStick and praying I would never suffer this poor woman's fate. And now here I was, all these years later, in danger of having labia lips!

The ER surgeon who treated me was confident to the point of arrogance, but that was all right with me if he knew what he was doing. After numbing my lip with a giant shot of Novocain, he stitched it up while chatting with Carl at my bedside. His obligatory question, "What do you do?" led to an animated conversation about *Seinfeld*. The surgeon, like everyone else, had tons of ideas for *Seinfeld*.

He assured me that the wound would heal quickly and my scarring would be minimal. I silently thanked God that I would not need a transplant from my nether regions.

"Wha' abou' my teef?"

He referred me to a cosmetic dentist who would replace them with crowns. Then he ordered an EEG to see if I had a serious condition, like epilepsy, that might have caused me to lose consciousness. The test results were normal. I had passed out from the pain of the foot cramp, and it didn't help that I'd been anxious, sleep-deprived, and run down for weeks. In a way, this diagnosis was good news: I just needed to take better care of myself.

The problem was that I didn't really know how. En route to the hospital, I was already fretting over how to tell Dean I would have to miss work for a while. The stress that had consumed me since the overheard phone call was like a runaway train, and my mind was roiling with doubts and existential questions. Why was I letting a job I didn't care about kill me? And as long as we were pulling on that thread, why did I even come out to L.A. in the first place? Just to go on a handful of meetings with people who forgot about me the minute I walked out the door? Why the fuck was I doing this to myself?

When I returned to work a couple of weeks later, mostly healed, things were looking up. Dean, feeling sorry for me, was extra nice. And the long-awaited TV staffing season was underway. The hard work I had put into my *Buffy* spec paid off, and Larry gushed over it—well, as much as Larry ever gushed. He was cautious in his enthusiasm, not wanting to get my hopes up before deals were sealed. Many of the meetings I got from the spec were general ones, which to my mind were useful only because they were practice for staffing meetings. But I attended every meeting that came my way, no matter how pointless it seemed.

Then the impossible happened: I got a meeting at *Buffy*. Not at the studio or network, but the show itself. Usually when you write a spec for a show, it won't get you a meeting with the showrunner because, being so intimate with the material, they can tell how off your attempt to emulate it is. But two *Buffy* producers had read my spec and it passed muster. I would meet with them first, and if I made it through that hoop, they would pass my script along to the show's creator, Joss Whedon.

I don't remember much about the meeting except that I tried hard not to blow it. *Buffy* had become my favorite show, and I would've killed to write for it. After, Larry called me, excited—I had passed the test and the gatekeepers were giving my script to Joss. The next few days were miserable as I waited with bated breath for the phone to ring. By the time Larry called again, I was a massive ball of stress.

"He didn't respond to it." My heart sank. That was code for "he didn't like it," one of those industry euphemisms that makes no sense. Obviously, there was *some* response, just not a good one. "He thought it was well written, but that you were too green."

"What?"

"I know. I was like, of course she's green. She's never been on staff before."

Suddenly I was ashamed of the script I had just been so proud of. Self-doubt enveloped me, sucking me into a tailspin of insecurity. Was it true? Did my writing come off as green? What was I supposed to do about that? How do you write *less green*? Larry focused on the positive: I wrote a great spec that a lot of people "responded" to, got a meeting on a hit show, did well in that meeting, and was read by the actual showrunner. These small successes would lead to more opportunities. He assured me the future would be bright.

But I was haunted by Joss's words. Well, just that one: *green*. That word summed up the bind I was in. I had no experience as a writer, and I wasn't going to get any unless someone hired me. But they wouldn't hire me because I was too green. Now, I hadn't scored that high on the logic part of the SAT, but it didn't take a genius to figure out I was screwed.

Summer came and I didn't get staffed. *ATF* didn't get picked up, so Dean's deal with Sony ended and he went on hiatus. Which meant that I was jobless again.

I tumbled into a depression, spending the next two months moping around my sweltering apartment and literally sweating over my bank balance. When the heat became unbearable, I dragged myself to Fry's Electronics to buy (on credit) a portable air conditioner, at the time priced at a thousand dollars. The salesman said, with a patronizing smile, "You know these are expensive, right?"

Once I was no longer in danger of heat stroke, I attempted to write a script—a pilot, something in my own voice, just to prove I could. Blasting the air conditioner and sucking on Marlboro Reds, I squeezed out a drama based on my early days in New York as an aspiring writer toiling away at a corporate job. No matter how much I tinkered with it, the script just seemed like a bad imitation of the embarrassingly Gen X movie *Reality Bites,* so I never showed it to anyone. Despite Larry's pep talk, I didn't feel any closer to becoming a writer. Instead, I was filled with shame.

Then a ray of hope broke through. In mid-August, Larry told me that a new show on CBS called *Martial Law* was looking for freelance writers. I watched the videotapes he sent over, baffled by what I saw: a fat Chinese guy doing martial arts on a bad cop show. Not "bad" in a "so bad it's good" kind of way—just *bad.* The portly star was Sammo Hung, who had costarred with Jackie Chan in several Hong Kong action films. My brother and I used to watch *Kung Fu,* the culturally appropriated series starring David Carradine in yellowface.

This background notwithstanding, *Martial Law* was as far out of my wheelhouse as you could get. But it would be a paid writing job, so I did my best to come up with a few story ideas to pitch to the creator and executive producer, Carlton Cuse.

I went to the *Martial Law* office, located in a warehouse-like building in Van Nuys, to meet with Carlton. He was a tall, imposing figure with graying curly hair and a deep radio-host voice. He didn't appear to be impressed by my mediocre ideas, but he *was* impressed that I had memorized all of them for the pitch. I didn't know it was acceptable—in fact, customary—to refer to your notes in a pitch meeting. Despite my naïveté, I got hired to write an episode.

My first TV episode! I should've been ecstatic. Mostly I was in shock.

I scurried home and started pounding out the script, based on a flimsy idea I'd pitched about a kung fu showdown in a Chinese restaurant. Before I was even halfway done, Carlton offered me a staff job on *Martial Law*. He hadn't even seen my freelance script yet and he wanted to hire me full time. How did this happen?

Well, I found out later that half the staff had been fired after two months, and the show was now desperate for writers. This was not a good sign and certainly not the most auspicious way to kick off my TV writing career. But it's not like anyone else was asking me to the prom. Of course I said yes.

A little over a year had passed since those heady days of getting an agent, quitting *Letterman*, and moving to Tinseltown. And now I had what I came for. It took most people a lot longer to get their first break writing for television, and some never did. Though I had paid my dues, I couldn't deny that I'd been lucky. How did that old saying go? "Luck is what happens when preparation meets opportunity."

I had the opportunity. But nothing could've prepared me for what came next.

4

Baby Writer

On my first day as a television writer, my boss used me to fuck over one of the other writers. That writer, Barney, was in his late fifties and had been working in television for as long as I'd been alive. He had created a cheesy, inexplicably popular cop show when I was still playing with Barbies. And he was about to hate my guts.

That September morning in 1998, I came to work so nervous I could barely see straight. I expected to be introduced to the staff, perhaps at the morning meeting over bagels and coffee. But there was no morning meeting. The writers' offices were deserted; Carlton wasn't even there to welcome me. His assistant showed me to my office, a small room with not much more than a desk, a stiff loveseat, and a standard-issue halogen floor lamp. It had been recently vacated by one of the fired writing teams. Their names were still on the door.

For hours I sat at my bare desk, waiting for someone to tell me what to do. I passed the time by reading the first eight scripts of *Martial Law*, which I found stacked on an otherwise empty book case. These were the scripts that had gotten half of the writers fired. They looked fine to me. But what the hell did I know?

After what seemed like an eon, the assistant poked her head back in. "Carlton wants you to read this script and give notes this afternoon."

She handed me a new episode that Barney had written. I had no idea why Carlton would want my notes on another writer's script. I wasn't even sure what "notes" were. I assumed, correctly, that it's the industry euphemism for a "critique," which itself is a euphemism for "what's wrong with your script." But I was relieved to have an assignment and determined to do it well, so I hunkered down at my desk and went over the script with a fine-tooth comb. I didn't understand the political implications of a baby writer giving notes to a writer at Barney's level. It was my *first day* and I was about to critique someone with more than twenty years of experience.

Unlike the scripts I had just read, this one did not seem fine. The plot didn't make sense, the stage direction was confusing, and the dialogue sounded corny. All the characters had 1950s white-bread names like you'd find in a Hardy Boys book. I jotted my notes in the margins with a pencil, hoping I wasn't the only one who had unflattering things to say.

When I was called to Carlton's office, I walked into the huge, sparsely furnished room and was shocked to discover that the only people there were Carlton and Barney. And the only person giving notes was me. Scared, clueless, first-day-on-the-job me. I didn't know whether Carlton had already given Barney his notes or whether he would give them later, but he wasn't giving any now. He had called this meeting just to watch *me* give notes.

Barney, a stoic man with trim gray hair and steely eyes, was not happy. He didn't say much, but his anger was palpable. I'm not saying he would've felt better if I were a white man shredding his script to bits, but I suspect it didn't help that I was a young Asian woman. He glared at me like he'd been in the shit in Vietnam, and I was the gook who blew his legs off in a foxhole.

Carlton sat there silently, his mouth set in an implacable line, and watched this whole debacle play out. He didn't stick up for Barney, nor did he side with me. I plowed through my notes, trying to be as professional as possible, even though it was dawning on me that this situation was extremely fucked up.

I found out later that Carlton didn't like the script, either. My first day on the job must've presented an opportunity to kill two birds with one stone: (1) humiliate the old writer and (2) see what the new writer was made of. I would always be grateful to Carlton for giving me my first writing job, but I would never get over this ruthless initiation.

After the notes meeting, Barney's script was gutted and rewritten; what is known in the industry as a "page-one rewrite." In the writers' room, Barney glowered at me with silent vitriol, which made this unfamiliar place even less inviting. In the beginning, I had no idea what a writers' room was supposed to be like or what you were supposed to do in there. I never got any training, just like when I worked for Dean. I was starting to see a pattern: lack of communication was par for the course.

The writers' room at *Martial Law* was a conference room with whiteboards along the walls, its windows overlooking the parking lot and industrial wasteland beyond. It stank of Expo markers and baby back ribs from Dr. Hogly Wogly's Tyler Texas BBQ. Most of the ideas pitched in there were either met with icy silence or brusquely shot down, until no one dared say anything at all and we'd just stare at one another over our congealed takeout. At first, I mostly just listened. I heard later that Barney complained to the other writers that I had "nothing to contribute." Excuse me for trying to learn something before opening my mouth.

Most of what happens in a writers' room is called "breaking stories," which means plotting out an episode's scenes. At *Martial Law*, breaking stories was a torturous task that never got easier. I used to think coming up with ideas for TV shows would be fun. In college I had a weekend job as a short-order cook, and on my breaks, I'd jot down story ideas for *Beverly Hills, 90210*. (For example: "Brenda and Brandon give in to their incestuous urges, and Brenda gets pregnant with their two-headed love child.") But I just wasn't inspired by *Martial Law*, and the other writers didn't appear to be, either. Most of our brainstorming was pointless anyway, as ultimately the only important scenes were the martial arts. We joked that our show was like a porno movie: people fast-forwarded through the talking to get to the action.

Carlton was barely around, as this show was technically a side project for him. He was also the executive producer of another CBS cop show called *Nash Bridges*, starring eighties icon Don Johnson of *Miami Vice* fame. *Martial Law* was the network's attempt to capitalize on the success of *Nash Bridges*. Add the Carlton Cuse magic to a fat guy doing backflips and you've got a hit!

But it didn't work. The first mistake was putting one person in charge of two shows. Carlton was a seasoned showrunner, but everyone has limits. There are only so many hours in a day. The way it usually broke down was Carlton would spend most of the day at his *Nash* office in Burbank. At around six or seven p.m.—quitting time for most people—he would show up at *Martial Law*. By then, the rest of us had been there for eight hours and had to start our workday all over again.

We felt like neglected stepchildren. I understood why Carlton's priority was *Nash*, since it was a long-running hit show that the network was heavily invested in. A new show, on the other hand, needs to find itself, and the showrunner needs to have a vision. I don't think anyone had a vision for *Martial Law*.

When I joined the staff, I had already written an outline of the free-lance episode about the Chinese restaurant, which Carlton titled "Take Out." My story got re-broken in the writers' room without much help from me. Once the beats were laid out, I was dispatched to my office to write the script, which I did with the urgency of Pac-Man trying to outrun a mob of hungry ghosts. I had a week to finish the script before it went into preproduction, the phase when the director starts planning the shoot. This was the first time I had to write uncomfortably fast, and I'd have to keep doing it for the rest of my career.

After I turned in my first draft—technically called the "writer's draft"—Carlton gave it to Al and Miles, an experienced writing team who were his second-in-command. He made them do a pass on every script before he would even look at it. Another writer explained it to me this way: "Carlton likes to shop at Gelson's," she said, referring to an expensive grocery chain in Los Angeles. "Even though food from Ralphs"—a cheaper supermarket chain—"may be just as good, that doesn't matter. It needs to have the Gelson's name on it, or Carlton won't buy it." I was obviously Ralphs in this scenario.

After Al and Miles did their pass, Carlton would do his, implementing a bunch of lateral changes that made the script neither better nor worse, just different. The writers referred to this as Carlton "pissing on the script" because it was like a dog marking its territory. This pass would become the production draft—the version that got distributed to the staff, cast, and crew.

I'll never forget the experience of reading the production draft of my first episode. Here it was: the moment I'd been working for all those years, the first time something I wrote was going to get made by a real production company and aired on network television. Even though it wasn't a show I was proud of, I still couldn't wait to see my words in print.

My script was distributed on a Friday afternoon, and that weekend Carl and I drove up to a bed-and-breakfast in Montecito to celebrate. Our cottage was decorated in a quaint country style and appointed with every luxury. The bed's lily-white down comforter was so thick and fluffy, you could sink into it and make snow angels. I was a bona fide TV writer on a weekend getaway with her TV writer boyfriend, lounging around in a plush bathrobe and ordering mimosas and huevos rancheros from room service. I was living the dream.

After breakfast, I pulled the production draft from my bag and read it while soaking in the clawfoot bathtub. As I scanned the pages, I couldn't believe how little of my original work remained. After all the changes, the script was unrecognizable to me. My name was on the cover, as it would be on the screen when this thing aired—my first-ever "written by" credit. But I felt no connection to—let alone ownership of—the document in front of me. The huevos started to feel like a brick in my stomach and I wanted to retch.

When Al and Miles were busy, they would outsource their *Martial Law* rewrite work by farming out pages to the rest of us. We all became worker bees, writing disembodied scenes that would get stitched together into a Frankenstein of a script. During one of these communal rewrites—disturbingly known in the business as a "gang bang"—I was assigned to write a scene and had no idea where to begin. The outline was incomprehensible.

Luckily, a veteran writer named Pam had taken me and the other baby writers under her wing. I went to her office and asked for help. "Sure," she said. "We'll write it together."

Until then, writing had always been a solitary endeavor for me. I knew that writing teams collaborated on scripts, but I couldn't picture the mechanics of it. Pam guided me through it. She sat at her computer and typed while we talked through the scene, each of us pitching lines of action and dialogue. Every so often I'd start tearing my hair out, moaning, "This scene is idiotic! It makes no sense!" and Pam would nod and say, "I know. But we have to do it. Let's just shit it out."

The king of "just shitting it out" was a writer named Del, who also mentored me at the show. He cranked out scenes the way L. Ron Hubbard cranked out pulp sci-fi novels before turning them into the basis for Scientology. A playwright of gay Southern comedies, Del had no idea why someone with his sensibilities had been hired on *Martial Law.* I felt the same way. We were both fish out of water.

I suspected one reason *I* was hired was my ethnicity. Two of our lead actors were Chinese, and the show had martial arts in it. Thus, they needed at least one Asian writer for the optics, even though at the time, no one talked about diversity and inclusion. But my coworkers and I would joke about how I failed to represent my people. Once, when we were ordering lunch from Jerry's Deli, I asked for pastrami on rye and a chocolate egg cream. "Jesus, Patty," quipped one of the Jewish writers, "you're more Jewish than I am."

Given the differences in our backgrounds, we all got along well, with an exception here and there. One was Barney, who by this point had pretty much checked out. The other was a new writer, hired mid-season—in *his* mind, to save the show. A suburban punk kid in a middle-aged body, he had hair that was dyed canary yellow, the same shade as Tweety Bird.

At first Carlton treated Tweety like a partner, having private meetings with him and seeing him socially. Whenever Tweety had been to Carlton's house, he blabbed about it later to make us jealous.

Carlton seemed to have bought into the ex-junkie hipster persona that Tweety had cultivated. His indie film about a doctor addicted to heroin gave him lots of opportunities to mention his own former heroin habit. Dropping the H-bomb was his favorite way of trying to shock people and make them think he was cool.

Tweety made quick enemies by trying to assert his power. The first people he targeted were us baby writers. Instead of picking on someone his own size, he was like an insecure fifth-grade bully who stomps around the sandbox and terrorizes the kindergarteners.

It happened to me when I was assigned to cowrite an episode with another writer. We began breaking the story as a group, and because of my neat penmanship, I was put in charge of writing the story beats on the whiteboard. The "board writer" in TV rooms often ends up being a woman, not necessarily because we have better handwriting than men, but because we're still treated like secretaries. In fact, Carl told me a female writer he worked with on *Seinfeld* refused to do it because she thought it was sexist. But at this point in my career, I just wanted to be useful, so I grabbed that Expo marker with gusto.

Despite the usual hiccups, we got about half the episode's beats up on the board. The next morning, I arrived at work cautiously optimistic that we might finish the outline and be ready to pitch it to Carlton. A few of us were gathered around the table, waiting for the rest to arrive, when Tweety strode in with a smug look. Without saying a word, he grabbed an eraser and wiped the board clean, obliterating my tidy handwriting with a few dramatic sweeps of his arm.

The rest of us looked at one another, bewildered. Tweety turned to face me.

"You're off the hook, Patty. I'm cowriting this episode."

Off the hook? What did that mean? All I could get out was "Why?"

Turned out he had called Carlton the night before and told him that, based on what he'd observed, I was not excited to write this script. Taking Tweety's word for it, Carlton reassigned it to him. With a single phone call, Tweety had taken away my episode, my writing credit, my script fee, and any future residual payments I would've received for repeat airings. And perhaps even worse, he had made me look bad to my boss.

A tangle of confusion and outrage bubbled up in me. I had never once thought of backing out of the script. I wanted to do a good job, pay my bills, fulfill people's expectations. The idea that Carlton might see me as difficult and ungrateful—a first-year writer who thinks she can pick and choose her assignments—horrified me. Why would someone do this to me? What did I ever do to *them*?

Tears sprang to my eyes. Too shocked to defend myself, I just sat there speechless, willing myself not to blubber. When I was in kindergarten, there was an older girl who was mean to me for no reason. One day during recess, she grabbed me by the lapels of my pink cotton coat and *buttoned me to the flagpole*. I don't remember how I got free. Did another kid rescue me, or did I have the wherewithal to do it myself? Like most childhood traumas, this one shaped a core piece of my personality: fear of bullies. The incident with Tweety was pushing all my buttons, no pun intended. I felt like that little girl again, paralyzed and mute.

Del, bless his heart, jumped to my rescue. He rose from his chair and told Tweety that what he had done was reprehensible: he had stepped on me to promote his own interests. This led to a righteous, impassioned diatribe about basic human decency and dignity. "All anyone wants is to be treated with respect," he lectured, with a gravity out of character for a guy who was usually cracking bitchy jokes. By the end of his speech, the room was transfixed and Tweety had been shamed.

I never got my episode back, but Tweety got his comeuppance. It started when Al and Miles made some disparaging comments about him to Carlton. This raised Carlton's suspicions, and he started interviewing the other writer-producers to get their take. When he got to Del, any benefit of the doubt went right out the window. Del told him about the way I had seen Tweety intimidate and undermine people. He described the board-erasing incident, capping it with: *he made Patty Lin cry!*

The fact that Carlton now knew about this was embarrassing, but I was thankful that the truth had come to light. I heard that Carlton told Tweety to cut the shit and reduced his duties to two tasks: (1) showing up for work and (2) repairing his relationship with Del and me. How he was supposed to achieve the latter was left undefined.

At *Martial Law*, my stress level went through the roof. Now that I was a professional writer, I felt enormous pressure to succeed because the stakes were so high. I'd never been good at dealing with stress, as losing my front teeth had illustrated. But stress alone wasn't the problem—it was the fact that stress and success were linked in my subconscious.

I pulled my first all-nighter in my sophomore year of high school, writing a paper about *The Scarlet Letter*, a classic that made little sense to me until my teacher allowed us to watch the movie. I wrote the paper in a panic and then, euphoric with exhaustion, read it over and deemed it a masterpiece. I even kissed it before handing it in, inadvertently leaving lipstick on the page. When I got it back, my teacher had given me an A-plus. There was a smiley face drawn around the lipstick. From then on, I held a superstitious belief that I had to suffer to succeed, like a batter who thinks he needs to tap the plate three times before he can hit a home run.

As soon as I started at *Martial Law,* I had no life outside work. No time for exercise, hobbies, or leisure activities, though I needed those things now more than ever. I used to look forward to the day I could go to parties and tell people I was a writer. But now who had time for parties? My only friends in L.A. were my coworkers, and this would continue to be the case for most of my TV career. Could they really be called friends when you lost touch as soon as the show was over?

Meanwhile, Carl and I were barely seeing each other, even though *Seinfeld* had come to the end of its nine-year run the previous spring. I was looking forward to reconnecting with him, but instead of slowing down, he had signed a development deal with NBC and was now creating a pilot, consulting on a sitcom, and writing features on the side. I started to miss the days when he was at *Saturday Night Live.* At least I'd see him for a few fleeting hours on Sundays.

Over the holidays, I visited my parents and stayed in my old room, which they'd kept just as it was when I was a teenager, minus the Culture Club posters. Rummaging through my closet, I found the notebooks of Boy George fan fic that I wrote in middle school. I hadn't looked at them in fifteen years. I opened one, its cover frayed and falling off, and started reading.

In the first story, I'm married to Boy George and we have a young son. George comes home from his world tour wearing "masses of sequins and ragged hems," his hair a "disarray of striking colours." (My Anglophile phase included my spelling.) But our joyful reunion takes a turn when I broach a painful subject.

> *"George, I wish you weren't on tour so often," I said awkwardly. "I was so lonely without you here."*

"It's my job," George stated matter-of-factly. "I have to tour often."

I was disturbed by George's apathy. "You don't know what torture I go through every time you leave," I said, on the verge of tears. "Don't you understand that you're my everything? My friends and my job aren't enough for me. . . . I need you."

"I'm here and I love you." George shrugged carelessly. "What else do you need?"

"Stop it!" I cried. "You know that next year you're going on another tour. It's the same every time, George."

"So what should I do? Quit singing and be a janitor?"

I couldn't believe how eerily prescient this was. This could've been a conversation with Carl if you replaced "touring" and "singing" with "writing." *It's the same every time.* I had said these exact words whenever he promised to slow down. But Carl was the rock star, and I believed it was unfair of me to make demands on him. As much as I rued his neglect, I never wished he had a "regular" job, because his rock stardom was part of what I loved about him. Did my twelve-year-old self know I would have a relationship like this one day? Did my youthful fantasies lead me to *choose* it?

As I kept reading, my heart broke. Here's how the scene with George ends: he asks me to come on tour with him from then on. We'll even bring our son. "I don't have to be lonely anymore," I say. We embrace, tell each other "I love you," and fall into bed.

During my first week on the job, Carlton had smirked at the sparse outline I'd written for my freelance episode. I had clue-lessly filled in unknown plot points with the placeholder "and hijinks ensue." When he asked me to enumerate these hijinks, I had nothing. I saw him exchange an amused look with one of the other writers, the two of them bonded in their condescension. But over time, I began to figure things out. I started talking more in the room, pitching more ideas. The scenes I contributed to gang bangs were no worse than anyone else's. And little by little, I seemed to be earning Carlton's respect.

Then, toward the end of the season, he gave me a mandatory extra-credit assignment: watch every Hong Kong action film I could get my hands on and write a detailed synopsis of its plot. Why? So we could borrow their ideas. After months of arduous story breaking, Carlton decided it was time to find inspiration from some tried-and-true plotlines.

As I slogged through stacks of Blockbuster videotapes night after night, meticulously recording each story beat in a spiral notebook, resentment started to build. Yes, I was a lowly first-year writer, but Carlton should've given this task to a writers' assistant or, at the very least, split it between me and the other two baby writers. I assumed they didn't get stuck with it because they were white men. This wouldn't be the last time I felt like I wasn't taken seriously despite my title, credentials, and abilities.

I was sure that all this work would be for naught anyway since we were going to get canceled. But to everyone's surprise, CBS announced the show was being picked up for a second season, proving that you can never underestimate the taste of the American TV viewer. But here's the rub: the network was hiring a pair of executive producers to help Carlton run the show, and these guys were going to bring their own writers. Meaning that all of us first-season survivors were out.

When Carlton told me the news, he apologized for the turn of events and thanked me for my hard work. A few weeks later, he called me at home and asked me to fax him my notes from the Hong Kong action films. For use on season two. Which I would not be working on. As one last gesture of loyalty and obedience, I complied, but without bothering to type them up. He was lucky my handwriting was so legible.

My first reaction to getting fired was relief that I wasn't the only one. At least I could hold on to a tiny bit of self-respect. Still, when I told my parents the news, I could sense how let down they were. They had started to come around to the idea of my being a TV writer when I landed a legit job. With my writer's salary, I had been able to pay them back for moving expenses. For Christmas, I had given my dad a *Martial Law* windbreaker with the show's logo embroidered on it in English and Chinese, a jacket he would wear for years. My parents even took a picture of their TV screen when "Written by Patty Lin" appeared, then framed it and gave it to me as a souvenir. Yup: the worst part about getting fired was telling my parents.

My next reaction was abject panic. Would I ever be able to get another writing job? Everyone told me, "Getting your second job is harder than the first, because it costs more to hire you now." Plus, I was no longer a virgin without bad habits. *Martial Law* had broken my cherry in a fucked-up way, and I still had no clue how a normal show operated. Having *Martial Law* as the only credit on my résumé was almost as bad as having no credits at all.

5

The Staffing Hustle

After *Martial Law* wrapped in the spring of 1999, I got swallowed up by staffing season: the most miserable three months in a TV writer's year. This was the period from March until May when I had to be on call for meetings and read dozens of pilot scripts that my agent messengered to me. Every spring the floor of my apartment would become cluttered with lopsided stacks of scripts that I would trip over with irritating regularity.

Most of these shows would never get picked up, but some showrunners took meetings with writers just in case. If I landed a meeting, I had to be able to discuss the script. Since I was supposed to be on hiatus, sometimes I'd go out to lunch or to the beach, but I'd always bring at least one script with me, diligently whittling down the enormous "To Read" pile. Each script would then get put into one of four categories: Liked, On the Fence, Yuck (keep until staffing season ends, then recycle), or Seriously Yuck (keep for future ridicule).

The fact that I hadn't read a book for pleasure in more than a year gnawed at me. Had I become one of those semi-literate El-Lay people? At least I didn't read the trade magazines anymore. When I worked for Dean, I used to peruse his copies of *The Hollywood Reporter* and *Variety*, struggling to decode their insider lingo, until I realized that reading about some twenty-three-year-old "scribe" who got a million-dollar deal to "pen" a script for "helmer" Steven Spielberg wasn't helpful. All it did was annoy the shit out of me and make me feel like a loser.

Whenever a staffing meeting was scheduled for me, a UTA messenger would come to my apartment and drop off a videotape of the pilot. This usually meant a rough cut with a bad temp score (placeholder music) and missing scenes. I'd watch the tape, praying it was decent so that I wouldn't have to depend on my poor acting skills in the meeting. "The pilot turned out great!" (said too loudly with a forced smile). In addition to pilots, existing shows would also hire new writers. Once in a while I'd get meetings on shows I watched regularly. More often they were on shows I'd never seen. To prepare, I'd binge-watch an entire season in a day or two—less fun than it sounds.

All this preparation was a full-time job. Staffing season was a lot like applying to colleges, but instead of a stellar academic record, I had one lame credit. "Meeting" implied something more casual than a traditional job interview, but I was never relaxed in them. They felt like the piano competitions my parents forced on me when I was a kid. (I know, shocking: another Asian girl who played the piano.) No matter how much I practiced beforehand, performance anxiety would make me choke.

Over time, meetings got slightly less nerve-racking, and soon my agent started saying, "You're great in meetings." I had no idea what he was talking about. The few times I felt like I'd nailed it, I didn't get the job. So I stopped trusting my own instincts and started erring on the side of pessimism to manage my expectations. It was less painful than having my hopes dashed.

One night that spring, I was taking a bubble bath to relax when the memory of the bathtub in Montecito, where my writer's dreams were crushed, popped into my head. My thoughts spiraled into negativity, and the anxiety I'd been trying to keep under control came whooshing up to drown me. I was sure I'd never get another writing job again.

"Honey?" I called out to Carl, who was in the living room watching *The Simpsons.*

"Yeah?"

"Barney said I was a bad writer. He said I didn't contribute." Carl huffed. "Who gives a shit what he thinks?"

"Tweety called me a bad writer, too."

"So what? He's an asshole."

But even though I didn't respect either of these men, their opinions of me triggered my imposter syndrome, reinforcing my belief that I was unworthy. I never sat around obsessing about the *good* things people said about me, but one unflattering remark would stick in my brain and get replayed again and again.

I'm a bad writer. Here's proof.

One day in late April, Larry called and asked in an urgent voice if I had read a pilot titled *Freaks and Geeks.* I rummaged through the stack next to my desk and found it in the "Liked" pile. I had read lots of high school shows, but two things stuck out about *Freaks and Geeks.* First, it was a period piece that took place in 1980. Second, much of the pilot's plot revolved around an intellectually disabled character named Eli. My overall impression was that the script had some funny dialogue and promising characters, but I couldn't quite picture the show.

"It didn't blow me away, but it was kind of interesting."

He didn't care whether I liked it or not. "The writer, Paul Feig, has a deal with Judd Apatow to produce the show," he said, almost manic. "They want to meet with you."

As he rattled off Judd's credits, I understood his excitement. Judd was a hot producer, a wunderkind in his early thirties who had run *The Larry Sanders Show*, a comedy about a neurotic late-night host played by Garry Shandling. Judd had worked closely with Jim Carrey, Adam Sandler, and Ben Stiller, and seemed to have a hand in every comedy property in town. But he had me at *Larry Sanders*. That show prompted me to splurge on HBO back when I was struggling to pay rent; it was hilarious and so realistic. Judd was obviously a rock star.

My meeting with Judd and Paul was held at a bungalow across the street from the CBS Radford lot, a temporary space they were using for preproduction. When Paul introduced himself, Judd was busy talking on the phone in the next room. I was afraid this was a bad sign, but I ended up grateful to have time alone with Paul, because we really clicked.

A gangly Midwesterner in his late thirties, Paul reminded me of Peter Tork from the Monkees. He was so nice that I wondered if he'd only just arrived in Hollywood. But no, he'd been around for years, working as a character actor—he played the science teacher on *Sabrina the Teenage Witch*—before taking up writing. He wrote *Freaks and Geeks* on spec, meaning that he did it with the *hope* that a network would buy it. Luckily, Judd was looking for a pilot to produce. He read Paul's script . . . and here we were.

By this point, I was used to apologizing for my one credit, explaining that I never intended to write for an action show. But to my surprise, Paul said that he dug *Martial Law*. All those times

I wondered, "Who the hell is watching this?" the answer was: Paul Feig. With his nerdy penchant for martial arts, he appreciated the show more than I did.

We discovered we had a lot in common. We both grew up in the Midwest in the early eighties. We both liked classic rock and adored Styx, a Chicago band whose music Paul wrote into the pilot. "Come Sail Away," a bombastic prog-rock epic about aliens coming to Earth, was my favorite song when I was a kid. Like the show's lead character, Lindsay, I was an honor student and dated a pothead drummer in high school, allowing me to straddle both the freak and geek worlds. But I was a geek at heart, just like Paul.

The more we talked, the more I began to overlook my initial ambivalence. Paul had a clear vision for the show: realistic, character-driven, and funny. I liked the fact that he was weird. Talking to him made me feel like a kid again, the one who sang along to Billy Joel songs and made my *Star Wars* figures interact with my Muppet Babies. I'd stuffed that part of myself away, embarrassed by it, and this was an invitation to embrace it again.

Judd finally wrapped up his calls and joined us. He had dark curly hair and heavy-lidded eyes, and he talked in a fast surfer-bro lilt. His brisk, efficient manner made me nervous—but he was also very funny. It wasn't until years later that I saw a stand-up act he had done in 1992 on HBO's *Young Comedians Special* and realized that underneath the über-producer persona, he was just a dorky guy who lived and breathed comedy.

After taking meetings, Judd and Paul auditioned their prospective writers by making us submit ten story ideas for *Freaks and Geeks*. They were trying to suss out whether we got the show. After my long talk with Paul, I felt like I understood the kind of stories he wanted to tell. Bizarre stories. Embarrassing stories. Stories you didn't normally see on television. These were the three pitches I was most proud of:

> *One of the geeks gets an after-school job at a funeral home. When a woman's corpse is brought in, the geeks use this as an opportunity to look at a naked woman's body for the first time.*

> *One of the freaks tries to commit suicide by sitting in his car in the garage and leaving the engine running, but he forgets to close the garage window and ends up alive and even more depressed. He soon discovers the silver lining: chicks are turned on by screwed-up guys, and his suicide attempt makes him a babe magnet.*

> *Eli takes a shit in the school's swimming pool, causing an emergency evacuation. Everyone mercilessly ridicules Eli. Taking pity on him, Sam lies, telling everyone that he planted a phony turd, à la* Caddyshack. *When the principal threatens to suspend Sam, he has to decide whether he wants to save his own ass or help Eli.*

These also happened to be the three ideas my agent objected to when I sent him the list.

"These ideas are sort of . . . out there," Larry warned.

"I know, but I really think Paul and Judd would go for them. Especially Paul."

"I just think they're too . . . edgy."

"But isn't edgy good? It's an edgy show."

"Yeah, but some of these are *too* edgy."

He advised me to cut my three favorite stories, repeatedly using the words *out there* and *edgy*. But my instincts told me that Paul and Judd would not be offended. Even though I wasn't in the habit of trusting my instincts—or disagreeing with my agent—I stuck to my guns and refused to cut anything.

"If I'm gonna miss the mark, I'd rather do it being outrageous than playing it safe."

Larry protested with everything he had, but he finally accepted my decision. Paul and Judd loved my submission. Years later Larry told me, "One of the biggest mistakes I made as an agent was trying to get you to cut those ideas." This was an important lesson for me: to trust my own instincts and fight for them if necessary.

Next, I was summoned to meet the development executive at DreamWorks who was overseeing the production. He was a hipster with a shaved head who said "cool" a lot. After a brief chat, he sat me down in an empty office and left me alone to watch a tape of the near-completed pilot.

Any lingering doubts dropped away. The execution of this pilot was stunning. The casting, music, directing, acting, cinematography, costumes, set design—all of it was inspired. I almost jumped out of my chair with glee as I watched the geeks wandering awkwardly through the cafeteria, their conversation peppered with *Star Trek* and *Star Wars* references. Boba Fett joke? William Shatner impression? You could actually *do* those things? Most high school shows had conventionally attractive actors in their twenties or even thirties playing teenagers. But the kids on *Freaks and Geeks* were young and funny-looking. They looked real.

The most exciting scene was one where the lead geek, Sam—played by a skinny, wide-eyed thirteen-year-old named John Francis Daley—gets pummeled with dodgeballs in gym class. In the script the scene was funny; onscreen it was electrifying. It was like watching a great action movie—Indiana Jones getting chased by a boulder, if Indiana Jones were a geek—which, come to think of it, he was.

Halfway through the tape, the hipster popped back in. "What do you think?"

I struggled to peel my eyes off the screen. Where to begin? I went on and on about the cast, the music, and one of the best things about the show: the pacing. Most shows had a frenetic pace that catered to short attention spans. Not this one. The director, Jake Kasdan, who would go on to direct several more episodes, knew when to let scenes breathe and when to pick up the pace. The result was a perfectly orchestrated ride, its ups and downs mirroring real life.

Clearly, this show was special. Never before had I been so eager to be a part of something. The minute I left the building, I whipped out my phone and called Larry.

"You gotta get me on this show."

I never begged, so he knew this was serious.

"I'll do my best," he said, and hurried off to do recon.

A few days later the TV networks announced their fall lineups. *Freaks and Geeks* was officially on the NBC schedule. Soon after, Larry called to tell me I was hired.

"Really?" I squealed. "Are you fucking kidding me?"

This was the elated reaction I should've had when getting my first job but couldn't manage to drum up (for obvious reasons). *Freaks and Geeks* was my do-over, the show I was meant to write for. I couldn't believe my luck. Not only had I gotten my second job, but I'd gotten it on one of the best shows I had ever seen.

Before the job started, Carl and I went on a vacation in Kauai. You'd think that while I laid out by the pool, basted with suntan oil and buzzed on piña coladas, I'd be flipping through gossip magazines or diving into a juicy novel. Instead, I read *How to Meditate: A Guide to Self-Discovery*, a spiritual self-help book with the Tree of Life on its cover. The path that led me to this choice was a long one.

My interest in meditation began when I was eleven, when I moved to New Jersey and was plagued by migraines and other mysterious symptoms. One day I was sorting through a box of old books in our garage and came across a paperback titled *Self-Hypnotism: The Technique and Its Use in Daily Living*. It was written by a clinical psychologist who claimed that many physical ailments are "caused by hidden influences from the subconscious mind." I tried the exercises in the book and discovered that counting to a hundred while staring at a candle flame did make my skull feel less like it was going to explode. The self-hypnosis methods were essentially meditation, though I didn't know it at the time.

Then, when I was a teenager, I became a huge fan of the Beatles and fell in love with *The White Album* while smoking pot for the first time. I later found out that they'd written the album in India while studying meditation with the Maharishi in 1968. The song "Dear Prudence" was written about Mia Farrow's sister, who was at that retreat with the Beatles and who became so devoted to meditating that she wouldn't come out of her room, not even for meals. I wondered what could make someone want to sit in the lotus position, alone and in silence for days on end, missing out on all that delicious curry. Another seed planted.

Cut to my early twenties in New York, when I listened to Howard Stern's radio show every morning. Between mocking his producer Baba Booey and leering at women's breasts, Howard often talked about how his daily meditation practice helped him cope with stress. The mental image of the shock jock ohm-ing in his limo on the way to work was absurd, but something about it spoke to me. By the time I headed to Kauai with *How to Meditate* in my suitcase, I was tired of living with constant stress and longed for an alternative.

This was not a "For Dummies" book. I didn't understand everything, though I tried, underlining passages and reading them over and over. But as the author says, there's no substitute for the *experience* of meditating. He suggests doing it for fifteen minutes to see what it feels like. So, stretched out on my chaise longue, I closed my eyes and started counting breaths, trying to block out the sound of kids screaming in the pool. I didn't even get to three before my mind was racing with thoughts.

This is so stupid. Why am I doing this instead of getting a massage? Should I buy that orange sarong in the gift shop? I hope Paul and Judd don't realize they've made a huge mistake. . . . Trying to shut off this stream of mental chatter was like waving a red flag in front of a bull— the thoughts just grew louder and more insistent. It was shocking to see how little control I had over my own brain.

I had clearly fucked up my first attempt at meditation. I gave myself a pass and concluded that to do it right, I would need to "figure it out" first, perhaps by rereading *How to Meditate* several more times. But after Hawaii, that book went right onto the bookshelf, its contents forgotten as the new job took over my life.

6

Laughs and Gaffes

Before *Freaks and Geeks* started, Paul Feig made us all read the bible. The series bible, that is. A bible is usually an overview of a show's premise, characters, and story arcs, written solely for the purpose of selling a pilot to a network. But Paul's wasn't some throwaway to appease the executives. It was a massive collection of detailed character biographies and enough story ideas to last several seasons. *Martial Law* never had an ounce of this kind of planning.

Our other homework was to fill out a questionnaire meant to get us thinking about our teenage memories and inspire ideas for the show. Questions like, "What was your most embarrassing high school moment?" I remembered mine clearly. When I was a freshman, I drew a portrait of a junior I had a crush on, a skater dude who, with his long face and spiky mullet, looked like Ric Ocasek from the Cars. I submitted the drawing to my school's literary journal. What was I thinking? When it was published, the whole school knew I was in love with skater dude and he never spoke to me again. Normally, I wouldn't reveal this to a bunch of people I had just met, but the questionnaire encouraged us to open up. No personal pain was too trivial or mortifying to mine for material.

Many of those high school memories got put to use when we brainstormed for the second episode, called "Beers and Weirs," following the rhyming trend set by the series title. In this episode, Sam and Lindsay Weir, the earnest siblings at the heart of the show, throw a keg party when their parents go out of town. You've heard this setup before, I'm sure. But unlike standard teen fare, we weren't going to have beautiful, popular kids mixing with nerds and burnouts, *Breakfast Club*-style. This party would just be the nerds and burnouts.

After we finished outlining the episode, we broke into small groups to plot out the next few. *Freaks and Geeks* had eight writers on staff, including Paul and Judd. I was the only person of color, and one of two women in the room. Our show was a "dramedy"—a cross between a drama and a comedy—but the only other drama writer besides me was Mike White, who had written for *Dawson's Creek* (and who would go on to create the Emmy Award–winning series *The White Lotus*). The rest came from comedy. I was intimidated by everyone's credits and experience.

I got put into a group with Paul and a wisecracking bald guy named Bob who had written for *The Drew Carey Show*. After the writers' room at *Martial Law*, I was terrified of having "nothing to contribute," especially in a gathering of three where I'd have nowhere to hide. But my fear melted away when it seemed like Paul and Bob didn't know what they were doing, either.

"I've never been good at this part," said Bob, seconds after he had me rolling on the floor. "Breaking a story, figuring out what happens next. I just never know how to do it."

"Me neither," said Paul.

My whole body relaxed. They were human—thank God, I stopped feeling like a five-year-old in a college class.

Freaks and Geeks provided the kind of structure I'd craved at my last job. We had daily writers' meetings, led by Judd and Paul, in a conference room at Raleigh Studios, our permanent home across from the Paramount lot. The atmosphere was the opposite of what I was used to: everyone was encouraged to participate. Our ideas didn't have to be fully baked; even a dash of something funny or interesting was welcomed.

Sometimes Judd would set a kitchen timer for ten minutes and tell us to jot down as many ideas as we could, no matter how small or stupid. He made it into a game. This short-circuited our inner critics, and without the pressure of producing quality, ideas came easily. The writers' assistant would then gather everyone's pages and make photocopies. We'd sit around reading all the crazy stuff that came from people's streams of consciousness, laughing our asses off. And, like magic, within a few weeks we had several binders filled with ideas.

But we ended up basing many stories on the personal experiences of Paul Feig. As twisted as our childhoods might be, they couldn't compare to, say, young Paul wearing a disco jumpsuit to school and getting teased mercilessly for it. He was a fount of anecdotes about cringeworthy rejections from girls and locker room humiliations. After he kept mentioning the term "dogpile," one of the writers finally asked, "What the hell is that?"

"It's when a bunch of naked jocks pounce on a geek in a locker room." Paul explained that this was a common occurrence where he grew up. As far as I know, nothing that homoerotic ever happened in *my* school, but I could be wrong.

I was assigned to cowrite my first *Freaks and Geeks* script with Paul. But he became busy with production duties, so Judd sent me off by myself to flesh out some ideas I'd pitched in our brainstorming sessions. I wanted to write a story where Sam discovers that Cindy Sanders, the perky cheerleader he has a crush on, is not the perfect dream girl: she eats junk food, burps like a frat boy, and has a little bit of a mustache. After noodling with the idea, I went back to Judd for feedback. He seemed unsure about it and told me to ask Mike White for help.

Mike and I happened to have adjoining offices. Mine was bigger, with a couch and a picture window facing Melrose Avenue. They'd offered it to Mike first, but he wanted to be farther from the hallway, since he was writing a feature in his downtime and needed privacy. I knocked on the door between us.

"Hey, Mike? You got a minute?"

He came in and sat on my couch, resting his sneaker-clad feet against the coffee table. I liked Mike a lot. He had a skittish, intense way of talking, and he was kind of a genius. After pitching his first episode, he came in *the next morning* with a complete outline where every beat was laid out, great new characters were introduced, and snippets of clever dialogue were sprinkled throughout. No doubt I could've used his help with my episode.

But I wanted help with *my* idea, not a brand-new one. When I told him that Judd was on the fence about my story, Mike pitched a different one, laying out plot points so fast that I couldn't believe he was talking off the top of his head. I transcribed it all on a legal pad, my hand cramping. After he left, I looked at my notes and thought, *I can't write this.* The story had nothing to do with my personal experience. I'd have to knock on Mike's door every five minutes and ask him what came next.

I reported back to Judd. "Did you talk to Mike?" he asked.

"Yes. And he came up with a really funny story." Before I could chicken out, I added, "But Mike should write that story, not me."

To my relief, he agreed to shelve Mike's idea. But I worried that my refusal made me look uncooperative, the way Tweety's phone call with Carlton had done. Why couldn't I just shut up and do as I was told? That night I barely slept, worried sick even though Judd didn't seem upset with me. But in the end, I was glad I'd held out for what I wanted. Judd eventually approved my idea, and I got to write a script I was excited about, which turned out much better than if I'd written one that someone else had pitched.

The next few weeks were heaven. I got my assignment and my deadline, and everyone left me alone until I was done. I left my office only to attend the morning meetings and forage for snacks. Because the show's subject matter was so personal, I was able to use material from my own life. The maudlin poetry that Cindy submits to the yearbook club was based on some pretentious dreck I wrote at the depths of adolescent despair. In a scene where Lindsay's parents corner her for the sex talk, I borrowed a line from my own mother: "Your virginity is a gift." She told me this when I was twenty-three, by the way. Let's just say her advice was a little late.

After Paul and I each finished writing our half of the script, titled "Girlfriends and Boyfriends," we camped out at his desk and worked together to finesse it. The process was easy and full of laughs. Despite my greenness, Paul treated me as an equal. I can't remember a single time he shot down my ideas. I'm sure it happened—not all of them were gold—but he must've done it with such kindness that it didn't even leave a mark.

I cowrote my second episode, "The Garage Door," with Gabe and Jeff, a team who had come from sitcoms. They treated me as an equal, just like Paul did. But I discovered that Judd was harder on them than he was on me. I don't know if this was because they were men or because he sensed that I was insecure and needed a gentler hand. The notes I got from Judd on my first script were direct but never mean. On this script, however, he scrawled notes like, "PEOPLE WILL BE TURNING OFF THEIR TELEVISION SETS." Yes, in ALL CAPS. Gabe and Jeff tore that page out and hung on to it as a souvenir.

My relationship with Judd turned a corner when he asked me to make notes on a script that Bob, the *Drew Carey* guy, had written. I didn't know if this was some sort of test, like what Carlton did to me on my first day at *Martial Law*. Bob was a talented writer and a kind person. The last thing I wanted to do was make him look bad. But there were things I would've done differently in his script. Should I be honest about that?

I decided to go for it, hoping Bob wouldn't take it personally. Judd liked most of my suggestions and instructed Bob to use them in his next draft. To my knowledge, Bob didn't gripe. We remained friends, and if anything, I looked up to him even more because of the graceful way he handled the situation.

From then on, Judd had me give notes on every episode. He'd say, "Do what you did to Bob's script." Seeing my ideas appear in the next draft made me feel useful. In any job, the best moments were when I felt useful.

All the *Freaks and Geeks* writers produced their own episodes, whether we were at the producer level or not. This meant that we were involved in casting, location scouts, shooting, and editing. Judd and Paul insisted that a writer always be on set to collaborate with the director and to make sure the show's vision was intact.

We started shooting "Girlfriends and Boyfriends" in October 1999. On the first day, I showed up at the location, a sporting goods store in Monrovia, feeling unsure of what I was supposed to do. (At *Martial Law*, the writers never went to the set, except to score lunch from the catering tent.) Thankfully, Paul was there to lead the way. While the crew was setting up, he turned to me and said, "You've been doing a great job, Patty. I just want you to know it hasn't gone unnoticed."

My heart soared. In a way, I wanted to please Paul even more than I did Judd. They were both parental figures to me, but Judd was like a dad and Paul was like a mom. I didn't realize until later in my career how rare it was for someone in his position to be so complimentary. Most showrunners are either too self-absorbed or too protective of their own power to dole out crumbs of praise to their minions. Paul was one of a kind.

The director of our episode was Lesli Linka Glatter, who would go on to become one of the most sought-after TV directors and the president of the Directors Guild of America. At first, Paul was the one giving Lesli notes during the shoot, usually about how the actors were interpreting a line of dialogue or a physical action. But then he got pulled into other business, leaving me to collaborate with Lesli. She made it easy for me. After every take she'd lean over and ask, "What'd you think of that?" If I had any notes she didn't agree with, we discussed them. But we agreed most of the time.

That shoot was the best eight days I would ever spend on a set. To be honest, I preferred being alone at my desk, writing. That's just my nature. But that week was magical.

When Judd gave an introductory pep talk to the cast, he joked, "I don't want to see anyone end up as an *E! True Hollywood Story*." It was a testament to the show's casting that many of the young actors went on to be not only successful but well-adjusted. Most of them were humble, hardworking, and thrilled to be there. *Freaks and Geeks* was the only show I ever worked on where I became real friends with the actors. Maybe it was because we were all around the same age, or because we spent so much time on a set that looked like a high school.

While I adored most of the actors, I became especially close with Jason Segel. He played Nick, the drummer freak who is Lindsay's love interest. Jason would go on to have a fruitful career, starring in the TV comedies *How I Met Your Mother* and *Shrinking*, as well as writing and starring in *Forgetting Sarah Marshall* and other films. Only nineteen at the time, he wasn't the type that made girls swoon, but he was cute. He had warm brown eyes, a goofy smile, and a tall, lanky frame—like, basketball-player tall. In fact, he used to play basketball, just like his character.

He was also a pothead, just like his character. That was something we had in common. While shooting "Girlfriends and Boyfriends," we sussed out our mutual interest and became stoner buddies. We never got high at work, but occasionally we'd smoke a bowl in the evening with Seth Rogen, who played one of the freaks—his first acting job ever. Back then he was just an unknown seventeen-year-old Canadian. You might judge me for smoking pot with a minor, but trust me, I didn't introduce Seth Rogen to marijuana. I can't take credit for that.

Even at that age, Seth was a riot. One weekend Busy Philipps, who had also just been discovered, had a party at her Manhattan Beach apartment. Seth started cracking jokes in his deep, mumbling deadpan about the rubber duckie–themed decor in Busy's bedroom. There were yellow ducks everywhere, in the form of stuffed animals, pillows, candles, soaps. Seth said, "You ever notice how girls just pick an animal and go with it?" (It's true. I did it with pigs.) He kept riffing for ages, pumping out joke after joke. It was as natural for him as coughing after a bong hit.

But sometimes Jason and I hung out without Seth. One night after a shoot in Newhall, we had a late dinner at the Outback Steakhouse, before and after which we toked up in his car in the parking lot, passing a small brass pipe back and forth and sharing deep thoughts. And that was when I started having feelings for Jason, despite our nine-year age gap and the fact that I already had a boyfriend.

It was impossible not to like Jason. He had a positive attitude and did his job without any complaints. Not only was he an intuitive actor, but a budding writer and musician as well. We lounged in the front seats of his Land Rover, the weed making time stretch like taffy. We talked about acting and writing, our career goals, his fear of fame, our love of privacy, and the need for solitude. It was the kind of conversation that makes you fall in love with someone. Judd once told me he'd had a conversation like that in a car with the actress Leslie Mann, when they were working on *The Cable Guy*. They ended up married.

Eventually I had to pee. By now the parking lot was empty except for us, and the restaurant had closed, so Jason drove me to a Hampton Inn nearby, where I ran in to use the lobby restroom. As he drove me back to my car, I asked, "How'd you know about that hotel?"

"I saw the sign from the parking lot."

"Oh. I thought maybe you'd had a rendezvous here or something."

Jason laughed. We started talking about hotels where people go to hook up. He surmised the only reason there was a Ritz-Carlton in Pasadena was for rich Hollywood guys to have affairs. *Affairs*. As we pulled up to my car, I noticed how the conversation had taken a suggestive turn, and I had a wild impulse to ask Jason to spend the night with me at the hotel where I'd taken a leak. Granted, the Hampton Inn was no Ritz-Carlton, but I'd had sex in worse accommodations. Tethered by a shred of propriety, I stamped out the urge to kiss him and gave him a hug instead.

"See you tomorrow," I said, feeling his stubble graze my neck.

Zipping down the freeway in my Camry, I replayed the whole evening in my head. I felt intoxicated by Jason's attention, even though I knew it was wrong. Carl and I had been together for six years. But he was more work-obsessed than ever, and my frustration had been growing. I hadn't told him I was going to dinner with Jason, maybe because I knew in the back of my mind that it wasn't entirely innocent.

Carl was the jealous type. When we first started dating, we ran into a few guys I'd slept with. After that, whenever I introduced him to a guy, he'd say, "Did you fuck him?" as soon as he was out of earshot. It pissed me off that he had the gall to be both possessive and neglectful, but I was too afraid to confront him. He could get mad about the smallest things—he once flew into a rage when I'd gotten my hair cut short, refusing to talk to me for hours. In fact, every time I changed my hair, he'd yell, "You ambushed me!" If this was how he reacted to new bangs, I could only imagine what he'd do if he found out I was attracted to someone else.

That night, I woke up at three a.m. with my bed shaking. For a split second, I thought it was Carl: somehow he found out I'd gotten stoned with a cute actor, had barged into my apartment, and was now standing at the foot of my bed, jostling it angrily. Either that or I was possessed by the devil and was about to spew green vomit while my head spun around.

But it was just an earthquake. I lay there on my shuddering mattress, trying to remember the emergency protocol. Was I supposed to stand under a doorframe? Go outside? Crawl under a table? Before I could do any of these things, the shaking stopped. Nothing fell or broke. I was fine, just freaked out. But of course I looked for the symbolism. My very first earthquake, and it happened on the night I was tempted to cheat on Carl? Was this some cosmic warning that I was headed down a dangerous road?

If so, I ignored it. The next day I went to visit Jason in his dressing room during a break in shooting. Costumed in a polyester shirt and corduroy pants, he was reclining on a loveseat with a phone pressed to his ear. He waved me in.

"I'm on hold with Pottery Barn. Ordering chairs for my new dining table."

I sat next to him and he shifted so that his head was resting on my lap. I took this as my cue to give him a head rub. He closed his eyes and purred, "I think you should break up with your boyfriend and massage my head all day long—yes, six of the Stella dining chairs in Tuscan chestnut."

After he hung up, I asked him the question that had been eating away at me. "What would've happened if I had asked you to check into that hotel with me last night?"

Jason shrugged. "We would've effed."

So the chemistry between us wasn't just in my head! He felt it, too. . . . But before either of us could make a move, I heard the bell signaling that the shoot had resumed, and we had to report back to set. I was saved by the bell. Literally.

My birthday came later that week. Carl had to go out of town for work, so I used that as an excuse to make dinner plans with Jason. All day long I toggled between guilt and anticipation. Then I noticed Jason flirting with Linda Cardellini, the actress who played Lindsay. Linda was in her mid-twenties, with a heart-shaped face and a wide smile. She was just starting out in a career that would later include roles in *ER, Mad Men, Brokeback Mountain*, and *Dead to Me*. My heart sank when Jason came up to me and asked, "Where do you want to go for your birthday dinner? And is it okay if Cardellini comes?"

He explained something about her going through a hard time and not wanting to be alone. I couldn't say no. It wasn't like this was a date. Not officially, anyway.

The two of them came over to my place for a pre-dinner smoke. While Linda explored my apartment, Jason handed me a small birthday gift wrapped in tissue paper. I ripped it open to find a blown-glass pipe with a blue swirly design.

"It's from me and Seth."

"Aw, you guys."

I loaded the bowl with a fresh tuft of weed and the three of us got baked. As usual, the pot relaxed my overly analytical brain, and soon I forgot about my earlier worries and was having a blast—until Linda pointed to pictures of Carl on my bookshelf.

"How did you guys meet?"

I felt awkward talking about Carl in front of Jason. But I went ahead and told them the story of When Carl Met Patty, from the day I asked him for *Letterman* tickets to where we were now. I should've known that any chance of hooking up with Jason died when I mentioned "you should get a bigger button." Linda's reaction was typical: *how romantic, it was fate, you were meant to be together.* Yet here I was spending my birthday with two coworkers I hardly knew instead of my boyfriend. Something was wrong with this picture.

We ate dinner at Fred 62, a hipster diner in Los Feliz, sitting in a horseshoe-shaped booth with Jason in the middle. For dessert, Jason and Linda got me a brownie sundae with birthday candles. When I blew them out, I made a silent wish: *kiss me, Jason Segel.* But all I got when he dropped me off later was a brotherly hug.

The next day on set, Jason stopped by video village, the cluster of monitors behind which the crew gathers, and sat in the chair next to me, his brow creased with unease. Lesli was off giving notes to the actors, and we were momentarily alone. He gestured to a string of wooden beads around my wrist.

"Are those the prayer beads Lesli gave you for your birthday?"

I nodded. "My wish still hasn't come true," I said, fingering the bracelet, "and now I'm praying on the beads."

"Six years is a long time. I don't want to ruin your boyfriend's life."

"His life isn't gonna be ruined."

"It *will* be if he loses you."

I was crushed like a lovesick teenager. Maybe Jason was being honest, and if so, his moral code was impressive for a guy his age. But I had a feeling that whatever had been brewing between us was barely a blip compared to what was going on with Linda. And I was right: before long they were a couple, their union deemed by everyone as cute and inevitable. Linda was beautiful and talented, not to mention a cool person. I never stood a chance.

My excitement about being on set didn't last long. The problem was that not every director was Lesli Linka Glatter. One director got upset with me for speaking to the actors—something only the director is supposed to do. There were countless unwritten rules I learned the hard way. In this business, you can't go directly where you want to go; there's always some circuitous route you need to take to avoid stepping on toes. You can't even move a piece of tape on the floor because that's a specific person's job. But no one told me this stuff. I had to figure it out for myself.

When I was due on set for my next script, "The Garage Door," I was relieved that my cowriters, Gabe and Jeff, would be there as allies. Our director was Bryan Gordon. He had to endure not one but *three* writers' notes. Sensing his frustration, we designated Jeff as our spokesperson so that he wouldn't feel outnumbered, but he still seemed to resent our being there.

On all the shows I've worked on, most directors treated writers like a nuisance. I once heard a writer refer to this part of her job as being the "designated set bitch" because she had to fight the director on everything. Interestingly, I never had to take on that confrontational stance with Lesli or the other female directors I worked with. But there weren't many of those at the time—directing was notoriously a boys' club.

I tried to stay out of Bryan's way. But once again, I committed a set no-no. It happened when we were shooting a scene in a Sears department store where Sam is shopping with his mom, played by Becky Ann Baker. The first shot is always a master shot; it's a wide shot that includes all the action in a scene. (The medium shots and close-ups will have to match the master, or you'll run into continuity problems in editing.) During the master, I noticed Becky carrying a black plastic shopping bag that looked wrong for Sears. It was the kind of bag you'd get buying a dirty magazine from a liquor store. The take was riddled with other problems, and Jeff was making his way over to Bryan to deliver our notes when I remembered the bag. I considered chasing after Jeff, but, given the chaos, decided I'd talk to the props guy myself.

He gave Becky a different bag, one that looked more appropriate. After the second take, the usual pandemonium ensued as Bryan ran around barking orders at people. Over the din I heard him bellow, "And what happened to the bag she had before?"

My cheeks burned. I saw Bryan grilling the props guy and knew I was in trouble. He stomped back to video village and got up in my face. "DON'T EVER CHANGE SOMETHING WITHOUT RUNNING IT BY ME!"

Terrified, I stammered an apology. Bryan spun back around, plopped down in his chair, and never talked to or even looked at me again. I'd heard of men giving the cold shoulder to women who piss them off at work. It's the ultimate fuck-you. Yes, I made a mistake, but there were other ways he could've handled it. Did I deserve to be demeaned and dismissed?

As the crew got back to work, I sank down in my chair and whispered to Jeff, "We're still in the master and the first take was unusable anyway." In other words, the new prop wouldn't affect continuity. But the bottom line was that I angered the director. I failed to bow down to his authority, an inexcusable transgression for a woman to make. Would he have screamed like that at Gabe or Jeff or any other penis-bearing individual? I doubt it. Looking back, I wish I had reported the incident to Judd or Paul or human resources, but I was too ashamed. Gabe and Jeff reacted with raised eyebrows and silence. So much for allies. And they weren't the only ones who saw Bryan yell at me and did nothing.

That is how powerful men in Hollywood are able to get away with what they do for so long. That is the culture that allows men to behave badly.

Freaks and Geeks, despite its critical acclaim, was not doing well in the ratings. It would go on to be a cult classic and launch many a career, proving it was ahead of its time and paving the way for shows like *Stranger Things*, a series based on eighties pop culture and the lives of geeks. But when it first aired, *Freaks and Geeks* bombed. Why? Here's my theory.

Our show was about painful memories of being a teenager; we didn't sugarcoat the awkward or humiliating. The scene of Nick serenading Lindsay on their first date, earnest and slightly off-key, still makes me wince . . . in the best way. To enjoy our show, you had to embrace the cringe factor, and that was easier if you were old enough to laugh about it. But NBC didn't market the show to Gen Xers like me. I don't think they had any idea who our audience was.

Still, we had a small but rabid following from the start, loyal fans who bombarded our website with good-natured complaints whenever an episode had a title that didn't rhyme. But even hard-core fans had trouble tuning in every week because the network kept moving our time slot in search of better ratings. Pretty soon *I* didn't even remember what night it aired.

People who've been in the business a long time talk about the good old days when shows were allowed to grow. The famous example is *Seinfeld*: though it had dismal ratings at first, NBC left it on the air. As the show found itself, it established a faithful audience and became a giant hit. But networks were no longer so patient. They either canceled shows after a few episodes or tinkered with them endlessly.

We got a lot of nervous notes from NBC. They wanted us to tone things down and make the show less "provocative." Remember, this was 1999, the year of the Columbine High School massacre, and there was a common belief that the two teenage shooters committed this heinous crime because they were social outcasts. *Freaks and Geeks* sympathized with social outcasts.

With the threat of cancellation looming, Paul started writing the series finale, "Discos and Dragons." He cared too much about the show to leave it dangling. So he went for it in this last one, tying up as many loose ends as possible. In this final chapter, he added a guest character named Sara—played by Lizzy Caplan—to be Nick's rebound girlfriend after his breakup with Lindsay. Other than her love of disco, Sara didn't have much of a personality. Paul and Judd asked me to do a "Sara pass" to make her more interesting. I made her insecure but relatable, someone trying too hard to be liked and accepted into the group. She became a character instead of just a joke.

I've always found it curious when male writers have trouble writing female characters, because the opposite isn't true. People assumed that, as a woman, I must be the "voice of Lindsay." But I felt most in my element writing for the geeks—I just wrote the way my brother and I talked when we were kids. Paul once told me, "You write the geeks *really* well." I chose to take that as an unequivocal compliment.

When we all took off for the holidays in December, our future was unclear. And I don't just mean the show. The whole world was worried that when the clock turned over from 1999 to 2000, critical industries and government functions could stop working. Here I was on the cusp of a new millennium, with the best job I'd ever had, and it could come crashing down in an instant, like the world's grid when hit by the Y2K bug.

Over the Christmas break, Carl and I flew back East. We wanted to spend New Year's Eve in New York and party like it was 1999, which it actually was. People got all symbolic about the new millennium, and it seemed like everyone was getting engaged. I listened to all the cute proposal stories and congratulated everyone while secretly thinking that proposing on New Year's Eve 1999 was unoriginal and cheesy as hell.

Of course, that would've been the perfect time for Carl to propose. New Year's Eve was the anniversary of our first sleepover date. A couple of weeks after we'd ice-skated at the *Letterman* party, Carl took me to the Hilton in Midtown for a romantic tryst. We ordered filet mignon and champagne from room service and watched the Times Square ball drop on TV. Later, as we lay in the dark, he kept saying in the high-pitched voice of those creepy little girls in *The Shining*, "Come play with us, Danny," until I got so scared that I slept with him.

Back then marriage seemed like a long way off. Now I was nearing thirty, the age when women are supposed to start worrying about their biological clocks. Carl was nearing thirty-five, the age when guys are supposed to stop acting like they're still in college and settle down. But the two of us were clearly not on that schedule. We rarely talked about marriage, not even at the weddings we attended. As we watched each of his Jewish friends take their vows, I'd think about whether the two of us would ever stomp on a lightbulb under a chuppah and get lifted up on chairs to "Hava Nagila." And then I'd think of the old adage, "Shiksas are for practice."

I knew my parents were also wondering why we hadn't gotten engaged yet, though I avoided the topic with them. My parents' feelings about this were the least of my problems. There was that pesky little issue of monogamy and my near fling with Jason Segel. I figured that since I was still attracted to other guys, I wasn't prepared to commit to Carl. It didn't occur to me that my wandering eye might have something to do with how unsatisfying our relationship was. I just thought I wasn't ready to get married. Which was a moot point, since Carl didn't ask.

In February we got the word: NBC was pulling the plug on *Freaks and Geeks*. Dire phone calls from agents rolled in. Everyone started hustling to find a new job. The best show I would ever work on had lasted all of eighteen episodes.

We had a prom-themed wrap party at the Hollywood American Legion, a drab event hall spiced up with balloons and streamers. I wore a baby-blue taffeta dress (ironically purchased from Sears) and a matching wrist corsage. Carl, never one to dress up or get into the spirit, wore a boring old suit. We posed for a prom picture, holding hands in front of a mottled backdrop. At most wrap parties, the producers give you a parting gift, usually a sweatshirt or a baseball cap with the show's logo on it. At ours, we got a *Freaks and Geeks* yearbook containing pictures of everyone who worked on the show, awards like Best Dressed and Worst Attendance, and tons of candids taken on the set. A gift made with love.

For some, this was just another wrap party. But for me it was the end of an exhilarating time fulfilling my creative potential and working with people I loved and admired. All night I was a blubbering mess as I walked around getting people to sign my yearbook, which didn't feel much different from when I did it in high school. By now, most of the awkwardness with Jason had dissipated and we had resumed our platonic friendship. But when he wrote in my yearbook, "You are a special woman," I felt a pang in my chest. There was so much about working on this show that transported me back to my tender teenage years, which speaks to its authenticity.

When I went to say goodbye to Paul's wife, she gave me a big hug. "You know, Patty," she confided, "Paul was making himself sick, worrying about the show. And then you started coming to the set, and it was such a relief because he knew he could trust you."

All that time I was worrying about doing things wrong, Paul had trusted me. And he wasn't the only one. The morning after the wrap party, I flipped through my yearbook and saw that Judd had scribbled with a red Sharpie, "Patty, you are hilarious." I believed this about as much as I had believed in myself as an artist. Here was the king of comedy telling me I was funny, and I couldn't think of a single line I'd written that I would consider an actual joke. I read Judd's words over and over, trying to convince myself they were true before heading back out to pound the pavement, looking for someone else to hire me.

7

A Well-Oiled Machine

Freaks and Geeks had become an industry favorite, especially among writers. When my agent told me that the *Friends* team wanted to meet with me, I was stunned. The last time I'd set foot in the *Friends* office, I was interviewing for an assistant job with the head writer Michael Borkow, who was no longer there. When I told him that I didn't want to write for the show, I never imagined that one day it might be a real possibility.

So, did I want to write for *Friends*? It was, without a doubt, America's most popular sitcom and most popular TV show, period. *Friends* wasn't just a show; it was a juggernaut. Therefore, whether I *wanted* to write for it was irrelevant. What kind of fool would pass up the chance? Still, that didn't stop me from arguing for my limitations.

"I'm not a joke writer," I insisted to Larry. "The comedy on *Freaks and Geeks* was character-based."

"They don't need another joke writer. They want someone who's good with story and character."

This made me feel only slightly less petrified. Writing for *Friends* after only two years of experience seemed like going straight to the

Olympics after just learning to skate. This show was as high-profile as you could get. If I screwed up, it could ruin my career.

What made the situation even more uncomfortable was that NBC had just launched a diversity program, a sort of voluntary affirmative action. The network was urging its showrunners to hire at least one writer of color per staff. On principle, I support affirmative action policies because I believe that overcoming institutional racism without them is impossible. But in practice? When you're the one benefitting from affirmative action, it's a major mindfuck. You don't know if you're getting the job because of your talent or your race. Naturally, I wondered whether *Friends* would have considered me if the diversity program hadn't put pressure on them to look outside the usual comedy writing pool of white Jewish males. But dwelling on that question wasn't going to help my career.

Friends had many writer-producers in decision-making positions, and because it was important for new writers to fit the culture, I had to be vetted by a total of eight people. These included the creators, Marta Kauffman and David Crane, and a bunch of erudite Harvard and Yale grads that a writer's assistant later described as "all young and smart and rich and shit."

I managed to survive the gauntlet of interviewers and, after, heard that they called Judd Apatow to inquire about me. I saw him a few days later at a *Freaks and Geeks* panel discussion at the Museum of Television & Radio in Beverly Hills. After the panel we chatted in the airy modern lobby as fans milled around, eyeing Judd and waiting for an opening to pounce. Even though he had vouched for me with the *Friends* people, he warned me about taking the job.

"The show's been on for, what? Six seasons? It's a well-oiled machine." He shrugged. "You're not going to learn that much."

Easy for him to say, with a list of credits as long as his arm. It still amazes me now that his focus was on how writing for *Friends* would fail to serve me, rather than how I might fail at *Friends*. His faith in me far exceeded my own. But despite his warning, I knew that if the show wanted to hire me, there was no way I could refuse. Sure enough, when Larry told me they were offering me the job, he didn't even give me the option of saying no.

My first day at *Friends*, in July 2000, was a nerve-racking blur. The staff had fourteen writers, which was unusually large, but this show had a big budget, many episodes to produce, and high expectations. Five of the writers were women. I was the only minority. The other new hires—all dudes—had previously been writers' assistants on the show, so they were familiar with the staff and the culture. They weren't brand-new like me.

We gathered in the writers' room, an enormous sun-drenched corner office with a huge oak table and floor-to-ceiling windows overlooking the San Fernando Valley. Before we did any work, Marta and David announced we'd be going out for the "annual welcome lunch" at Ca' Del Sole, an Italian restaurant in Toluca Lake.

The lunch had the forced feeling of Thanksgiving dinner with relatives you don't like. I could tell the old-timers were on their best behavior but would rather be gossiping over burgers from In-N-Out. Despite the mild weather and the scent of garlicky pasta wafting across the patio, I, too, wanted to be anywhere else. Sitting stiffly at one of the large round tables, I kept a smile plastered on my face and picked at my fancy watercress salad, feeling guilty about being treated to such an expensive meal before even putting in a day's work.

In all of my fears about the new job, I never predicted one of the challenges I would face was that the *Friends* writing staff was cliquey, more so than at any other show I would work on. They reminded me of the preppy rich kids in my high school who shopped at Abercrombie & Fitch and drove brand-new Cabriolets. The welcome lunch was only the beginning. During preproduction the staff went out to lunch every day, and the stress of figuring out whom to sit next to stirred up troubling memories of the middle school cafeteria, where I'd walk around with my pork roll sandwich and milk carton, trying to find the table with the least hostile body language. Now I understood why the *Friends* writers had interviewed me so rigorously. Personalities were a huge part of the job. I guess this made sense, given that we had to spend twelve hours a day together.

Each day started in the giant conference room. At ten a.m. people would trickle in to eat breakfast, read the newspaper, and bullshit. Then we'd break into two teams of seven and go to separate rooms, where each team worked on a different episode. We had to produce twenty-three shows that season. It was brutal. Having one team work on the current episode while the other worked on the next was the only way to keep up with the schedule.

Every morning a few senior writers would go off to confer and come back minutes later to assign the teams. The teams varied each day and seemed to be picked at random. But they were of utmost importance, because the people you were stuck with determined whether you would have a decent day or want to slit your wrists by lunchtime.

David would always lead one room and Marta the other. I was scared of them both, for different reasons. David, a workaholic who was impossible to please, was always looking for a better line or joke. Behind his soft-spoken demeanor, he seemed to be judging everyone with eagle eyes. He was the most genteel person in the room, becoming visibly pained whenever the conversation turned blue—which happened often.

Marta was the Oscar Madison to David's Felix Unger. She had a booming voice and a laugh that could rattle windows. She would kick her bare feet up on the conference table, à la Steve Jobs, and do needlepoint while we worked. She often brought her kids to the office and let them run up and down the halls. Though proud of her East Coast roots, in some ways she was totally L.A. An outspoken liberal, Marta took the diversity mandate seriously, and I suspected she had more to do with hiring me than David did. Still, I would do anything to avoid being alone with her and having to chitchat, which always felt stilted.

While breaking stories, one person would be put in charge of writing the story beats on the whiteboard. They had an egalitarian way of assigning this task so that we all shared the burden. When it was my turn, the clean block letters I dashed off immediately drew attention. "Your handwriting's not only neat, but fast," one of the writers marveled. I began to wonder if I'd be better suited to cue-card writing than screenwriting. That way I could just make *other* people's ideas look awesome.

In theory, breaking stories on *Friends* should've gone faster than it did on dramas, since sitcoms are only half as long and have fewer story beats. Even so, there was a lot of sitting around the table in silence. Trust me, any show that makes it to season seven is hurting for ideas, one plotline away from jumping the shark.

Much of the time, the writers' room was like an endless cocktail party where we had run out of polite things to talk about. And so we talked about sex. Constantly.

That year a former writers' assistant had launched a lawsuit against Warner Bros. for racial discrimination and sexual harassment, claiming that racist jokes and sexually explicit talk made the *Friends* writers' room a hostile workplace. Though I don't recall hearing racist jokes, the sex talk was pervasive. But the California Supreme Court would ultimately rule that talking about sex in the writers' room did not constitute harassment, and that for an "adult comedy" that revolved around sexual themes, it was necessary for the creative process.

Harmless, maybe. But necessary? Now, *that* is hard to justify. I remember exactly one time that details about our sex lives were used on the show, in "The One with Rachel's Book," where Joey finds a book of erotica that Rachel uses to get off. (Several of us had such a book in our nightstand drawers.) But mostly we talked about sex just to amuse ourselves. What kind of birth control did we use? Did we have sex on our periods? Did we ever fall asleep during sex? When I answered no to the latter, one of the married writers quipped, "That's because you're not married."

None of these conversations bothered me. I was proud of my ability to laugh at obscenities and not take offense. In comedy, this toughness—or, put another way, lack of sensitivity—was considered a requirement. But given how much has shifted in the last few years around sexual harassment and racial injustice, I'd probably feel differently if I were sitting in a writers' room today. Can people be funny and sensitive at the same time? I'd like to think so.

On rare occasions, the silly things we did to kill time while trapped in the room led to a story idea. Like the fifty states game. Here's how it works: you make a list of the fifty American states from memory. Easy, right? But people always forget at least one. I was unable to master the game and became obsessed with it. The writers' room table was littered with sheets of paper listing forty-eight states, followed by an angry expletive and a doodle of my head exploding.

We turned my fixation into a B-story (subplot) for the episode I would write, "The One Where Chandler Doesn't Like Dogs." This was going to be the Thanksgiving episode, and the A-story (main plot) was about Phoebe sneaking a dog into the apartment and everyone having to hide him from Chandler.

What I was most worried about was writing jokes, so I took meticulous notes in the room even though the writers' assistant was already typing up every word. After we broke the story, I went home to write for a week—what is known as "going off on script." Working my own hours, braless and in stretchy pants, I relished the solitude, free from the peculiar social obligations of the *Friends* office. But I felt immense pressure to write a good script, or at least one that wouldn't get me fired.

Fearful of making a wrong move, I stuck closely to the detailed outline. Thankfully, there were very few holes in the story. We had a name for such a hole: "WP," which stood for the "writer's problem." This term would come up when everyone was exhausted and sick of pitching ideas. As in, "How does Monica go from being pissed off at Chandler to kissing him at the end of the scene?" "WP."

I didn't have trouble figuring out story beats by myself. But I got anxious whenever I had to write my own joke—not just a funny line of dialogue but a *joke* joke, especially a strong one at the end of a scene or act. Not trusting my own instincts, I needed to bounce my jokes off someone else. I didn't realize at the time that *every comedy writer does this*. Even Carl was still asking, "Is this funny?"

By this point in our relationship, I dreaded showing my work to Carl because I'd always take his criticism too hard and we'd end up fighting. When your mentor is also your romantic partner—a situation I suspect is quite common—things can get complicated. But this time I deferred to his expertise, knowing he wouldn't allow me to embarrass myself with an unfunny script. He was the comedy sensei and I was his Grasshopper.

I called him when I finished my rough draft. "Can you take a look at this and tell me if it's total shit?"

This was what he lived for. If I needed help fixing a leaky faucet, he'd have plenty of better things to do. But help punching up jokes? He was there within minutes, ready to rock. He hovered over my shoulder at the vintage Steelcase desk that used to be his, eating snacks and pitching lines, while I typed and my neighbor blasted Cat Stevens records. To this day, the song "Peace Train" reminds me of Cheetos powder and panic.

When I got to the tag (the short scene after the end credits), I hit a major WP. The room had not been able to decide on the final joke. Earlier in the episode, Ross makes a bet with Chandler that he'll be able to win the fifty states game; if he can't, his punishment is he won't get to eat Thanksgiving dinner. But Ross can remember only forty-nine. In the tag, Chandler tortures him over his hubris, and Ross is supposed to remember the fiftieth state in some random, hilarious way. I was beating my head against the wall, trying to figure out how to make Wyoming funny, when Carl came up with a great idea.

                    CHANDLER
          Are you aware how wrong you were when
          you said this game was, and I quote,
          "insanely easy"?

                    ROSS
               (defeated)
          Yes.

                    CHANDLER
          And you're aware how acting all cocky
          makes other people feel stupid?

                         ROSS
Yes, I'm aware.

                         CHANDLER
And you're aware how annoying you are
and how you'll never finish this game
unless I give you the answer?

                         ROSS
Yes, Chandler, I'm well aware! So just
give me—
          (freezes as it hits him)
Well aware . . . Delaware!! Delaware!!

A couple of days after I handed in my script, one of the senior writers called me into his office to give me notes. Amazingly, they weren't too bad. I pulled it off—I didn't get fired!

But after my second draft, the script got turned over to the group. At *Friends* we rewrote every script together in the room, line by line. No one's was immune. When your script was getting gang-banged, you had to let go of all sense of ownership or your ego would end up in tatters. You were forced to watch the carnage happen right in front of you and pretend like it didn't faze you. Unlike with *Freaks and Geeks*, I didn't have much attachment to my *Friends* script, but the process of watching it get rewritten was painful and demoralizing nonetheless.

There was one thing I loved in my first draft even though I didn't come up with it: the Delaware joke. When the room was done with my script, only one word of the scene remained: *Delaware*.

After each script was completed, we'd have a table read in a Warner Bros. conference room, where the cast would read the script aloud in front of the producers, writers, executives, and various depart ment heads. Table reads at *Friends* were a big deal and served three purposes: (1) for the actors to judge the script (so they could gripe about it later), (2) for the showrunners to decide what didn't work and needed to be rewritten, and (3) for the writer of the episode to feel both bloatedly important and sickeningly self-conscious.

At first, I was excited about table reads because I got to be in the same room as the cast, who were Big Stars. Plus, there was a catered breakfast buffet, a spread that made IHOP look like child's play: fluffy scrambled eggs, crispy bacon, pancakes, waffles, pastries of all kinds. On the way to the table reads, I would start salivating like one of Pavlov's dogs.

But the novelty of seeing Big Stars up close wore off fast, along with my zeal about the hot breakfast. The actors were clearly unhappy to be chained to a tired old show when they would rather be branching out. Each had a one-track mind: *How is this script going to serve ME?* They all knew how to get a laugh, but if they didn't like a joke, they seemed to deliberately tank it, knowing we'd rewrite it. Dozens of good jokes would get thrown out just because, say, Lisa Kudrow had mumbled the line through a mouthful of bacon. David and Marta never said, "This joke is funny. The actor just needs to sell it."

Once the first rewrite was finished, we'd have a run-through on the set, where the actors would rehearse and work out blocking with the director. Then everyone would sit around Monica and Chandler's apartment and discuss the script. This was the actors' first opportunity to voice their opinions, which they did vociferously. This part was like being in hell, except instead of a cavern filled with fire and brimstone, we were in a brightly painted living room furnished with overstuffed couches and an abundance of throw pillows.

By now the actors had had enough time to stew over their complaints about the script. They rarely had anything positive to say, and when they brought up problems, they didn't suggest feasible solutions. Seeing themselves as guardians of their characters, they often argued that they would never do or say such-and-such. That was occasionally helpful, but overall, these sessions had a dire, aggressive quality that lacked all the levity you'd expect from the making of a sitcom. The cast behaved as if they weren't just Big Stars but also Serious Actors—even though *Friends* was never going to be *Citizen Kane.*

The run-throughs were followed by more rewrites. We hunkered down in the writers' room and worked into the wee hours, endlessly rewriting stuff that was funny the first time. Someone would pitch a joke and everyone would laugh, but whoever was running the room would ask for more pitches. We'd pitch dozens of alternates before they would decide to go with the first pitch. This happened so often that we had a saying for it: the Allen Ginsberg quote, "First thought, best thought." And yet this frustrating process continued. One night I fell asleep with my head on the table, and when I woke up they were still working on the same joke.

I tried to contribute to the rewrites, but my strength was fixing story problems—not pitching jokes. Comedy rooms favor writers who are quick on their feet and good at performing: class clowns. That's not me. Sometimes I'd think of a joke that I could clearly picture Chandler or Phoebe saying to hilarious effect, but I'd wreck it in the pitch because I was so nervous. Some comedy writers took improv classes for this very reason. Even if they had no interest in doing stand-up or acting, they thought improv skills would help them write jokes faster and pitch them with more conviction. Just the *idea* of taking an improv class made my crotch sweat.

Being surrounded by an elite cadre of comedy writers had eroded my self-confidence. Judd's "you are hilarious" comment seemed like a distant memory. In fact, he had recently recommended me for a roundtable rewrite of the stoner movie *How High*, but a roundtable was a writers' room on steroids—I'd be like a gazelle getting mauled by a pack of lions. I turned it down, claiming I was too busy. Which was the truth, but not the whole one.

After the rewrites and rehearsals, we would finally tape the show on Friday night. While sitting in the audience of a sitcom starts out fun, it ends up feeling like the longest night of your life. At five p.m. the audience would be revved up and punchy, but after six hours of sitting in one place, watching the same scenes over and over, they'd be hungry and tired and no longer laughing.

Which is why it made no sense that we had to rewrite jokes based on the studio audience's response. During the taping, the writers sat in a tense cluster off to the side of the bleachers. Between takes, we would huddle around David and Marta to pitch new jokes when the ones in the script didn't get a big enough laugh. And when I say *big enough*, I mean *uproarious*—the kind of laughter that is impossible to elicit after someone's already heard a joke. The element of surprise is crucial. A joke might get a hearty laugh on the first take, but on subsequent takes the laughter would taper off, sending David and Marta into a tizzy.

Not funny enough! Need better joke! Huddle!

The huddle was by far the most stressful part of the job. Being a good performer was everything, even more so than in the room, because in this high-stakes time-pressure situation, David dropped the pretense of diplomacy and listened to pitches only from his three go-to joke writers—who all happened to be men.

There is a long-running stereotype in Hollywood that women aren't funny, which is why, even now, most comedy rooms are male-dominated. Some of the funniest people I've known are women, and I bet the same is true for you. That doesn't mean all funny women are class clowns—that's like saying every good cook has a show on Food Network and a catchphrase. Humor comes in different forms. But in our society, men have traditionally made the rules about who and what is considered funny.

The one time I ever got a joke in during the huddle was when Marta liked it. In the Christmas episode, "The One with All the Candy," Monica makes holiday treats to put out for the whole apartment building. When Chandler asks her why, she says, "We can learn their names and get to know our neighbors." Chandler's response to this, as written in the script, did not garner the sidesplitting laughter required. The usual suspects pitched some alternate lines, all met by David's silence.

Then I pitched, "Wouldn't it be easier if we just moved?"

Marta let out a full-throated laugh, which in that moment was the most wonderful sound I'd ever heard. David seemed unconvinced, but there were no other pitches he liked, so Marta got her way and I got a joke in by default.

That also happened to be the episode in which I was tapped to be an extra, playing one of the angry neighbors who stalks Monica and Chandler's apartment, demanding more candy. I escaped from the dreaded huddle and stepped onto the set, joining the rowdy mob packed into the hallway. David Schwimmer, who was directing the episode, came over to give instructions.

"Patty, can you scooch closer to the door?"

I scooched, thrilled that instead of saying, "Hey, you," Schwimmer addressed me by name. Really, it takes so little for a celebrity to seem like a decent person. That night was the high point of my *Friends* experience. For once, I felt like I had something to do with the show.

When I went home for Thanksgiving, I invited my old friend Melissa over to watch my *Friends* episode, which aired on the holiday.

My parents left us alone but listened from the kitchen while they put leftovers away. Even though Melissa laughed in all the right places, the viewing was anticlimactic and an almost dissociative experience. After so many gang bangs, it was hard to remember who wrote what, but I always remembered what I *didn't* write.

When Joey says, "It's a moo point. It's like a cow's opinion—it doesn't matter," Melissa cracked up and grabbed my arm.

"Not my joke," I apologized. "It's really funny, though."

My dad appeared in the doorway. "What does that mean . . . 'moo point'?"

I thought I would feel different that weekend—a writer on a megahit, the local girl made good. But I just felt like the same old me, trimming green beans for my mom, standing in line at Dunkin' Donuts, and sleeping in the twin-size bed that I'd slept in as a child.

Carl hadn't come with me on the trip, choosing to visit his own parents instead. We rarely spent time with each other's families— another bad sign that I glossed over, rationalizing it as healthy independence. On Sunday my mother drove me to Newark Airport so I could fly back to L.A. As we approached the departures gate, she turned to me with a pained expression that looked like she was passing a gallstone.

"Are you and Carl going to get married?" she said, pulling up to the curb.

"You had a whole week to talk to me about this, and you're doing it *now*?"

"It's just, you've been with him for seven years."

I huffed, throwing the car door open. "Why can't you appreciate everything I've accomplished instead of pressuring me into marriage?"

"If I was going to pressure you, I would've done it a long time ago!"

I jumped out of the car and yanked my bags out of the trunk, as my mother stood by with a helpless frown, other travelers staring. "Just because we're not married doesn't mean we're not happy!"

I spent the whole flight fuming. The thing that angered me the most was her timing, which guaranteed we couldn't have a proper conversation. But the reason she'd put it off was that she was terrified of my reaction, and I'd given her every reason to be. Because we never talked about uncomfortable things, there wasn't an established rapport to cushion our intense emotions. They would blow up into a shit-show every time.

Of course, I knew my mom wanted me to get married and have kids—no breaking news there. But it bothered me that my growing professional success hadn't staved off her anxiety about it, especially after I'd worked so hard to prove myself. It didn't occur to me that she might have been worried not only about my unmarried status, but also my actual relationship with Carl. That maybe she was seeing the signs I chose to ignore.

After a few strained phone calls, I made up with my mom, though we mostly just talked around the subject instead of facing it head-on. Months later, I finally stopped fixating on how she'd cornered me at the airport and started thinking about how defensive I'd sounded. *Just because we're not married doesn't mean we're not happy!* If we were, I wouldn't have had to scream it in front of the skycap.

The stress of working at *Friends* led to overeating as I tried to soothe my anxiety with comfort foods. The office kitchen was stocked with enough groceries to feed a small village. Lunches and dinners were brought to us in massive takeout orders coordinated by the food P.A. (production assistant). That's right, the task of feeding the writers was so important that it made up someone's entire job description.

The writers took turns choosing where to get takeout, which ranged from fast food to five-star gourmet. Peer pressure made this task a weighty responsibility because when it was your turn, you decided what the whole group would eat. I usually opted for either Ruth's Chris Steak House, an absurd indulgence, or the opposite end of the spectrum, KFC. The latter would elicit groans from the health-conscious writers who were on low-carb diets, though I suspect they were secretly elated to eat fried chicken and biscuits instead of raw walnuts and breadless sandwiches. When the food P.A. returned from foraging, he'd announce, "Food's here!" and everyone would drop what they were doing and descend upon the takeout bags like vultures.

On top of this, the office manager made snacks for us after the run-throughs to lift our spirits. For a while she was on a charcuterie kick, and all of that smoked gouda and salami made me constipated. In fact, the whole writers' room was obsessed with fiber. We would force ourselves to eat rye crackers that contained 99 percent of a person's daily fiber requirement; it was like gnawing on particleboard. To make matters worse, my constipation was accompanied by a stubborn case of hemorrhoids. I sat in a chair all day long, and this made my rear orifice very unhappy. Just as furniture movers are susceptible to hernias, hemorrhoids are an occupational hazard for writers.

I put on several pounds and had to buy bigger clothes. Some of the writers would go to the gym before work, but I was so tired all the time that I couldn't imagine getting up earlier than I had to. People would tell me, "Exercise actually gives you more energy," and I'd want to tell them to go fuck themselves.

On weekends I had no motivation to go out with friends or make plans. A party invitation would send me into a neurotic fit. My hours were so long, and my time so structured and packed with social interaction, that all I wanted to do was be alone and veg out when I wasn't working.

I tried to get out of town as often as possible. During the short breaks after lunch, I'd sit in my office and read travel guides, planning my escapes. Carl and I took a few weekend trips to Santa Barbara, Desert Hot Springs, Las Vegas. But I longed for something beyond recreation. I daydreamed about going to a spa near San Diego where Madonna reportedly went on lengthy retreats to get centered. I was convinced I needed this kind of drastic overhaul. My life was out of balance.

But there was one huge upside to the job: money was no longer an issue. Now I could afford to buy pretty much anything I wanted. No Rolexes or a Rolls-Royce—I had simpler tastes. I bought sweaters and jeans from the Gap, a dining room table, a bed frame, and a TiVo, the grandfather of DVRs.

At *Friends* there was a culture of spending, a rich person's mentality. One of the writers wore understated, luxurious clothing and the kind of jewelry that stores keep locked in the display case. I spent all winter admiring her Italian leather boots, which you could tell just by looking at them were like butter. Once, when she was dithering over whether to buy an expensive necklace, another writer encouraged her with, "You work hard. You deserve it!" And that was how I justified spending my newly earned money: I deserved all that stuff, and maybe it would make me happier.

Friends rarely won any Emmys, but they swept the People's Choice Awards every year. The writers were all invited to attend the ceremony (without plus-ones). Decked out in a crimson floor-length gown, I hitched a ride with a few other writers in a stretch limo. When it was time to accept the trophy for Favorite Television

Comedy Series, the whole staff was urged to go up on stage. I stood behind the others, feeling like I didn't deserve to be up there at all.

Even though I got along with everyone at *Friends*, deep down I felt like an outsider. I once heard the writers refer to the act of telling people they wrote for *Friends* as "dropping the F-bomb." The bomb was meant to impress and would usually be met with wide eyes, drooling, and babbling. But I had no desire to drop the F-bomb, because presenting myself as a *Friends* writer felt fraudulent and just kind of wrong.

For a long time, I justified my imposter syndrome because I was a drama writer working in comedy. And yes, that was part of it. But imposter syndrome, I later learned, is a common experience for racial minorities who work in fields where they lack representation. As the only Asian writer in those rooms, I felt so alone, buckling under the pressure to represent my entire race and to prove that I deserved a seat at the table—or a spot on that stage. With every joke, I had to prove it to my peers, my bosses, and my parents.

When the season wrapped in the spring of 2001, I was delirious with exhaustion. The marathon was over, and I crawled across the finish line with an Expo marker in one hand and a tube of Preparation H in the other. Once again, my future was up in the air. *Friends* had an option on me, which meant that if they wanted me back, I had to do it. As far as I knew, no writers left *Friends* of their own accord. I didn't really want to go back, but I didn't want to get rejected, either. No one had treated me differently during the last days, and I'd been included in all the season-end festivities. And yet I had a bad feeling.

To distract myself, I went shopping at the Beverly Center mall and stopped to have lunch. I was sitting in the food court, shoveling down a trough of chopped salad to get my daily fiber, when my phone rang. It was Larry.

"I want to warn you before David Crane calls," he said in his usual brass-tacks way. "They're not picking up your option."

"Oh. Okay." I didn't even try to act surprised. "Did he say why?"

"They need a joke writer for next year."

Well, that was that. A joke writer I was not. Thinking of all those times I felt invisible in the huddle, I was mortified and indignant.

Larry was pissed off, too. He had given David an earful. "I was like, 'You said you needed a writer who was good with story and character. You knew Patty wasn't a joke writer!'"

"Wow, you actually said that?"

"Of course. And now I can't watch *Friends* anymore."

"What? Why not?"

"That's my thing. You don't know about my thing? When a show fires one of my clients, I never watch that show again."

Why would Larry jeopardize his relationship with such a high-profile show on my behalf, not to mention miss out on a pop culture phenomenon? (How would he know if Rachel and Ross ever got back together?!) But that was the kind of agent Larry was: loyal and principled. He was not afraid of the David Cranes of the world. And besides, isn't that what agents are for? Telling people off so you don't have to?

Relief washed over me. No more all-night rewrites, anxious joke pitching, and feeling like a nerd at the popular kids' table. That said, it still sucked to be dumped. I was already scrambling to come up with a way to explain it to my family. "My option didn't get picked up" was just a euphemism for "I got fired." Even if my parents didn't quite grasp the popularity of *Friends*, they had a sense that with this job I'd finally "made it." There was no way to downplay this failure. I just hoped they didn't have any cruises with their friends lined up.

A few minutes after I hung up with Larry, David Crane called. He obviously assumed that I'd gotten the news already and this conversation was just a formality.

"This is an 'I'm sorry' call," he began in a soft voice, and I pictured his head cocked to the side in the universal sign for sympathy. I was so hung up on the preciousness of his opening that I can't remember how he explained—or even *if* he explained—why he was firing me. But I managed to pull myself together and put on a professional demeanor.

"I just want to thank you for the opportunity to work with such talented people on such a great show. It's been an amazing experience."

David seemed confused by my courteous response. He said an awkward goodbye and hung up, leaving me to wonder whether Marta had stuck him with this lousy task or if they had drawn straws for it. I shut off my phone, forced down the rest of my salad, and spent the next few hours buying shit with a vengeance. I consoled myself by purchasing a deluxe Cuisinart food processor with four blade attachments. After all the soggy takeout I'd been fed by the food P.A., I couldn't wait to make a home-cooked meal.

I found out later that one of the other new writers had also been fired. I felt bad for him, but I have to admit it was a comfort that I wasn't the only one, and that they'd fired a white guy as well. As far as I know, *Friends* dropped the diversity mandate the following year and went back to the status quo: hiring white people at will.

In the end, Judd Apatow was right: I didn't learn that much, except that I never wanted to work on a sitcom again. But the choice had been clear at the time. Throughout my career, *Friends* would remain my most recognizable credit. Plus, there was the money. I now had some nice furniture, high-tech housewares, and cute new clothes, albeit a size larger than I would've liked. And I would be forever grateful, especially in lean times, for *Friends* residual checks. Syndicated in every country, perpetually rerunning on cable, and now streaming on demand, *Friends* is the gift that keeps on giving.

8

Snow Day

After all that fantasizing over travel guides, when I was finally free to go on vacation, I chose New York. By this time, I had lived in Los Angeles for almost four years—Carl for five—and we weren't moving back East anytime soon. Our careers wouldn't allow it. Plus, the longer I lived in L.A., the softer I became. Now it was hard to imagine, say, dragging my laundry seven blocks in a cart— something I used to do without blinking an eye.

I couldn't say that I *missed* the day-to-day stress of living in Manhattan, yet many of my fondest memories of the city were intertwined with this difficulty. The rats and cockroaches, the taxis that nearly ran you over when you crossed the street, the soup vendors yelling at you for not ordering fast enough. Surviving all that stuff builds character and fosters an intense, if perhaps irrational, loyalty.

Each time I went back, I felt more like a tourist. I made pilgrimages to my favorite haunts, like the Joe's Pizza on Bleecker and Carmine, where I used to stop for a slice on my way home from work. But I also visited places I hadn't had time for when I was a resident:

the John Lennon memorial at Strawberry Fields, the Central Park Zoo, the Hayden Planetarium.

While Carl and I rode the subway to the Upper West Side to make these rounds, I reminisced about my first few days in New York, back in 1993. A real estate broker had taken me on the subway to see what would end up becoming my apartment. Wearing a baby-doll dress and combat boots, I'd thought I looked hip and was, as they say, feeling myself. But my bubbliness about moving to New York overrode any semblance of cool.

"Do I look like a New Yorker?" I asked the broker.

"No. You're smiling too much."

And now here I was, doing it again, a big smile on my face as I stood clutching a pole in the middle of a subway car, squished amid this sea of humanity—my former neighbors. I couldn't help myself. I would never stop loving this place.

I was still sightseeing that afternoon when I got a call from Lydia Woodward, the woman who would become my next boss.

"Are you in some bizarro place right now?" she asked.

"Um, sort of." I peered into a glass case at a diorama of Komodo dragons attacking a wild boar. "I'm in the reptile hall at the Museum of Natural History."

She laughed. "That's pretty bizarro."

She was calling to offer me a job on her new show, *Citizen Baines*. I'd met with her just before flying to New York, at the tail end of my busiest staffing season ever. Getting fired from a hit show was not the death sentence I thought it would be. It didn't ruin my career. In fact, my *Friends* credit opened a lot of doors, and not just in comedy. It now seemed like everyone in town wanted to meet me. No one asked me why I was fired; that's not the kind of thing people talk about to your face. I felt self-conscious about it until years later when I realized it was no big deal. In Hollywood, everyone gets fired all the time.

Still, there weren't many shows I was right for in the spring of 2001. Procedural dramas—about cops, lawyers, and doctors—were still trending. Relationship and character-based shows were rare. And that's how I ended up going from *Friends* to a show that most people have never heard of. *Citizen Baines* was a CBS drama about a longtime senator who loses his bid for reelection and must face the second act of his career.

With this underwhelming premise, it would've been an unlikely candidate for pickup, but it was a project from John Wells Productions. Wells was a prolific producer and the creator of *ER, The West Wing, China Beach,* and *Third Watch,* all popular and profitable shows. Lydia, who had written *Citizen Baines,* was a protégé of Wells, cutting her teeth on *China Beach* and running *ER* for several years.

When I'd met with Lydia, she was laid-back and easy to talk to. She was in her fifties, her hair in a brown bob with gray roots, and she was wearing a loose outfit and beat-up leather slides. What I remember most about our meeting was that I made her laugh a lot. She had a wonderful laugh—her head would tilt back, her eyes would squeeze shut, and her mouth would open so wide you could get a good look at her tonsils.

After we talked, she left me alone to watch the pilot. Like *Freaks and Geeks,* it blew me away. It had the production values of a feature film and a movie star cast. In the role of Senator Elliott Baines was James Cromwell, the distinguished white-haired actor who played Farmer Hoggett in *Babe* and the crooked cop in *L.A. Confidential.* But mostly I was won over by Lydia's eloquent writing. Her character development was so masterful that I cried, right there in her office, when Senator Baines lost the election.

So I took a risk on this staid drama starring a sexagenarian, knowing it wasn't a sure-fire hit. I loved it, and that was enough for me. After I accepted the offer, I hung up with Lydia and called my parents to tell them the good news.

"Out of all the shows I had meetings on, this is by far the best. Have you heard of James Cromwell? The guy from *Babe*? The talking pig movie?"

"Talking pig?" my dad said.

"Never mind. The point is, it's a great show."

"What is it called again?" my mom asked. I could picture her writing it down so she'd be able to report back to her friends. Despite my excitement, she seemed unimpressed, and understandably worried after what had happened with my first three writing jobs. "Do you know how long this one will last?"

"That depends on how well the show does."

She sighed. "I really wish you'd gone into something more stable."

How about a "congratulations, honey"? Was that too much to ask for?

I started working at *Citizen Baines* in June 2001. Our offices were housed in a production trailer at Warner Bros., not far from the *Friends* soundstage where I'd spent many a Friday night. A production trailer is like a double-wide mobile home, plunked down on a studio lot when there's not enough space to accommodate a new show. I tried to make my office, with its thin walls and fluorescent lights, seem less sad by keeping a big apothecary jar filled with jelly-beans on my desk.

We had writers' meetings every morning, and Lydia was always there, steering the ship. There were only three other writers. The small staff was a refreshing change from *Friends*. We shared a lot about our personal lives while breaking stories over bowls of micro-waved popcorn, Lydia's favorite snack. There wasn't any pressure to conform or compete. Weirdly, I turned out to be the comedian in the room, as the others had come strictly from drama. I was surprised by how easily I cracked them up without even trying. It wasn't hard to be the funniest writer on a drama that somber—*Citizen Baines* was as depressing as a Morrissey song. But, hey, I filled a niche, and in this business, that was the closest you could get to job security.

The day after I turned in my first script, "The Appraisal," I was walking down the hallway and ran into one of the writers, a serious guy named P.K. who had bushy eyebrows and gapped teeth. He used to write for *Party of Five* back when I was still putzing around with my spec script.

"I want to talk to you," he said, his expression inscrutable.

I followed him to his office, silently freaking out. P.K. was Lydia's second-in-command, so I regarded him with deference. My script must've been so horrendous that Lydia couldn't deal with it and had dispatched P.K. to tell me what a disaster it was. Oh, the shame! There were staffers milling around outside his office, watching us go in.

"Close the door," he instructed.

Okay, I was fucked. I shut the door and turned to face him, my heart knocking violently against my ribs. He picked up a copy of my script from his desk.

"You're a really good writer."

I started to breathe again. "Really? I mean . . . thanks."

"You're a specific writer. That's what makes you so good." He com-plimented me on the skillful ways I'd handled certain story points and character beats, gushing over lines of dialogue that moved him. By this time, I had been around P.K. long enough to know he wasn't an effusive person and he had discriminating tastes. In a writers' room, you learn a lot about people's artistic criteria. You listen to someone pick apart plotlines from *Six Feet Under* or castigate Christopher Nolan for *Memento*, and you realize how much it takes to satisfy them. Hearing P.K. rave about my script filled me with a sense of pride that I still haven't forgotten.

Lydia liked it, too. Her notes were minimal. I got to write a few more drafts on my own and never had to suffer the indignity of a gang bang. Like most showrunners, Lydia did a final pass on every script, but she didn't piss all over it like Carlton used to. She recognized what was good and left it alone.

I was thrilled to find out that I wasn't required to be on set for my episode. But I'd reached the point in my career where my title was co-producer, which meant that I did have a lot of other responsibilities I'd never had before, like attending producers' meetings. These were no fun. The non-writing producers—staffers on the business side of things—would take over the conference room and chew Lydia's ear off with minutiae about budgets and schedules and other topics that bored me to tears.

Being a producer also meant I had to deal with problems I used to be sheltered from. And by *problems*, I mean *actors*. When James Cromwell objected to a line in my script, Lydia sent me to his dressing room to talk to him. I went in bracing myself for the worst. I'd already heard that Cromwell, a classically trained actor, was pious and difficult.

His assistant, an Asian American woman around my age, offered me a bottled water, then drifted off to putter in the background. People got the two of us mixed up all the time, even though we looked nothing alike, other than our long black hair. Some staffer would start talking to me about Cromwell's lunch order before I cut them off with "I think you have me confused with the other Asian woman who works here." They'd laugh nervously and skitter away, and somehow *I'd* be left feeling embarrassed.

Cromwell dispensed with the small talk and dove right into his complaint, which was about the line "I'm sorry" in a scene where Elliott apologizes to one of his daughters. When I wrote the script, I never imagined anyone would object to such an unremarkable line of dialogue—but that was before I witnessed the cryptic logic of James Cromwell.

"The phrase 'I'm sorry' is so overused it's been rendered meaningless," he said in his crisp, aristocratic diction. "I'd like to replace it with 'I apologize.' It's more accurate."

I thought this was preposterous but tried my best to reason with him. "'I apologize' sounds stilted to me. Elliott is talking to his daughter. He should sound conversational, not like he's writing a form letter."

Cromwell fought me for what seemed like an eternity, spouting all sorts of philosophy to make his point. It felt like a debate against a New Age self-empowerment guru. I won the argument, but not without a fair amount of grief. And courage. It took a sizable pair of balls to stand up to the star of our show, a man with such gravitas. I couldn't help but see him as an authority figure, even though as the writer of the episode, I had as much say in the script as he did—technically, more.

I wondered whether Cromwell, like the others, had equated me with his assistant and expected the same obedience. Alas, I did not give in, maybe because I'd swallowed my voice too many times, or because he was so clearly wrong. I felt proud of myself for not backing down, but also shaky and exhausted. The fight had sucked the life force out of me.

By late August, I felt overwhelmed. Our hours were getting longer all the time, and I was always being pulled in multiple directions. My apartment was a mess, my TiVo backlogged with shows I never had time to watch. Exercise was just another chore to squeeze into a jam-packed schedule. When my friends wanted to see me, all I could manage was a rushed lunch during which I'd complain about how stressed out I was. I didn't even *think* about meditating again after my aborted attempt two years before. If I didn't have time to catch up on *Survivor*, I sure as fuck didn't have time to meditate.

One morning in early September, I woke up feeling sluggish, not looking forward to tackling the day. As I stood at the stove making breakfast, I looked down at my usual pot of heart-healthy oatmeal and it hit me that there wasn't enough joy in my life. It didn't occur to me that this might have something to do with my job—nope, not ready to open that can of worms. Instead, I needed a quick fix that wouldn't require me to look too closely at my life choices. I dumped my steaming gruel into the garbage, grabbed some eggs and thick-cut bacon from the fridge, and cooked myself a cholesterol fest while I sipped coffee from my favorite oversized mug. I resolved to treat myself to this indulgence every day to bring joy back into my life. As if bacon were the answer to all my problems.

On a Tuesday morning soon after that, I woke up to a news report on the radio announcing that the World Trade Center had been attacked and the Twin Towers had collapsed. The words did not compute. Groggy and disoriented, I slid out of bed and made my way into the living room, where I turned on the TV and saw the now-famous footage of the North and South Towers disintegrating in a cloud of rubble.

As I stood there, slack-jawed, the phone rang. It was our writers' assistant, a young hipster named Aron.

"Aron, oh my God. Are you watching the news?"

Of course he was. Everyone was. Poor Aron was given the task of telling the writers that we should report to the office as usual. Too shell-shocked to register the absurdity of this, I said okay, hung up, and got ready for work—showering, getting dressed, and eating my eggs and bacon, all performed in a surreal fog between bouts of staring at the TV, my mouth agape.

Since my TiVo had recorded three hours of earlier breaking news, I could roll back and watch the whole series of events as they unfolded: the first tower erupting into flames, a plane crashing into the second tower, both skyscrapers falling to the ground, bedlam at the Pentagon, reports of a fourth hijacked plane crashing in a field in Pennsylvania.

Within an hour Aron called me again. "No work today," he said this time. "No one's coming in."

A horribly inappropriate thought popped into my head: *snow day*. In all my years in the television business, I had never worked on a show that had an unscheduled day off. Nothing short of a national disaster would keep the show from going on. This is what it took.

Carl came over. We cried and held each other, then called our friends and family in the New York area, all of whom were okay, albeit shaken. Time seemed to stand still while we camped out on the couch and watched the news all day. What got to me the most were the people jumping out of the windows of the towers, diving into the shroud of smoke toward certain death. That visual would be forever seared into my brain. Their desperation, hopelessness, fear, and pain were incomprehensible.

I was suddenly aware of how precarious life was.

The immediacy of the 2001 terrorist attack, and the disaster movie graphicness of it, made it an unforgettable trauma for many people. For me it was a loss of innocence, the first time I faced the prospect of my own mortality and stopped blithely assuming I'd always be safe and protected. I went to bed that night shaken to my core.

The next day at work, no work got done. The office was simply a place to get together and process. A few days later, Warner Bros. held a memorial service for the victims of 9/11. On a sunny afternoon, the staffs and crews of various shows gathered on the lot, converging on a grassy cul-de-sac that served as an exterior suburban set. In the center was a wooden gazebo draped with red-white-and-blue bunting, rounding out this ironic picture of an old-timey America that no longer existed. A few studio bigwigs made solemn speeches and we all sang "God Bless America." I managed to hold it together until the funeral bagpipes kicked in. Then my shoulders started shaking with sobs, tears splashing against the lenses of my sunglasses.

I didn't know if I would ever laugh again. Then, on a Saturday night a couple weeks later, Carl and I went to the movies. We saw *Rock Star*, a comedy about the lead singer of a heavy metal tribute band, played by Mark Wahlberg, who gets hired to replace the actual singer in the band he imitates. Marky Mark's girlfriend was played by none other than Jennifer Aniston. Though the movie was not great by any stretch, parts of it were delightfully campy—like a scene where the couple gets trashed at a party, does some dirty dancing, and wakes up the next morning naked in a cuddle puddle. By releasing it right after 9/11, the studio might as well have tossed the film into a dumpster. But I'll always remember it, because it was the first thing to make me laugh after that horrible day.

It wasn't long before gallows humor kicked in at work. Everyone was so tense and distraught that we were desperate for comic relief. A lot of mushy "I Love NY" emails were being circulated, and I received one that was like a chain letter; you were supposed to add your favorite New York moment to the list and forward it to your friends.

I wrote "eating a slice of Joe's Pizza in the rain," then forwarded it to Carl. He added "the time that Hinckley guy shot John Lennon" and sent it back to me. After I peeled myself off the floor, I wrote back, "That would be hilarious except that Hinckley shot Ronald Reagan. Mark David Chapman shot John Lennon."

The exchange was so tasteless that of course I showed it to everyone in the office—except Lydia, who would surely disapprove, being a mature adult and all. But when she walked in on a bunch of us cackling, she forced me to tell her what was so funny. I read her the emails and she couldn't suppress a smile.

In Hollywood, it's never too early to joke about a tragedy.

The ratings for *Citizen Baines* were bad from the get-go, so we couldn't blame 9/11. Even though CBS executives were supportive of the show, everyone knew if we didn't get more viewers, we'd be toast. No pressure or anything.

For my second episode, the time crunch had begun. I had four days to write the first draft, and one of those days would be my thirtieth birthday. To me this was an important milestone that would mark my true passage into adulthood. Proof that I had survived my often-misguided twenties. I had always expected that by the time I hit thirty, I'd be happy, whatever that meant.

I wanted to do something extra-special to celebrate, but being so busy with work, the only thing I managed to plan was a weekend with Carl at a bed-and-breakfast in Santa Barbara. The only thing I had the bandwidth for was watching TV from a bathtub, which happened to be my favorite thing ever. But now even that plan seemed dicey, since my deadline was Monday morning.

On Friday I sequestered myself in my office and powered through as much of the script as I could. But Aron had to drag me out so everyone could sing "Happy Birthday" and stand around eating sheet cake off paper plates.

As Lydia was tucking into a slice, she asked in a chipper voice, "So, Patty, what're you doing for your birthday?"

I stared at her in disbelief. "Um . . . writing a script?"

She didn't respond. Obviously, her mind was on other things besides me.

On Saturday morning, I got up early and wrote like a fiend until Carl picked me up and drove us to Santa Barbara. I put my laptop aside for a few hours while we settled into our cottage and had a gut-busting dinner at the Wine Cask, followed by champagne and a bubble bath adorned with floating rose petals. But it was hard to relax with the deadline hanging over my head. This was a pattern throughout my career: going on fabulous vacations to escape the stress and being too stressed to enjoy them.

The next morning at dawn, I leapt out of bed, threw on a bathrobe, and started hammering out the rest of my script with the kind of single-minded focus I managed to whip up only when in a panic. Carl dragged a table and a chintz armchair over to the fireplace so I could write with some ambience. While I sat hunched over my laptop, he went to the movies, coming back between features to bring me greased-stained bags of Fatburger. The only breaks I took were to wolf down food, empty my bladder, and add logs to the fire. I must've burned an entire forest's worth of wood that day. Whenever the fire started to die down, I'd become anxious, as if my energy would run out, too.

I wrote for fifteen hours straight and finished at three a.m., feeling less triumphant than relieved. After a few hours of fitful sleep, I took a quick shower and we checked out and drove back to L.A. I went straight to the office and, with a zombie-eyed hello, handed my script over to Aron, let down by the lack of fanfare. Though I wouldn't have called the script my *baby*—it was only a TV show, after all—I felt as drained as if I'd just given birth. But to everyone else, this was just another Monday morning. Was this what thirty was supposed to feel like? Exhausted? Overworked? Unappreciated?

But one person did acknowledge the hardship I went through that weekend: Carl. Usually, he was the one who worked straight through our vacations. He once spent an entire week in Hawaii on the phone, arguing with a comedian he was collaborating with, while I read a book on the lanai, lonely and annoyed. The trip to Santa Barbara was a role reversal for us. Later, Carl would tell me, "That Sunday was the moment I knew you were a real writer." No more of that namby-pamby writing on a humane schedule and trying to find work-life balance! A *real* writer blew off everything to get the job done!

It was ironic—and telling—that Carl rewarded me for ignoring him, the thing he did to me that I couldn't stand. His reaction said volumes about his values. I had finally won his admiration by becoming just like him.

When Lydia called me into her office, I was prepared for a shit-ton of notes. What I didn't expect was for her to pretty much throw out my entire script, which focused more on the main character's brother. She explained in her cool, measured manner that because of the pressure to gain a solid audience, we needed to focus on the lead character instead of bringing in guest stars.

I suspected this had something to do with a squeaky wheel named James Cromwell. His character did come off like a tool in my script, and I understood why Lydia didn't want to further disgruntle him by giving someone else the spotlight. But that didn't make me any less angry. Why didn't she think of this when we were breaking the story, *before* I was sent off on script and killed myself to finish it on time? I was sick of people treating scripts like disposable napkins.

Swallowing my frustration, I headed back to the room to re-break my episode with Lydia and the other writers. On top of this, I had to supervise a publicity project, another of my dreaded producer duties—one that I was wholly unqualified to do. I had already bumbled my way through several publicity snafus and gotten yelled at by various executives and crew members. Now, as part of its post-9/11 public relations, CBS was going to run spots featuring its stars honoring the Big Apple. Picture Ray Romano from *Everybody Loves Raymond* talking wistfully about the autumn leaves falling in Central Park. They wanted the *Citizen Baines* cast to perform some spots, hoping the added exposure would boost our viewership.

I knew the cast wouldn't be happy about this extracurricular work. The scripts for the spots read just like the cheesy stuff in that "I Love NY" chain letter. The network let me rewrite the copy if I preserved the basic premise, so I tried my best to make it less saccharine. But it was the last thing I wanted to do. I had a whole new episode to write, for God's sake.

We were less than an hour into re-breaking that episode when one of the publicity execs called, summoning me to the set to supervise the CBS spots. This was the moment of truth. I looked at Lydia across the popcorn bowl and asked her point-blank, "Do you want me to go to the set or stay here?"

She mulled it over for a beat. "You'd better go over there."

Goddammit! That was when I should've said, "Was I hired to be a writer or a publicist?" But I'd already used up my balls talking back to James Cromwell. I hurried to the soundstage and then sat around for hours, waiting for breaks when I could pull the actors aside to film the spots. The vibe on the set was tense. When I approached the attractive but brittle actress who played one of Elliott's daughters, she gave the script a cursory once-over and snapped in her haughty South African accent, "Who writes this shit?"

Then she was called away for hair touchups, and I was left standing there like a kid who's just received a wedgie. We never filmed the spot. For days after, I would rewrite our conversation in my head, imagining that instead of letting her insult me, I had stood up for myself using an assortment of colorful language.

When I returned to the writers' room that evening, my coworkers had finished breaking the new outline for my episode. The most significant change was that *James Cromwell was in almost every scene* and came off like a hero instead of a curmudgeon whose family hated him. I still liked the original story better, especially the brother, but at this point I had stopped caring. I was sent off to write the new script, again with a ridiculous deadline. Never write a script in four days— you'll be expected to keep doing it.

After being humiliated by that actress, I had hit my breaking point with the publicity stuff. Bracing myself, I marched into Lydia's office and told her I needed to focus exclusively on writing if she wanted me to meet the deadline. She showed some mercy and let me work at home for the next few days.

Camped out at my Steelcase desk in my comfiest pajamas, sipping hot chocolate and listening to Bing Crosby to psych myself up to write a Christmas episode in October, I tried my best to recapture the pleasure of my little writing bubble. But nothing got me to a happy place. I was cracking under the pressure.

One night as I was scrambling to finish the script, my anxiety grew to a fever pitch. At ten-thirty I broke down and called my agent at home, something I never did.

"I'm so sorry to bother you, Larry. . . ."

"No worries," he said, as if it were normal to chat with clients at this hour. "What's up?"

"You gotta get me off this show."

I spilled my guts, describing the nightmare in detail. Because I usually kept my problems to myself, Larry had no idea how unbearable my job had become.

"It'll all be over soon," he assured me. "The ratings are still piss-poor. Word on the street is that CBS is gonna pull the plug."

I was so unhinged that I would've quit the very next morning if Larry had given me the go-ahead. But he advised against it. Breaking my contract would burn bridges.

"Hang in there." This was starting to become his standard sign-off on our calls. "It won't be long."

He was right. The day after I turned in my revised script, Lydia called a meeting with the entire staff and announced the show was being canceled. She'd had a "mature conversation" with the network and studio execs, and everyone concluded that to make the show viable, we'd have to change the concept far too much. The consensus was to call it.

The news was met with long faces as my coworkers pondered their looming unemployment. Trying to be respectful of their feelings, I pretended to be bummed out, too. Then I slipped into my office, closed the door, and jumped up and down with glee, making my jellybeans rattle in their jar.

I called Larry and told him the news. He wanted to find me another job ASAP, but I needed a break first. Despite my best intentions, I had found it impossible to find work-life balance while writing on a show. One of the *Friends* writers used to stock up on shampoo and other supplies when the season started, knowing she'd have no time to shop until the next hiatus. I hated living this way, sprinting for months at a time and coming out drained. All I cared about was having a life again.

I had been thinking a lot about how John Lennon had retired from the music business at thirty-five to play with his son and bake bread. I, too, was longing to ditch the rat race and slow down. My career felt like a treadmill, moving faster and faster . . . but toward what? The faster it went, the unhappier I became.

Before we vacated the premises, P.K. stopped by my office and we had a heart-to-heart. I told him that my worst fear—other than dying painfully at the hands of terrorists—was that I was losing my passion for writing. I looked back on my year at *Friends,* when I had to bury that passion to survive, and worried that I was on a downward spiral. There was no joy in the writing anymore, and no amount of bacon was going to fix that.

"I know exactly what you're talking about," said P.K. "I went through the same thing at *Party of Five.*"

"How'd you deal with it?"

"Started writing a feature over the hiatus and decided I was only going to work on it if I was having fun." He'd take his laptop to Starbucks and tinker with his screenplay while relaxing with a cup of coffee. That sounded cute, but I knew it wouldn't work for me. For one thing, how can anyone concentrate at Starbucks with the hissing of that milk frother?

"I have all these fantasies of quitting writing altogether. Maybe going to art school or cooking school." Funny how all my fantasies involved school—I knew I wasn't qualified to do anything else. "But I can't just quit. I've worked so hard to get where I am."

"Make a decision in your mind and see how it feels. That's what my therapist told me to do when I was trying to decide whether to propose to my wife. Once you make a decision, you'll know if that's what you really want."

The fact that P.K. was happily married proved this advice was sound. But even *hypothetically* deciding to quit television made my butt pucker with fear. There were a million reasons why I couldn't quit, the most obvious being that I'd already invested so much energy in a career that people all over town would've killed for. I was at the peak of my career, in a field where careers typically don't last long. To walk away now would be insane.

Plus, deep in my heart, I still believed that I was meant to be a writer, that I had the ability to touch people with my words. Later that day when I was packing up my jellybeans, one of the other writers, a guileless young woman with a Midwestern accent, trudged into my office and let out a sigh. This was her first staff job, and the poor girl didn't even get to write an episode.

"I just wanted to tell you," she confided. "In my rage, I threw away everything in my office except for one thing: your first draft about the brother. I loved that script."

After 9/11, I was experiencing fear on a daily basis. My thoughts were now riddled with words like *suicide mission, terrorist cell, car bomb*. Driving on freeways was the worst. I would picture the suspicious van next to my Camry blowing up and obliterating everything in a quarter-mile radius. Even opening my mail was scary after the anthrax attacks, when, shortly after 9/11, letters containing spores of the deadly bacterium were mailed to several news media offices and two U.S. senators. My cousin was a doctor, and I kept her number on speed dial in case I needed to get some Cipro on the double.

I decided to call Carl's best friend, Ezra, my old stoner buddy, to talk about my new paranoia. As a Jewish psychologist who lived in New York, he seemed uniquely qualified to give me advice in this situation.

"I don't know how to function anymore. How do people go on after something like this?"

Ezra told me about the time he had spent traveling in Israel. Terrorism was so common there that Israelis were forced to learn how to live without fear—or, more accurately, in *spite* of fear. The paradox was that a constant awareness of their mortality resulted in a zest for life; they lived every day as if it were their last. I knew I couldn't go back to my pre-9/11 ignorance, to the illusion of control. But could I be aware and awake, and not paralyzed by fear?

In December, I mustered enough courage to get back on an airplane so I could spend the holidays with my parents. During the trip, I felt drawn to go back to New York again and see for myself what had happened. The gaiety that had graced my visit the previous spring was replaced by grim resolve.

On a gray and frigid day, I took the bus into Port Authority and caught a cab down to the World Trade Center site, now called Ground Zero. Unable to see anything past the construction plywood surrounding the area, I ducked inside an Au Bon Pain across the street to hide from the cold and watched from the window as people slogged through the mud-stained snow to place handwritten signs, flowers, candles, and photos of their loved ones along the fence. While I wept into a napkin, everyday life went on around me: people eating sandwiches, babbling on their phones, bitching about the weather. At first, it was unthinkable to me that someone could sit there nibbling on a scone, reading the sports section, just steps from where thousands of people had died a gruesome, senseless death.

Then I remembered how tough I used to be when I lived here. How tough everyone was. Once, I watched a customer in a Park

Avenue wine shop casually shake a large cockroach off his pant leg as he paid for his pinot noir. New Yorkers were resilient. The people in that Au Bon Pain were the epitome of what Ezra was talking about. This was how it had to be. At some point, you had to get on with it. You had to try your best to forget, while, at the same time, never forgetting.

9

Lazy

As staffing season approached in the spring of 2002, my agent took me to dinner to discuss my future. I managed to put off talking business until the dessert course, because the thought of finding a new job made me want to cry into my fresh mint tisane. In the months following 9/11, it seemed like everyone I knew was getting either engaged or pregnant. People were figuring out what was important to them, and I was asking myself the same thing: *What did I want?*

When I looked back over my career, I saw a string of stressful, soul-crushing experiences and only one job I truly enjoyed. Those were not good odds. Larry determined that my career had "peaked too early" with *Freaks and Geeks*, as most writers worked a bunch of bad jobs before they hit the jackpot. Hearing this made me feel even more hopeless. The track I was on was supposed to lead to bigger, better-paid producer positions and eventually a development deal where I could create my own show. But that track had never appealed to me. I had serious doubts about whether I wanted to run my own show.

This wasn't some sort of "leaning out," a failure to step up and claim my rightful creative power. Running a show was truly more responsibility than I wanted, and it involved doing all sorts of things I had no interest in or aptitude for—as I'd learned at *Citizen Baines*. I had never met a happy showrunner. Lydia had her moments, but in the end, the pressures had gotten the better of her. Even Judd and Paul grew frazzled as they juggled all their duties, negotiating with the network and fighting to keep the show alive. No thanks. My goal was to write for shows I loved, not to claw my way up the producer ladder.

But the more pressing issue was that I was burned out in every way. I'd been so chronically anxious over the past few years that I developed a habit of grinding my teeth while I slept. Carl first noticed it in the summer of 2000, when we were on vacation in Paris and I fell asleep in the airport taxi. No coincidence this happened a few days before I started at *Friends*. Ever since the foot-cramp incident in 1998, I'd had recurring nightmares in which I would lose my teeth in some gory fashion, so the discovery of this new habit freaked me out. By now the grinding had gotten so bad that I'd been diagnosed with temporomandibular joint syndrome, commonly known as TMJ. Many mornings I woke up feeling like I'd been punched in the jaw. Add to that a host of other stress-related ailments, including the ever-present hemorrhoids, and I was a serious mess.

Despite my efforts to appear functional, Larry could tell I was headed for a nervous breakdown, probably because I'd barely touched the profiteroles we were sharing. He put down his fork and asked me a question I never imagined coming out of his mouth.

"Do you want to take a year off to go on sabbatical?"

I froze with my teacup halfway to my lips. I had heard of sabbaticals only in an academic context. Other than professors, did anyone take extended periods of time off work? No one I knew, that's for sure. Was that even allowed? In our world, that was called being "between jobs," the euphemism for unemployment, when you passed the time by working on a passion project like a novel or a play that you'd abandon the minute a paying job came along.

"A sabbatical? I could do that?"

As I considered the possibility, tendrils of fear began to wrap themselves around me. If I took myself out of the game for a year, wouldn't everyone forget about me? Hollywood had brainwashed me into believing that if nobody sees you, you don't exist. But to be honest, my unflagging drive to do one thing after another started long before I worked in TV. When I graduated from high school, I envied the kids who were taking a gap year to go backpacking through Europe or do charity work in Chile . . . but I never even considered doing something like that because it would mean starting college late. I was raised to be competitive, and you couldn't win the race if you took a year off.

Now I was tired of the race. There was nothing I wanted more than a break from it. I had enough saved that I could take a year off, maybe even more if I was really careful about money. Yet the thought of having a nice long rest seemed too good to be true, like I didn't deserve it. I stared at Larry, dumbfounded, as my mind went into tilt mode.

After a few moments he said, "Do you want to think about it?"

"Yeah . . . okay. . . . Let me think about it. There's just a lot to consider."

While Larry took care of the check, I excused myself to go to the restroom. I peed, washed my hands, freshened my lipstick, and returned to the table.

"Okay, I thought about it. Yes, I want to take a sabbatical."

The minute I made the decision, it felt like an enormous weight had been lifted. I could breathe again. I knew I did the right thing because my TMJ went away overnight. Like quitting *Letterman*, going on sabbatical was an exhilarating leap into freedom.

It was also one of the scariest times in my life. Every few minutes a voice in my head would scream, *YOU CAN'T DO THIS!* and I'd feel a shot of adrenaline rocketing through my veins, signaling that something was horribly wrong. These fearful sensations made me worry that I was making a huge mistake. But I was determined not to give in to the fear. I had no idea what was going to happen to me out there in the void of voluntary unemployment. I just knew that the alternative would kill me.

For the first few weeks, I didn't tell anyone but Carl about my sabbatical. I wanted to savor my decision before having to deal with others' reactions to it. I knew certain people, most important, my parents, were not going to understand or approve. Even Carl was less than enthusiastic—no surprise, since he was never not working, and his self-esteem was directly proportionate to how overextended he was.

"If you're going to do this, you should tell people you're taking time off to work on features," he urged. "It's easier to explain."

"Than what? That I'm burnt out and need a break?"

"Yeah, that sounds like bullshit. Showrunners won't like that."

"I'm not going to lie. There's nothing wrong with taking time off."

"You can tell yourself that," he said with a shrug. "It's your career."

Despite his scare tactics, I resisted his advice. I was taking a step toward living authentically. The last thing I wanted to do was lie about it. So I instructed my agent to tell potential employers the truth, no matter the consequences.

Bowing out of staffing season was pure bliss. No piles of scripts to read, no constant calls from my agent, no having to be "on" for all those meetings. For once, I was having a real hiatus instead of hustling to find my next job. When I went to the movies, I didn't have to leave my phone on vibrate in case Larry called. When I went to the beach or out to lunch, I didn't have to bring a script. I could read a book or people-watch . . . or do nothing but sit there and enjoy my food. What a concept.

The first thing I noticed on sabbatical was how accustomed I had become to rushing. My default mode was to haul ass whenever I was driving, walking, eating, talking—doing anything. Racing against some invisible clock to maximize my productivity was a deeply ingrained habit that had no doubt contributed to my anxiety. As I began to slow down, I felt a sense of spaciousness and ease that was completely foreign to me, as I suspect it is for much of our fast-moving society. But once you get used to a slower pace, it's amazing.

With no obligations in front of me, I set out to have as much fun as humanly possible. My whole life I had worked hard, and now I was going to play hard.

This was no small feat. My family valued work ethics and practicality over everything. As a kid, I never went to summer camp. Instead, my brother and I spent our summers at home, watching reruns and hanging out with our friends, but our parents also made us scrub the kitchen floor with heavy-duty brushes until the tiles looked brand-new again—a project that took weeks to complete. When he was in college, Harry had summer gigs at Burger King and Arby's. Even my dad moonlighted for a while, delivering newspapers to make extra money for Harry's tuition. Picture that: my dad, with a PhD and a white-collar job, chucking the *Star-Ledger* onto driveways, alongside ten-year-olds who were saving up to buy video games.

When I could no longer avoid the inevitable, I flew home to tell my parents about my sabbatical. My mother cooked her famous crispy duck, which I knew had taken three days of prep, making me feel guilty for what I was about to spring on them. While I was polishing off seconds, I noticed my mom evaluating me across the table the way she used to when I had experimental haircuts as a teenager.

"You know, you can extend your eyebrows with a pencil," she said. "I need to tell you something. I'm taking a break from work."

My parents looked at each other, confused and alarmed. "Why?" asked my dad.

"I thought you were doing well," my mom said.

Not as well as your friends' kids, I thought, but kept it to myself. "I am. But I've been working nonstop for years and I'm totally stressed out. I'm tired of not having a life. Don't worry," I assured them, though I knew it was pointless. "I have enough savings in the bank."

My dad, not quite believing this, offered to give me money. I insisted that I was okay. But money wasn't the only issue. "Just don't relax too much," he warned.

That was all he had to say; I knew what he meant. Too much relaxing could start me on the sinful road to hell. We weren't religious, so that's not how my dad would put it, but he truly believed that being lazy was the worst thing a person could be.

No surprise that I began carrying around an incredible amount of guilt. It was like a constant white noise in the background, but it would rear up big-time whenever I saw someone working—a gardener, the car wash guys, even a random woman sitting in a cubicle, glimpsed through an office window on my way to my neighborhood coffee shop. A voice in my head, echoing my dad's, would say, "That responsible person has been busting her ass since nine a.m.—in heels—and you're going out for a latte. You should be ashamed of yourself."

But, eventually, the part of me that felt trapped and deprived, and that had been treated like a workhorse for so long, came out with a vengeance. And then fun was all I cared about. I felt like I was going through a second adolescence, without having to ask for an allowance or permission to do things. An early midlife crisis, if you will.

When I was fourteen, I had begged my parents to let me go to a Culture Club concert, and they said no because I had already seen them the year before.

"You've had enough fun," my dad chided.

You've had enough fun? FUCK THAT.

I was an adult now and, for starters, I was going to every rock concert that struck my fancy. I even splurged on Paul McCartney tickets, assuming that he was too old to be performing much longer. (Boy, was I wrong.) Back in those decadent pre–Great Recession days, UTA had a concierge that could get their clients the best seats, which was how I got to see McCartney from the twelfth row at the Staples Center. Even though Paul was my third-favorite Beatle (after George and John, respectively), he was still a Beatle. Seeing him perform live more than made up for the Culture Club show I missed.

With all my free time, I was able to dive into my Beatles obsession unfettered—watching all ten hours of the *Anthology* box set, reading biographies the size of the *Iliad*, and going to see tribute bands, most of whom I forgave for their dopey mop-top wigs. Carl took me to one of these concerts as a goof and couldn't believe it when I continued to go by myself. I even got to know the names of the guys who *played* the Beatles and would shout them out at shows, breaking the illusion for everyone around me. But to me that was a lot less weird than screaming "Ringo!" at a guy who was obviously not Ringo.

I was astonished by how busy I was on sabbatical. But when people asked me, "What do you do all day, now that you're not working?" I found it hard to come up with an answer that didn't sound embarrassing.

Here's the truth: I was making up for all the time I'd spent in a tunnel-vision pursuit of success. The childlike part of me that wanted to play had been shoved aside for so long, she was now my top priority. Whatever she was interested in, we'd investigate. Wherever she wanted to go, I took her there. Even if that meant driving two hours to Laguna Beach to see an art exhibit, rearranging my apartment to improve the feng shui, or shopping for days to find the perfect pair of motorcycle boots. No impulse was too frivolous to indulge.

I had given myself one year off, and so I said yes to everything, trying to squeeze in as much fun as I could before going back to the grind.

Fun was an essential medicine for what ailed me, but there was also a critical need for self-care—healing my body, mind, and spirit—that would take me in a radically new direction. Enter: yoga.

Yoga had always been something other people did, like bungee jumping or paintball tournaments—not for unathletic types like me. And I didn't think I was crunchy enough for yoga. But as it became more popular, I started to get curious. One day while shopping in the bougie neighborhood of Hancock Park, I stopped at a yoga studio and took a class on a whim. It was taught by a chunky, baby-voiced woman who encouraged us to spread our toes wide by saying, "Birkenstocks are sexy."

My transformation didn't happen overnight. Even after going to classes for weeks, I was on the fence, not sure whether I was into it or not. Every so often I'd go to a class taught by a robotic trainee or, worse, a drill sergeant who barked out instructions and tried to force my body into pretzel-like contortions.

Then I took a class with a petite, bright-eyed teacher who explained the poses in a way that made me feel safe and confident, as if I could do anything. Folded at the waist, head hanging over my

feet, I realized the stretch in my hamstrings actually felt *good*. Sunlight streaming through the window warmed my Spandexed but-
tocks, and I even began to enjoy the "earthy" smell of my classmates.
I was having an epiphany, possibly because all the blood had rushed
to my head. That's when I finally got what all the fuss was about.

I started reading books about the mind-body connection—
Deepak Chopra, Jon Kabat-Zinn. Suddenly it all made sense: the
canker sores, frequent colds, hemorrhoids, TMJ, even that fateful
foot cramp. For years I'd been ignoring the signals my body was
sending me, the ones that said, "Slow down!" Yoga forced me to
pay attention. I never became one of those five classes-a-week or
daily-sun-salutations people, but even when I got busy and fell off
the wagon, I always got back on at some point, rolling out my yoga
mat like a blank slate. Yoga brought me back to myself. It was my
touchstone of self-care.

The next big step was going to therapy. As with yoga, I used to
think of it as something for other people. What pushed me over the
edge was being stuck in a car with my family for five hours straight
on a road trip to Las Vegas that summer. It was one of those ill-
conceived family vacations where people who never talk are supposed to enjoy each other's company for days on end—unlike the
Bradys, who would've talked nonstop and had a blast. Squeezed
between my parents in the backseat, with my nose buried in a paperback to escape the deafening silence, a thought arose, clear as the
desert sunshine: *I need a shrink.*

A friend's therapist referred me to a colleague named Bonnie. She
had curly brown hair and wore tunics, long ropy necklaces, and no
makeup. Her office at Cedars-Sinai was so small that I suspected it
had once been a utility closet. But she made it cozy, and there was
always a box of Kleenex within reach.

My initial goal in therapy was to improve my relationship with my family, but that turned out to be the tip of the iceberg. I spent most of my early sessions venting about my career, sometimes expelling so much repressed anger that I felt high when I walked out. I didn't, however, go there to talk about Carl. In fact, I'm embarrassed to admit that when I first described our relationship to Bonnie, I borrowed the cliché "If it ain't broke, don't fix it." I later came to realize that it *was* broke. Very broke.

Now that my interests were expanding, Carl and I were growing apart. We bickered constantly and had some vicious fights—often in New York hotels, since traveling back to the city where we used to be happier tended to exacerbate the tensions between us. At one hotel he yelled at me for "grilling" one of his white friends about the guy's penchant for Asian girlfriends. At another hotel he exploded because I'd been *too* chummy with his friends and didn't pay him enough attention.

Our ugliest fight happened at the Four Seasons, the one where the *Seinfeld* party had taken place years before. I have zero recollection of what this fight was about. I just remember it involved yelling. Carl came from a family of yellers; in the few times I'd seen his parents, they went at it like Archie and Edith Bunker. *My* parents rarely fought. Every time I got into a fight with Carl, I felt like I was being dragged into an alien land, forced to be a caricature of a pissed-off girlfriend. That day at the Four Seasons, I got so blisteringly angry that I stormed out of our room with no idea where I was going.

Carl chased me into the hallway and grabbed my arm, just as a well-dressed elderly couple emerged from the elevator and regarded us with concern. In an absurd gesture, Carl nodded to them and said, "Hey." After they were gone, he managed to herd me back into our room, where we continued our argument. A few minutes later there was a knock on the door.

I opened it a crack. A burly hotel security guard peered in. "Ms. Lin? Is everything all right?" He eyed Carl, no doubt trying to figure out if this was an O.J. situation.

"Yes, we're fine," I replied, my face flushing with shame.

I shuddered to think of how we must've looked. That couple from the elevator was so worried *they called security*. Holy fuck. This was a wake-up call—one that made me see, if for only a split second, how bad things were. When there's that kind of rage between two people, something's not right.

But I repressed this moment of clarity. I pushed it away because I was so invested in the fantasy of our relationship. I told myself that one day we'd be free of all the external stressors in our lives, and we'd go back to our honeymoon phase when it was all sex and laughs and deep bonding conversations. From then on it would be smooth sailing, an extended version of the sweet snippets we still had every so often.

We did have them. There was the trip to Kauai when Carl made me laugh so much that I kept a list of his greatest hits; the afternoon in Paris when we drank half a bottle of wine and left the rest on Jim Morrison's grave; the Halloween when we sat in the car listening to ghost stories on the radio; the night he danced with my cat to "Baba O'Riley"; the times we snuck into movies at Universal CityWalk and rowed boats on the lake in Central Park. If our relationship were the stock market, it would be an overall downward trend, but with enough highs to keep us from panicking and pulling out.

By the time I started therapy, I had been with Carl for almost ten years. I couldn't imagine *not* being with him.

We were on the cusp of moving in together. Or, at least, that's how it seemed. After sustained pressure from his accountant, Carl was planning to buy a house to reduce his income taxes. I would live in it with him, though we didn't talk about that part much. By now I was willing to overlook most of his annoying bachelor habits; I was ready for this next step.

We spent our Sunday afternoons driving around, attending open houses. This gave me a glimmer of hope, even though he rejected every house for the slightest infractions. Any home with more than one staircase was "too vertical," and in the Hollywood Hills, where everything's on an incline, this pretty much eliminates all of them. Yet week after week, we kept looking. And week after week, I skirted the topic of Carl in therapy.

My therapist was the objective ear I needed. I couldn't be completely honest with anyone else in my life because they didn't want to hear about it (like Carl), or they had an agenda (like my agent), or they were simply too busy to talk (like my TV writer friends). Sometimes Bonnie could barely get a word in edgewise; I had a lot to unload and just needed to be heard. Since she allowed me to direct our conversations, it would often take a while to get to the heart of the issue. But we always did—eventually, we even got around to Carl. She was brilliant at analyzing dreams and seeing patterns that I was blind to. Patient and nurturing, she gave me the unconditional acceptance I felt like I wasn't getting from the rest of the world.

One day Bonnie asked me, "What do you like about yourself? I mean, other than your achievements?"

This question was a real doozy, given that I had both low self-esteem and childhood conditioning that forbade me from saying anything nice about myself. I racked my brain, but everything I could think of was an accomplishment, a goal I had succeeded in reaching. Anything else sounded false. Even though people described me as smart, funny, and creative, each compliment would evoke a sarcastic "yeah, right" in my head and a long list of evidence to the contrary. My identity as an achiever had come to a crashing halt, and now I had to ask myself: *Without doing, who am I?*

It's no coincidence this question sounds like a Zen koan because the third part of my personal growth trifecta was an exploration of spirituality. My interest in meditation had thus far led only to reading books about it. But once I got into yoga and therapy, I began to *experience* moments of stillness and intentional mindfulness. Both practices taught me to slow down and pay attention to what was going on inside me—without judgment.

I got over my fear of doing meditation "wrong" and just started doing it. Most of the time my mind still wandered all over the map, but instead of beating myself up and declaring it a waste, I tried to see it all as practice. Meditation was an antidote to the goal-oriented way that I approached everything. Soon I would be going on retreats, studying Buddhist philosophy, and applying these lessons in my daily life.

You could say that my spirituality was an indirect result of 9/11 and a direct result of my career. The constant angst and unhappiness that I grappled with while working in television had driven me to seek a healthy way of coping and a deeper sense of meaning. And as an artist, it's impossible to avoid spirituality if you're interested in going all the way, because at some point you realize you're not the one coming up with ideas, you're just the one channeling them. Realizing you're not in control is an essential part of Buddhism and many other faiths, and it's also the most freeing thing you can do for your art. The sooner you open that door, the better.

This openness, of course, was easier said than done. Though I was supposed to be taking a break from writing, the ambitious taskmaster in me planned on using my free time to get my creative juices flowing again. This was the implicit purpose of my sabbatical, so that when I went back to work in a year, I'd be good to go.

But that plan wasn't going well. In trying to establish a writing routine, I realized that I'd never actually had one. Most of my life, I wrote only when I had to, either out of emotional desperation or when someone was paying me to do it. Because I no longer had those motivators, it was impossible to get myself to write on a regular basis. A screenplay I'd started—a semi-autobiographical story about a commitment-phobic couple—languished in an unfinished limbo. To my mind, self-discipline meant nothing short of getting up at dawn every day and writing for hours before even having coffee. I heard there were writers who did this, but I didn't know any of them personally. They were mythical creatures, like unicorns. And if they did exist, I hated those fuckers.

When I told a friend about my writer's block, she recommended that I read *The Artist's Way* by Julia Cameron, a book designed to help people get in touch with their creativity. It had inspired a cult of followers; there were *Artist's Way* workshops all over town, advertised on flyers stapled to telephone poles and tacked to coffee shop bulletin boards. Desperate for advice, I read the book from cover to cover and did most of the exercises, even if they seemed silly.

The book makes you figure out what it is that you do to *avoid* making art. For some people it's drinking or drugs. For others it's crazy-making relationships. For me it was shopping. I didn't buy that much stuff, but I could kill days or even weeks searching for a specific item, like that perfect pair of motorcycle boots. If I managed to find the holy grail, I'd get a rush, a feeling of accomplishment. But if I didn't, I'd get depressed and hate myself for wasting all that time and energy. The binge, the high, the self-loathing. It was an addiction, all right.

What if I stopped shopping and spent that time writing instead?

I thought about my mom, who used to love writing when she was in school. When she got married and had kids, she gave all that up and followed the old-fashioned script for a wife and mother, devoting herself to domestic life. From what I could see, she no longer had any urge to write . . . but, man, could she shop.

Shopping was my mother's favorite hobby. The salespeople at Nordstrom were on a first-name basis with her. Her walk-in closet was overflowing with clothes she never wore, designer handbags bought on sale that still had their tags attached. One day when I was looking for something in there, I came across eight identical black jersey-knit skirts, and it dawned on me that *this* was what my mom did instead of writing. If I didn't stop doing the same thing, I would end up with eight pairs of motorcycle boots and a lifetime of regret.

Another important lesson I learned from *The Artist's Way* was that the professional artist has a responsibility to stay inspired after the business side of things sucks them dry. In other words, it was my job to feed the well of creativity. The book confirmed what I knew intuitively: if you don't have a life, you'll have nothing to write about. That's why TV writers trapped in the grind run out of ideas. Their wells are empty.

My well was drier than a stoner's cotton mouth. So I set out to refill it using Julia Cameron's bag of tricks. One exercise in the book was to write a letter to a person who had wounded you creatively. Not actually send the letter, just write it to get things off your chest. I thought about Carlton Cuse smirking at my first outline, Barney saying I had nothing to contribute, David Crane blowing off my pitches . . . but ultimately, I chose my fourth-grade teacher, Ms. Merck.

My third-grade teacher, Mrs. Aschauer, had been my biggest cheerleader. But things changed in fourth grade. I was assigned to Ms. Merck, a new teacher with frizzy hair and a shiny T-zone, who was in over her head and often resorted to shouting when she couldn't control the class. Ms. Merck didn't seem to think my writing was special.

When I turned in a story about an "aged woman"—I thought *old* was too boring an adjective—she called me up to her desk. She was in a sour mood, as she so often was. I found out later she'd been going through a divorce, but as a little kid, I knew nothing of her personal life and assumed her crankiness meant she didn't like me.

She stabbed a finger at the first line in my story. "What is this? 'Once there lived an *agg-id* woman'? What's *agg-id*?"

I stared at her, speechless. I had seen the word *aged* dozens of times in the books I'd read. I thought I knew what it meant and how it was pronounced. How was it possible my teacher didn't know? Had she never seen a label on a wedge of cheese? Because I was brainwashed to believe my teachers were infallible, her error did not compute.

"Um . . . it's aged," I said in a tiny voice. "An aged woman. Like . . . she's really old?"

Ms. Merck didn't argue, but she didn't agree with me, either. She did not pull out a dictionary and turn this into a learning opportunity. Instead, with no further comment, she sent me back to my desk, an interminable walk of shame that I made with eyes lowered, lest my friends clock the humiliation on my face.

From then on, I began to second-guess everything I wrote. I would think twice before dipping into my large vocabulary to express myself—it was safer to use words like *old*. Ms. Merck's criticism, misguided as it was, had a chilling effect on my creativity.

The inner critic that was born in the fourth grade got stronger and louder as I grew up. I learned to write with that critic standing over my shoulder, scrutinizing every word through the eyes of someone who would hate it and rip it to shreds. People commonly refer to this as "perfectionism," but in a lot of cases it's a self-hating neurosis. Writing a TV script was perfectionism at its worst because I wasn't just trying to make it perfect in my own eyes, but also trying to meet someone else's ambiguous standards.

During my sabbatical, even though I was no longer working for someone, I'd write a sentence or two and the critic in my head would shriek, "It's shit!" like my coworker Miles from *Martial Law* used to say about every script we wrote. "This is completely unoriginal" was another constant refrain in my thoughts. Other popular hooks were "No one wants to read this" and the short and sweet "You're a hack!"

But after doing *The Artist's Way*, I felt freer from the critic's abuse. Julia Cameron recommended writing "morning pages," a daily practice where you vomit out three pages of stream-of-consciousness writing, for your eyes only, as a way of clearing out the cobwebs. I'd been keeping diaries my whole life, but wrote in them only when I had something to say. Writing three pages every day, regardless, helped me let go of the belief that everything I committed to paper had to be important enough to justify my sabbatical and *represent me as a writer*. (The pressure!) Morning pages welcomed me and my unimportant writing. Before long, I flipped through my notebook of daily vomit and had to admit I wasn't blocked anymore.

I began writing short stories again for the first time since college. I enrolled in a fiction-writing class at UCLA Extension and joined a writers' group with people who, refreshingly, did not work in showbiz. I wrote personal essays. I even wrote a spec pilot, and though it never got sold, at least I put it out there instead of hiding it in a drawer. All of this was a small miracle, given how much I had come to dread writing when I was in television rooms. Writing for TV is like working in a sausage factory: the last thing you want to do after that is eat sausage.

But my creative renaissance wasn't limited to writing. One day, on a whim, I bought a sewing machine. After it took me half an hour just to thread it, I realized I needed some lessons, so I took a class at a small sewing studio in Silverlake. Within weeks I was making pajama pants for everyone I knew. Sewing used a different part of my brain than writing did—it was more instinctive, less intellectual. It felt like drawing and painting, the things I used to love before I gave them up.

Unlike with writing, I didn't expect myself to be good at sewing, so I could just enjoy it. This is what's known in Zen as "beginner's mind." Even after I progressed to more advanced projects, I was able to do them without the compulsive need to control the result. With sewing, it was easier for me to bring awareness to my perfectionistic, striving tendencies and let go of them. I thought about my old friend Paula from *Letterman*, who painted in her free time, and how I had pooh-poohed her unambitious approach to making art. Now I finally understood that she'd been onto something.

None of this would've been possible if I hadn't made the deliberate, unusual, and very fortunate decision to stop working, which gave me the time and mental space to reconnect with my artistic urges and finally have fun again. Taking a sabbatical saved my life. I got to live like a human instead of a machine that pumped out scripts. Being lazy, it turned out, wasn't the road to hell. For me, it was the road out of it.

10

Meddlers and Sycophants

After my year off, I felt like I had only just started to take care of myself and never wanted to work again. But I knew the internalized parental voices in my head—not to mention my actual parents—would go apeshit if I didn't get back to being a so-called responsible adult.

During my sabbatical, Larry had called frequently with inquiries from prospective employers. Rather than ruining my reputation, taking a break had given me a sort of mystique. But as the staffing season of 2003 ramped up, I made it clear I wasn't going to do this the way we had in the past. I wasn't going to read every pilot script out there. I wasn't going to meet with everyone who expressed interest in me. I would take a job only on an exceptional show that I felt passionate about.

I naïvely assumed I'd be able to find work under these strict conditions and had no plan B, since I still had some savings and treated it like "fuck-you money." Money means different things to different people. For some, it's a house, a nice car, travel, their kids' college education, security in their old age. For me, money meant the freedom to not take jobs that sucked.

But the truth is, the idea of *any* staff job still scared me. The thought of going back into a writers' room filled me with dread. My solution? Go into development instead. I still wasn't hot on the idea of running my own show, but I decided I'd cross that bridge when I came to it. In retrospect, I can see that's kind of like applying to law school when you have no intention of practicing law. I was young and shortsighted—and desperately trying to convince myself that I hadn't wasted the last six years of my life.

Since I didn't have any specific idea to pitch, I chose to pursue a blind script deal, which is when a production company or studio hires you to write a pilot without knowing what you're going to write. They agree to pay you a certain amount and you develop the idea together. It's like a mini-development deal. No office, assistant, or other perks, but it's a guaranteed paycheck.

Larry got me a meeting with the development executives at Brillstein-Grey, the company behind two of my favorite shows, *The Sopranos* and *The Larry Sanders Show*. Nervous but excited, I met them for lunch at Barney Greengrass in Beverly Hills. The head of development, Peter Traugott, was charming and funny, a caricature of the Hollywood player. He had a fit body and a Coppertone tan, but underneath his slick persona I saw a formerly overweight Jewish kid who counted calories like a teenage girl. He was a misfit. I hit it off with him right away.

As was the custom, no one spoke of the reason for this meeting. The phrase "blind script deal" never came up. We just sat there eating smoked salmon salads and sipping Arnold Palmers, chatting about the adventures I'd had on my sabbatical and my fervent Beatles obsession.

Even when meetings are going well, they always feel like a first date—you're there to sell your personality. I must've been doing a decent job of it, because they sent me a gift after. It was a book titled

A Hard Day's Write, which explains the story behind every Beatles song. Damn, these people were good! In the card they wrote, "We would love to do something together," and signed it "Your fans at Brill-stein-Grey." I was so flattered that I put the card up on my fridge and didn't take it down for months. To think that I would be courted this way after dropping out of the scene for a year was a huge ego boost.

When I started working with them during the summer of 2003, I had no idea how development was supposed to go. No one explained it to me. As with all my showbiz jobs, I was simply thrown into the deep end and expected to swim. Even if I had asked Carl what steps I might encounter, I assumed his experience would be different from mine, since his was a sitcom. I never considered asking Judd Apatow or Paul Feig for advice either, even though they would've been great mentors. I'd learned as a child not to bother anyone for help and still thought I should be able to do everything on my own.

When it came to development, there was no structure at all except for a vague sense that we had to have something to "go out with" (pitch to networks) by the end of August. That gave me roughly two months to come up with an idea. But all told, the amount of time I spent putting something on paper was less than it would take to wash a car. The idea-generating phase was spent mostly hanging out at their swank offices on Wilshire and Doheny, eating takeout and waiting for everyone to finish their phone calls.

Finally, near the end of July, I got down to pitching. I wish I could say that I swaggered in there with a groundbreaking vision. But the truth is, I was just trying to give these people, who had taken a chance on me, something they liked and something I knew I'd be capable of writing. Thus, most of the ideas I pitched were for youth-oriented relationship shows. Fortunately, high-concept shows were in vogue, and I had a few ideas in that vein.

High-concept shows are based on a unique premise, often playing with alternate realities. I'd been fascinated with alternate reality stories ever since I saw a film called *Julia and Julia* in 1987. It starred Kathleen Turner playing two versions of the same woman, caught in a love triangle with Gabriel Byrne and Sting, back when he was hot and tantric. Eleven years later Gwyneth Paltrow starred in *Sliding Doors*, a movie with the same basic concept. In one version of the story she misses a train, and in another version she catches it, sending her life in two drastically different directions.

Along those lines, I pitched a high school show based on the premise that the trajectory of your life depends on which lunch table you sit at on your first day. One road leads to being popular and cool, and the other to geekdom. In the twenty years since I pitched this idea, similar "high school *Sliding Doors*" shows have been attempted, but at the time it hadn't been done.

Everyone was into it, especially Lisa, the youngest of the Brillstein execs and my closest ally in the bunch. She suggested merging the *Sliding Doors* idea with another one of my pitches, a fish-out-of-water story about a Jersey girl who moves to New York City. In one reality, the main character, Cleo, would be a popular but jaded Jersey girl struggling to branch out from the suburban mold. In the other, she would be the insecure new girl from the 'burbs learning how to be cool in the big city. The same person would play both Cleos, a wet dream for a talented young actress. I knew I could write the shit out of this show, and everyone agreed it was the one we'd go out with. I named it *Bridge and Tunnel*.

With no office of my own, I worked from home. One afternoon, when the a/c couldn't put a dent in the heat, I took a break to hit the beach in Santa Monica, dragging Carl along for some muchneeded R & R. While I stretched out on my towel with my feet in the sand, Carl fidgeted under the umbrella, pestering me to try out my pitch on him.

"I'll tell you if it works."

I sighed without opening my eyes. "Can't you just, like . . . read a book or something?"

But I gave in. As I did my pitch, Carl kept interjecting with tips like, "Make sure you tell 'em she's got big Jersey hair in one world and a cool New York haircut in the other. I'm telling you, the hair's gonna sell it."

Everyone was single-mindedly focused on the sale, rather than telling a good story. It shouldn't have surprised me—I saw *The Player*—but it bummed me out anyway.

Once I was done writing the pitch, the process stopped being loosey-goosey and the micromanagement began. I couldn't even sneeze without getting it approved first. An idea has a nascent stage when it's tender and vulnerable and needs to be handled with extreme care. I've heard this called "protecting your muse." But when you're a TV writer, you're not allowed to protect your muse. In fact, if you even say the word *muse* without irony, you will be mocked. An idea can't grow organically when people are poking and prodding it all the time. That's the inherent problem with development.

And then there's the pitching . . . oy, the pitching.

First, I had to get the Brillstein team to approve the pitch. Then we had to pitch it to the studio, 20th Century Fox, and massage it until they were happy. Finally, we'd pitch it to the networks. Every step involved a series of arduous meetings, where I'd be sweating balls as I tried to make the pitch sound fresh for the hundredth time. By the time I did the network pitches, there were no fewer than sixteen eyes drilling into me. The performance anxiety was crippling.

My *Citizen Baines* coworker P.K. once said, "Writers are introverted by nature. Pitching is the worst forum for us." I knew that was true from working on *Friends*, where I had flubbed many of my own jokes. Worried that I would choke under pressure, I got ready for each meeting by memorizing the pitch verbatim and rehearsing it until my throat was raw—which pretty much guaranteed it wouldn't sound fresh.

We hung most of our hopes on Fox, the network known for other youth-centric entertainment such as *Beverly Hills, 90210* and *Melrose Place*. The Fox pitch took place on a sweltering, sticky afternoon in late August. Escorted by the Brillstein and 20th execs, I made my way across the blazing-hot asphalt, entered the overly air-conditioned building, and took the elevator up to the breeding ground of drama development.

The Fox execs were a couple of young preppies: a guy whose face showed no emotion whatsoever, and a woman who was halfway down the road between sorority girl and soccer mom. I heard she went by the nickname "Peaches." The cutesy moniker did not suit her. Before we were called in, Peaches confided to Lisa that she'd been in so many back-to-back meetings, she hadn't gone to the bathroom all day. It didn't ease my nerves to know that her focus would be split between my pitch and not pissing her pants.

I pulled out all the stops, hoping my desperation would come off as enthusiasm. I followed Carl's advice and emphasized the two hairstyles. To illustrate the Jersey mall-rat hair, I even passed around a visual aid: my student ID from 1988, in which my permed 'do was teased four inches high and I looked like an extra in a Whitesnake video.

The smiling Brillstein and 20th execs flanking me on the couch were like a bunch of stage moms. I could feel the encouragement seeping out of their pores. They laughed at my canned lines, trying to create an atmosphere of excitement—like hip-hop hype men, Flavor

Flav to my Chuck D. This was a tall order. The Fox preppies were a tough room. In fact, the male was so stiff and expressionless, I suspected he might be an android.

After, Lisa babysat me in the hallway while the other execs conferred behind closed doors. Only a few minutes passed before Traugott emerged, smiling, and announced that Fox wanted to buy the pilot. This was how it often went down, he said. If a network loved your pitch, they'd "buy it in the room" rather than wait to hear other pitches. I was thrilled. It felt like a badge of success. Lisa gave me a big hug and told me she was going to cancel our meeting with ABC, scheduled for the following morning.

"This show belongs at Fox," she said.

"I agree."

But mostly I was just relieved that I wouldn't have to pitch anymore.

From the get-go, there were too many cooks in the kitchen. This became even more evident after I turned in my outline of *Bridge and Tunnel* at the end of September. On a conference call with six execs—all of whom were either driving or otherwise multitasking—everyone vamped, throwing random things in just to have something to say. And I was taking all these notes seriously, even though many were contradictory or made no sense. By the time the call ended, I was thoroughly confused and had no idea how to proceed.

I hung up the phone and buried my face in my hands, debating whether I should beg my agent to get me out of my contract or put a quicker end to my misery—maybe a handful of Tylenol PMs chased with toilet bowl cleaner. Did I *have* any toilet bowl cleaner? A minute later the phone rang again. It was Traugott.

"I'm so sorry, Patty. That was such a clusterfuck."

"Oh my God, Peter. My head's exploding."

"I know. Forget everything you just heard, okay? Let's talk again in a few days after we've had a chance to get our shit together."

That was Traugott's special talent: knowing when to step in and get real. From that day on, I always respected him for being willing to admit when he and his people had fucked up. Hollywood is teeming with so much bullshit, it takes only a single moment of honesty to set someone apart.

But the stupid notes didn't stop, and I still had to address most of them. You see, development isn't about unbridled creativity; it's about pleasing a lot of people at once. In that way it was even more laborious than working on a staff, where all I needed to do was satisfy the showrunner—it was *their* job to deal with the network and studio. Now having had a taste of the showrunners' plight, I had more sympathy for their perpetual grumpiness.

My brother and his wife, Cynthia, who had been living in L.A. for several years, had their first baby that November. My mom came out from New Jersey for the birth, and since Cyn's parents were staying at their small house in Los Feliz, my mom crashed at my apartment. Even though she split most of her time between Harry's house and the hospital, I still felt claustrophobic with her in my space, worried she was scrutinizing my every move. When I was the one visiting my parents, I could hide in my old room and come out for meals now and then. But here, I felt pressure to entertain my mom, and her presence at my usual haunts was incongruous and disquieting.

Meanwhile, Peaches was pushing me to finish my script before Thanksgiving because her boss, Fox president Gail Berman, would be reading pilots over the holiday. Having mine in that pile would give my show a better chance of getting picked up. Once again, I put my entire life aside and worked around the clock. Every night while my mom was snoring on the sofa bed in my living room, I was hunched over my desk a few feet away, banging out my script until two in the morning.

It was during that visit that my mom realized how hard I worked at a job that, until then, probably seemed like a joke to her. She showed her appreciation with food, whipping up my favorite noodle dishes and stir-fries, to keep me fueled as I toiled away. I felt vindicated but bitter—like when Carl kept patting me on the back for that writing marathon on my birthday. Why were the people in my life only impressed by total sacrifice? They didn't value balance or taking care of oneself. They never said, "Patty, you're working too hard," or, "Maybe this isn't a healthy job situation." No one in my life recognized this, except for my therapist.

I managed to meet the deadline. After my script made the rounds among the cubicles at Fox, I was told that all the young assistants had declared *Bridge and Tunnel* their favorite pilot of the season. Peaches called me and raved about my script in hyperbolic terms; it sounded like she would've given me an Emmy right then and there if it had been in her power. But it was all about Gail Berman now. She had the final say on which pilots Fox would pick up. My future was riding on the opinion of this one person whom I had never met.

Thanksgiving came and went. I ate overcooked turkey at my brother's house and watched him learn how to change diapers. I didn't hear back from Fox. A week went by, then two. Soon it was mid-December and the whole industry was shutting down for Christmas. I was promised through a series of middlemen that Gail would read my script over the holiday . . . *this* holiday. It was like waiting for a guy to call after giving him my number at a party. After a certain point, I just knew it wasn't going to happen.

And then my parents decided to retire and move to L.A.

This was good news for Harry and Cyn because they needed help with the baby. While my parents were in town for the birth, they went shopping for a house. *Good luck with that*, I thought. I knew from house hunting with Carl that the market in L.A. was insultingly unaffordable. So imagine my surprise when my parents bought a house within one week of their search. It was in Azusa, a working-class suburb east of Pasadena. Which would put them a mere forty-five-minute drive from my apartment.

Six years had passed since I'd lived near my parents. Though the geographical distance hadn't exactly improved our relationship, it at least created a buffer. My mom was planning to apply for early retirement; she would move to L.A. the following spring while my dad stayed in New Jersey for a few more months until he could secure his pension. I knew I should've been happy about this, but it scared the hell out of me. I figured that with no job or husband to care for, my mom would have nothing to do but nag me and smother me to death. I obviously didn't foresee how much time she would spend babysitting my nephew.

One day in early December, when I was stressing out about all this, I injured myself at the gym. No, I didn't tear a tendon while bench-pressing or something macho like that. I was simply squatting down on an exercise mat to do some stretching when I felt a shooting pain in my right hip flexor. Then I couldn't even walk a few paces before my hip would start to hurt. Sitting cross-legged, which used to be a breeze for my flexible hips, was now excruciating.

I went to several doctors and had an X-ray, MRI, and ultrasound. Fortunately, at that time the Writers Guild health insurance had very good coverage, and I never fretted over medical bills. But none of the doctors could tell me what was wrong. I had just tweaked my hip—that was all. I had a strong suspicion the injury was psychosomatic.

Let's see, I find out my mother is moving nearby and my hip goes out. . . . Coincidence? My yoga teacher was always saying that the hips are closely related to emotions. Yup, I was pretty sure this pain wasn't random.

Carl and I spent our Christmas break in Hana, a remote town on the eastern coast of Maui. We stayed at a resort that had no cellphone reception or other modern distractions. While on vacation, I had plenty of time to think about my future and the possibility of my show getting made. The prospect still freaked me out, but—just like when I applied to colleges—I was more focused on getting accepted than on what came after. Thus, I found myself hoping for "good news." If enough people pump you up about something, you start believing you want it.

Meanwhile, Carl and I were celebrating our ten-year anniversary. It was hard to believe a decade had passed since we ice-skated at the *Letterman* Christmas party and fell in love. We'd been through so much together: our late-night jobs in New York, relocating to L.A., *Seinfeld* and *Friends*, 9/11 . . . but we were stuck in a holding pattern. He still hadn't bought a house, and the delay seemed more about postponing our cohabitation than anything else. His attitude toward marriage hadn't changed, even after most of his friends back East took the plunge. With each wedding he'd rant about how his friend was "settling" and how marriage would squash their potential.

Carl would sometimes talk about wanting to break up for a while before we got married. Not so he could fuck around—that, I would've understood. Rather, he had this notion that before "giving in" to marriage, he needed to be alone and search his soul, like an Aborigine on walkabout. I thought this masculine fantasy was ludicrous. Would marrying me be such a prison sentence? I'd get pissed off every time he brought it up, which is why I tried to avoid the topic as much as possible. I wanted Carl to *want* to marry me, not to be cattle-prodded into it.

When I allowed myself to think about our future, I saw our married life much as it was now, just with more togetherness. We'd still have fun, watching TV and movies, eating out, and going on vacations. Having kids was more of a theoretical thing. I figured we'd have a family, but the particulars remained vague. Either way, it seemed like a good life. It wasn't so much the certificate of marriage or the wedding that mattered to me. It was what marriage would symbolize: intimacy and commitment. If we'd had those things already, I wouldn't have cared about a piece of paper or a ring.

But we couldn't even talk about any of this without Carl freaking out. On the day of our anniversary, we were strolling through the open-air hotel lobby when Carl stopped and sank down onto a bench next to a gurgling fountain. I sat next to him, breathing in the sweet scent of plumerias before I turned to see a brooding look on his face.

"Tell me why I should marry you," he said.

"Are you fucking kidding me?"

"No. I really want to figure this out."

"We've been together for ten years. You need me to make a case for why you should marry me?"

Carl was dead serious. He had no idea how insulting it was to make me *pitch myself*, as if he were a network executive I was trying to woo. I should've broken up with him on the spot and hopped on the next plane back to the mainland. But in the moment, I didn't fully register how cruel his behavior was. Sadly, I was accustomed to being treated that way and brushing it off—a coping mechanism I'd adopted to protect myself.

We argued for a while, Carl insisting that marriage would get in the way of his career ambitions, and me reminding him that I had never held him back before. Growing angrier by the minute, I finally got up from the bench.

"You can sit here and keep coming up with reasons not to marry me," I said, slinging my purse over my shoulder. "I'll be in the gift shop."

As soon as we left the island, I checked my messages. Not one person had called me about the pilot. Not even my agent had left word. In the TV business, radio silence is par for the course. But to me it's just plain rude. It shows no understanding of an artist's need for feedback, and no respect for the people who poured their hearts into a project.

At last, in early January—seven weeks after turning in my final draft—I got a call from Peaches. The last time I had spoken to her, she was over the moon about my script. Now I pictured sweat forming dark circles in the armpits of her J.Crew button-down shirt, its sleeves rolled up in anticipation of the task ahead of her: delivering bad news, not just to me, but to a bunch of other hopeful writers on her call list. For a moment, I almost felt sorry for her for having such a hideous job.

"Gail didn't respond to the script," she said.

Maybe it was the stress that had built up over those seven weeks of waiting, or maybe it was the cowardice I could smell on Peaches beneath her professional manner—but for whatever reason, I didn't receive the news with my usual aplomb.

"First of all, it's unacceptable that I had to wait seven weeks to get an answer. Why did you pressure me to finish the script before Thanksgiving? I was killing myself for no reason."

"You did a great job—especially with so little time."

This backhanded compliment did nothing to assuage my anger. "You were *gushing* over this script. All the assistants in your office said it was their favorite pilot. They're the demographic for this show. If you're not gonna listen to them, who *are* you gonna listen to? I understand that in the end it's up to Gail, but if you were so gung ho about this pilot, why didn't you stand up for it?"

Peaches backpedaled like crazy, blathering "executive speak," an irksome lingo that reminded me of the coded language in *Variety*. It was clear to me now that most execs were either meddlers that gummed up the creative process or useless sycophants. Until they had yes-manned their way up the ladder to Gail Berman's level, they had no real influence. Their sole motivation was to not get fired.

After I let loose on Peaches, I sat frozen at my desk, in shock. I thought about my old friend Del from *Martial Law* saying, "All anyone wants is to be treated with respect." Development was supposed to be my escape from the abusive world of staff writing. But now I knew it was a cop-out, a way that I could keep working in the business and not have to find a new profession. The only thing I managed to do was shift the details around. I was still in an abusive relationship.

After we got back from Hana, things with Carl went downhill. He was going through a rough time—to be blunt, he was a total wreck. Not only was the marriage issue hanging over him like an anvil, but he was also stressed about his career. While he'd had huge success in both TV and features, as soon as he reached one goal, he became fixated on the next. He'd recently sold a screenplay about a workaholic who loses the love of his life because of his career obsession. Though ostensibly a comedy, I didn't find it funny at all.

At my urging, Carl agreed to start therapy. He went kicking and screaming, but he knew he needed to get his act together or he was going to lose me. Therapy turned his world upside down; it was like peeling the layers of a rotten onion. He would come back from a session with his identity in little pieces around him. He kept saying, "I'm working on this as fast as I can," to assure me that he would soon be "cured" and we could live happily ever after. But I knew from my own experience that therapy wasn't something you could muscle through. He was in for a long, rocky ride.

Believe it or not, we were still looking at houses every Sunday. We were the window shoppers, the ones hanging at the back of the crowd, trying not to catch the real estate agent's attention. Sometimes they'd manage to corner us anyway and name-drop a celebrity who had lived there. Even now when I hear certain names, I associate them with architectural features. *Paul Thomas Anderson: screening room. Renée Zellweger: clawfoot bathtub. Jane Fonda: tree growing in foyer.* At one house in Laurel Canyon, the realtor pointed to an expanse of green canvas that protected a nearby estate from public view.

"That's George Clooney's tennis court," she told us.

I didn't think Clooney would appreciate that.

We saw a house in Los Feliz that looked like a storybook castle, on a street called Chislehurst. It was on the market for months. Every Sunday after doing the rounds, we'd end up at Chislehurst again, exploring its nooks and crannies. It had a charming little turret room with blond wood floors and a bay window, where I pictured myself writing morning pages and doing yoga. But even though Carl loved the house, he had a litany of complaints and refused to make an offer. Why he tortured me by taking me there week after week, I'll never understand. There were always cinnamon-scented candles burning at the open house, and to this day when I smell that fragrance, it triggers an autonomic response of longing.

One day in May, we found a beautiful Country English house in Hancock Park. It had more than enough space, a swimming pool, and room for a basketball court in the driveway—something Carl insisted on even though he never played basketball. This house checked all his boxes except that it wasn't Spanish, which he had decided was his top must-have. I took one look and gave him my blessing. I'd seen enough to know it didn't get better than this.

After some hemming and hawing, Carl told his broker to make a bid, not expecting anything to come of it. He had bid on several houses before and always lowballed. That night he showed up at my apartment looking shell-shocked.

"Guess what," he said in a shaky voice.

"We got the house?"

"I got the house."

I, not *we*. He had been doing this all along, making me feel like I wasn't truly part of this decision. Yes, he was the one buying the house, but I was willing to contribute financially and, knowing Carl, I'd be doing most of the cooking, cleaning, and general upkeep. Yet this whole time he'd been thinking of the house as his and his alone.

As the prospect of commitment loomed, he appeared to be panicking like a caged animal. He went on a nitpicking frenzy, grasping for anything about the house that could be seen as a flaw. He even warned me not to get excited because he might back out of the deal. "There's a Mediterranean-style house coming on the market in a few weeks," he told me, after he'd grilled his broker about other options. Sure, the Hancock Park house was impeccable, but his dream house was Spanish . . . or, at the very least, Mediterranean.

After a day or so, we began to ease into talking about what we would do to the house. Despite Carl's admonitions, I started to fantasize. The kitchen had a breakfast nook featuring a U-shaped booth lined with red gingham cushions. I pictured lazy Sunday mornings in that little nook, eating pancakes and reading the paper—even though Carl usually spent Sunday mornings watching a talk show on AMC where a couple of showbiz weasels discussed the industry and interviewed celebs. There was no reason to believe he would give up this loathsome ritual after we moved in together.

Our friend Ezra, the New York psychologist, had recently moved to L.A. Carl and I had a running joke about making him our "Kato Kaelin"—letting him live in our guesthouse so he could take care of the property the way Kato did for O.J. while he was traveling (or, you know, out killing his ex-wife). The Hancock Park house didn't have a guesthouse, but it did have five bedrooms. When Carl brought up the idea of renting one out to Ezra, I realized he wasn't joking anymore. This was not the vision I had for us as a couple heading toward marriage.

"You're not seriously considering this, are you?"

Carl mulled it over for a beat. "I guess the only way I'd let Ezra live in the house is if we broke up for a while."

Here it was again, the threat he'd been lording over me for years. After all the therapy and so-called progress he'd made, Carl was still talking about breaking up? Just as we were on the cusp of a tighter bond, he was throwing this dagger at me again?

"I'm sick of hearing about this! Let's just fucking do it already!"

And that was how it started. The beginning of the end.

For the next two days, we talked about breaking up. On Monday night we had dinner at a tapas bar, where we ran into my agent's former assistant and his beaming fiancée. They had just gotten engaged and told us their cute proposal story. Painful. On Tuesday afternoon I went to therapy and cried. On Tuesday night we had dinner at an English pub on Sunset where we'd had many good times. We had gone there the day George Harrison died and played Beatles songs on the jukebox. But *this* sad situation couldn't be soothed with music and shepherd's pie. This time when we talked about breaking up, I knew it was the only option.

It was midnight by the time we got back to my place. Carl loitered, distraught, while I brushed my teeth, washed my face, and changed into pajamas. Then I climbed into bed, looked at him, and said, "That's it."

How does it feel when a ten-year relationship ends? Like how I imagine it feels to cut off your own arm. Carl couldn't understand the nuts and bolts of the breakup. How were we going to stop talking to each other? Were we allowed to communicate at all? I didn't see how we could have any contact without it being weird and, more important, defeating the purpose.

"I'm not saying, 'Don't call me until you have a ring.' That's not what this is about."

"But I *should* have a ring."

He knew where he wanted to end up. He just didn't know how long it would take to get there. The problem, however, ran much deeper than his fear of commitment: we had grown completely, irrevocably apart.

I would always be grateful to Carl for helping me get a foot in the door in television. He had been my role model, someone who started with nothing and made his dreams come true. But as my disillusionment with the business grew, I began to see him as a cautionary tale. It was clear to me that his professional achievements had come at the expense of his relationships, health, and overall engagement with the world. He had isolated himself in a solipsistic universe that I was longing to break away from.

Once it sank in that this was really the end, we both started crying. The kind of ugly, snot-filled, convulsive crying that makes you feel like you can't breathe. I kept begging him to leave, but he couldn't bring himself to do it. He stood by my bed and asked, in a gentle voice that broke my heart, "Are you gonna be able to make it through the night?"

I honestly didn't know. But I said yes because I couldn't take his being there any longer. At last, after a lot of sobbing and half starts toward the door, Carl hugged me as tightly as he ever had. Then he left.

I thought I would cry all night long. But the strangest thing happened. After a short while, I started to feel calmer. Relieved. I got out of bed, sat cross-legged on a cushion in the corner, and meditated. I was doing it purely out of desperation, to quell my anxiety. But as I sat there watching my breath, I connected to a deeper part of myself, a solid core of strength and well-being that was untouched by all this drama. This was the sense of peace that I had striven for so many times in meditation, often to no avail—and here it was, gracing me at my darkest, most turbulent moment.

Soon my tears dried up. I rose from the cushion and climbed back into bed, nestling under the covers as my eyelids grew heavy. Drifting off to sleep, I knew in my heart that I had done the right thing. I was free.

11

Lord of the Housewives

Right after I broke up with Carl, I got an offer to write for *Desperate Housewives* and accepted it with very little thought about the warning signs I'd seen in the meeting. I was too preoccupied with the upheaval in my personal life to make a clearheaded decision. No matter how troubled a relationship is, losing it leaves a void. And that's one of the reasons I went back to writing on a TV show: it was familiar, safe, and all-consuming enough to keep me distracted from the loneliness and grief that would otherwise swallow me up.

Desperate Housewives was a darkly funny nighttime soap. The pilot was written on spec by Marc Cherry, who used to write for the classic sitcom *The Golden Girls*. Marc was known as a "cold" writer, meaning he'd been out of work for a long time—like, ever since *The Golden Girls* went off the air in the early nineties. For years no one knew or cared what Marc Cherry was up to. Then he put out this pilot and the whole town was abuzz.

When Larry sent me the script in the spring of 2004, I was hunkered down in my unemployment and post-breakup cave, clad in sweats and closer than ever to being done with TV. But the script won me over, and I soon found myself putting on pants that buttoned and going to meet with Marc. He was friendly enough, but I could tell he took himself quite seriously. The fact that I had written a pilot seemed to give me some cachet with him. When I complained about the way the network handled it, Marc could relate. After his cold streak, he identified with the "Hollywood screwed me" point of view.

In staffing meetings no one ever asked me about my marital status. Sometimes the fact that I had a boyfriend would come up, but this was unsolicited, as it should be. Marc, on the other hand, asked me point-blank, "Are you married? Do you have a family?" Apparently, he didn't get the memo that you weren't supposed to ask that.

"No," I said.

"Good. We like people who have no lives."

He was joking. But not really.

We started work on a sunny day in June. Before we even set foot in our offices, Marc treated us to lunch at the Arnie Morton's in Burbank so we could all get to know each other. We sat at a long banquet table in the private party room and tucked into steaks and lobster tails at one in the afternoon. The writing staff consisted of ten people, including Marc. Surprise, surprise—I was the only person of color.

Bloated from lunch, we moved into our offices on the NBCUniversal lot. Mine had no windows, a clunky PC, and a chair across from the desk that would turn into a confessional of sorts as the season wore on and my coworkers would come in to vent.

But before this happened, we had our honeymoon period—the preproduction phase when we sat around the writers' room and chatted about character arcs, jotting down ideas on index cards and pinning them to the corkboards along the walls. The minute Marc saw my handwriting, I was stuck being the board writer and spent the rest of my time there with a Sharpie in my hand. My fate was impossible to avoid.

During those early days, everyone got a chance to speak, and the room felt surprisingly democratic. I didn't expect it to last—not with this many big personalities. The biggest was Marc's. I had never encountered overt racism until I worked for him. One day at lunch, the topic of Margaret Cho came up, and someone mentioned *All-American Girl*, Cho's short-lived sitcom about a Korean American family. Marc turned to me and said, "Patty, you should write a show like that."

I love Margaret Cho, but please don't lump us together just because we're both Asian women in show business. This wasn't the first time in my life I was subjected to this kind of "harmless" racism. In college, whenever I told people I was majoring in communications, they'd start talking about Connie Chung.

As soon as Marc wrote the first episode after the pilot, it became obvious to me that he didn't have a vision yet of what the show was going to be. This uncertainty, paired with his obsessive tendencies, amounted to a showrunner who was impossible to please. "No, that's not it" was his mantra. He rewrote even his own material with a maniacal drive.

The only writers he trusted to punch up jokes were Joey and John, a loyal team who had known Marc for many years. The three of them made up their own little comedy room filled with inside jokes and fraternal squabbles. Meanwhile, the rest of us were given the busy-work of writing the marginally funny material—like the voice-overs of Mary Alice, the deceased character who narrates the series with clever quips. Once, Marc sent me off to rewrite a single line of Mary Alice dialogue no fewer than six times. He was incapable of articulating what he wanted. It was maddening.

But I had another boss named Liam who was even worse. He was what the trades call a "top lieutenant," an experienced writer-producer that a network pairs up with a first-time showrunner. Marc was considered the *artiste*, while Liam managed the day-to-day operations of the writing staff. Unfortunately, that meant I had to take most of my orders from him.

Since scripts are usually assigned in order of seniority, Liam was first in line to write an episode after Marc. But he kept putting it off and then assigned it to a senior writer named Everett, who was hilarious and beloved. When Everett turned in his script, Marc began to treat him like a persona non grata. He was forced to do several rewrites without clear instructions, and a few days later Marc and Liam called an emergency meeting with the writers—everyone except Everett. We gathered in Liam's office and Marc closed the door with an ominous thunk.

"We've all got to gang-bang Everett's script," he announced. "We're gonna fire him. He just doesn't get the voice of the show."

I felt sick to my stomach. Everett got the show as well as anyone; he was just a scapegoat being punished for Marc's lack of vision. But what really appalled me was that Marc and Liam were telling us first. Why did they do that? The only reason I could fathom was that they wanted to put the fear of God in us. Let us know it could happen to us, too.

"If you see Everett," Marc instructed, "don't tell him."

That was when I lost any composure I had left. Marc was putting us in a horrible position. Anyone with an ounce of compassion would want to give Everett fair warning, but to do so would be disobeying our boss. My disgust must have been written all over my face because Marc paused and called on me.

"Patty? You look like you want to say something."

I try not to entertain regret, but that was the one moment in my career that I regret with all my heart. If I could go back in time, I'd tell Marc and Liam what I was really thinking: "What you're doing to Everett and what you're asking of us is fucked up and unfair, and I refuse to be a part of it." The next thing I would do is tell Everett. And then I would quit.

But at the time, I felt scared and trapped—and apparently so did all the other writers, because nobody said a damn thing. Glancing at their drawn faces, I was reminded of the group psychology experiments I learned about in Psych 101: mind control, submission to authority, herd mentality. People beating or electrocuting other people simply because they were following orders. Marc and Liam's fear tactics had worked. Instead of speaking up, I mumbled, "I'm just worried about how we're gonna get caught up on scripts. We're already so behind."

Which was true: thanks to Marc and Liam's stellar time management, we had missed every preproduction deadline, and this was only the second episode. No skin off *my* nose, but I was trying to cover for the real reason I felt like throwing up. Marc assured me we would all pitch in. Which was also true: from then on, we would gang-bang every script.

Throughout this meeting, Liam sat silently behind his desk, like a skinny Don Corleone, letting Marc do the dirty work. While Marc may have been an awful boss—demanding, unprofessional, and not very nice—I blame Liam for firing Everett. It's not uncommon on a new series for the first writer up at bat to be ousted for "not getting the show." By forcing Everett to turn in his script first, Liam ensured that he himself would not become the sacrificial scapegoat. That's some sneaky shit.

My mom moved into the new house in Azusa that summer. While my dad was helping her settle in, they asked me to go shopping with them for a dining room set, since I was the decorating expert in the family. I took them to lunch first at a seafood restaurant in the Gower Gulch, a strip mall with a façade that was once used in Westerns. A barbecue joint would've made more sense there, but L.A. strip malls were full of incongruities and surprises.

"I wanted to tell you in person," I said, picking at my poached salmon. "Carl and I broke up."

Neither of them seemed surprised. I'm sure my mom had been expecting this to happen ever since I'd flipped out on her at Newark Airport. But she was kind enough not to say so.

"Are you okay?" she asked.

"Yeah, I'm fine. I mean, I'm sad. . . . We were together a long time." I could feel my stomach clenching. I never confided in them about my love life, so I tried to keep it simple. "He just wasn't ready for a commitment."

My dad glanced at my mom, then back at me. "We knew something was wrong when you two kept going to weddings together and never got married."

The idea of weddings being some sort of contagion would've made me laugh if I hadn't been so depressed. "I just don't want you to worry about me, okay?"

They nodded, and I went back to talking about furniture, grateful they didn't say anything about my wasting the best years of my life on a dead-end relationship. Given that my mom had been waiting for me to get married since I was twenty, I was impressed by her discretion. It was possible I wasn't the only one relieved that Carl was out of the picture.

A few hours later, as we were trying out chairs at Crate & Barrel, I began to feel unwell. I raced home and barfed up what was left of my lunch, then moved on to bloody diarrhea and stomach cramps that had me in tears. The next morning, I had to call in sick—I could barely function. After hours of alternating between writhing on my bed and sprinting to the toilet, I finally went to the ER.

This time it was my parents, not Carl, who accompanied me to Cedars. They were the only people in the world inured to my diarrhea, having changed my diapers and wiped my ass countless times. The doctor took a stool sample and diagnosed me with salmonella poisoning, then put me on antibiotics and sent me home. A health inspector was dispatched to the seafood restaurant in the Gower Gulch, and soon after, this purveyor of spoiled fish disappeared like the city of Atlantis. I'm sure mine wasn't the first complaint.

The food poisoning may have been random, but the debilitating illness reflected my current emotional state. Between the breakup and the dawning nightmare of my job, I was not feeling strong. And even though I had implored my parents not to worry, I'm sure that watching me doubled over in pain and shitting myself didn't ease their minds.

When I returned to the office two days later, I had lost five pounds. The only food I could keep down was Saltines, so I brought a box to work and nibbled on them in the writers' room while everyone else was lunching on Mexican takeout. Marc helped himself to my crackers without asking. He polished them off within minutes, licking the tip of his chubby index finger and pressing it on the plastic sleeve to pick up every last crumb.

As soon as Everett was gone, Liam wasted no time bringing in his pals, hiring two new writers he had worked with before. He was on a mission to turn the writing staff into his own personal clubhouse, calculating that the more allies he had, the safer he would be from getting pushed out by Marc and his posse. Marc, Joey, and John were an insular trio that Liam was excluded from, which no doubt made him nervous.

But nothing could protect him from the spotlight of Marc's criticism. At the end of July, Liam turned in his long-awaited script while I was out of town for my cousin's wedding. On the second day of my trip, I called one of the writers to find out what was happening at work.

"We were sent home," she said.

"What do you mean 'sent home'?"

"Marc and Liam gave us the rest of the week off."

"Why?"

"So they could work on Liam's script."

The impromptu vacation was Liam's idea. After the writers had spent a whole day in the room watching Marc tear his script apart, Liam convinced Marc they should send everyone away, for efficiency's sake. But really, it was to save face. How would anyone respect Liam's authority after witnessing such a humiliating bloodbath?

His script turned out to be a page-one rewrite, executed by gang bang.

Gang-banging scripts at *Desperate Housewives* was dysfunctional and sloppy. Every scene was written hastily by a different person. Marc would barely be involved in the first few drafts, but once the script was in semi-decent shape, he'd take it from us, climb into a golf cart, and drive off to his "writing bungalow" to do a pass. He was given this detached room in an undisclosed location because he had a short attention span and tended to involve himself in all sorts of office minutiae. Keeping him in solitary was the only way to get this goose to lay any eggs.

After Marc finished his pass, he would return to the writers' room to punch up the script with Joey and John. The only ones who knew how to wrangle Marc, these guys had the unenviable task of keeping him focused and not allowing him to get fixated on every line. When they managed to wrench the script from his hands, it would get turned over to production, usually just before the table read and sometimes just before the first day of shooting.

With this wildly inefficient system, it's a miracle that any episodes of *Desperate Housewives* ever got made. The quality that had attracted me to the pilot—the dark humor—was lost in the slapdash, assembly-line approach to what was supposed to be a creative process. We were putting out schlock. The fact that it became the hottest show on TV, won multiple awards, ran for eight years, and earned more revenue than God still boggles my mind.

My hours got even longer when the show went into production in August. We were expected to arrive by ten a.m. even though Marc and Liam spent most of the day on set. The writers weren't barred from the set, but we weren't exactly welcome. Usually we'd see the cast only at table reads, where we'd sit quietly in the back and try not to make eye contact with Teri Hatcher.

We'd often have nothing to do until Liam called a meeting at dinnertime. Eight hours wasted. Why couldn't we tend to our lives earlier in the day and come in when they were ready for us? Oh, right: we weren't supposed to *have* lives.

And for the most part, I didn't. The little free time I had was spent trying to process the breakup with Carl. I wrote in my journal, called my friends, read self-help books, even upped my therapy to twice a week—at least until my work schedule got so intense that I had to cut back. But my recovery wasn't going well, mostly because I jumped back into dating too soon.

After ten years with the same person, I had wild oats to sow—but I've never been the kind of person who can have sex without getting attached. I was always looking for a boyfriend. Unfortunately, the guys I liked were not what you would call boyfriend material. One was a loser I met in my writers' group. On Friday nights we'd smoke a Cheech-and-Chong amount of pot, order lots of greasy food, and have sex with one-sided foreplay in which I'd go down on him but he wouldn't go down on me. I was also chasing an old flame who split his time between L.A. and New York, a setup that gave him a convenient escape hatch from any real intimacy. Both these dudes were commitment-phobes, like Carl.

I was also infatuated with one of our production assistants, a hot guy in his early twenties named Nick. With his brooding looks and retro sneakers, he was cooler than I ever was, even at his age. All the writers knew I liked him and teased me about it. One night when we were bored, waiting for Liam to call a meeting, I jumped up and said, "That's it, I'm asking Nick out."

Everyone got excited and started running around, yelling, "She's gonna do it! She's gonna ask Nick out!"

I lost my nerve and went to the kitchen to get a snack instead. When I returned with a pack of Corn Nuts and no story, everyone was disappointed. My messed-up love life was a source of entertainment for them, most of whom were in steady relationships. I used to be one of them, living vicariously, wishing I were single and free. Well, guess what? Single and free isn't all it's cracked up to be. A lot of the time it just sucks. I feared I would never find the right person and I was doomed to be alone.

One day I was in my office, writing some dumb scene, when Carl's assistant showed up in my doorway with a big cardboard box in his arms. Though I tried not to think about it, Carl still had an office at NBCUniversal, just a short walk from mine.

"This came to Carl's apartment." He set the box on my desk and left.

When I opened it, I found some skin care products I'd ordered. I used to have stuff shipped to Carl's place sometimes because he had a doorman to receive packages; the vendor had mistakenly used the old shipping address. But there was also a long letter from Carl and a bunch of gifts, small trinkets that weren't my taste at all. How could he know me intimately for ten years and think, *Boy, I bet Patty would love this cat-shaped picture frame*?

I knew it wasn't a good idea to read his letter at work, but how could I not? Unlike the scribbled birthday cards he'd given me over the years, this twelve-page single-spaced missive had been typed on a computer and printed on pink floral stationery. That paper made me sadder than anything else.

He told me he'd sold the house in Hancock Park before ever moving in, because he couldn't bear to live in it without me. "I kept seeing you in every room," he wrote. (Well, he'd seen Ezra in at least one of them.) He told me how much he had changed. He was no longer obsessed with work; all he wanted to do was marry me and shower me with affection every day for the rest of our lives. I was the most amazing woman he'd ever known and the best thing that ever happened to him.

He was saying everything I'd always wanted to hear—way too late. I knew the only reason Carl had come around was that I didn't want to be with him anymore. If I took him back, it wouldn't be long before the pendulum swung the other way.

Reading that letter was like watching a car crash; my body cringed with every sentence. Nobody knew how to get to me like Carl. I was a mess of conflicted emotions, including deep sadness about the death of a relationship that I had assumed would last forever, and fiery anger about the way he had chosen to deliver his message: buried in a box of moisturizer. He'd sent his minion to my office in the middle of a workday to drop this bomb. It was, to use one of Carl's favorite words, an ambush.

I tucked the letter back into the box, took it home that night, and filed it away in a drawer, not prepared to respond but knowing that one day I'd have to. I already felt it hanging over me. The letter had reopened wounds that had hardly begun to heal, and I felt as fragile as a teacup with a crack through the middle.

This personal melodrama was compounded by the one going on in my professional life. Taking the job at *Desperate Housewives* to distract myself from painful feelings turned out to be a gross miscalculation. The job piled on *more* pain when I was already so vulnerable. I picked exactly the wrong job at the wrong time. Instead of retreating into a warm, comforting embrace, I had walked naked onto a minefield.

Liam had created a *Lord of the Flies* situation. He would poke his head into the room and gather everyone but me and two other writers whom he had decided were the useless ones. He'd point to each of his favorites and say, "You . . . you . . . and you," leaving the three of us sitting there, humiliated. Anyone who's ever been picked last for a team in gym class knows how awful that feels. I'm sure Liam relished that power, since he was a dweeb who'd probably been picked last plenty of times.

Even though Liam was my nemesis, I was getting no respect from Marc, either. As far as he was concerned, my only talent was neat handwriting. He once sent a P.A. to summon me to his bungalow to "do his cards." Not to collaborate and come up with ideas, but to simply take dictation. Something in me snapped.

"Tell him I'm writing a scene." I was in the middle of toiling away on the assembly line that Marc pretended to have no knowledge of. He wanted to believe first drafts grew on trees.

One day he dropped in on a gang bang to read our pages, and when he got to one Mary Alice voice-over, he gushed, "That is a *great* line." He had no idea I wrote it.

Another writer tried to make sure I got credit. "Way to go, Lin," she said.

Marc acted like he didn't hear her. He moved on without comment. He had already made up his mind about me, and that was that.

One Monday morning in mid-October, I found out that all the writers had been called in to work over the weekend—except for me and my two "useless" cohorts. I knew our days were numbered. I had to remind myself over and over that I hated this job and wanted out. But there was that pesky pride thing in the way. No one enjoys getting canned, and the only thing worse is waiting for it to happen.

The network would soon be announcing whether they were ordering an additional nine episodes that season. In industry jargon this is called a "back nine." Everyone was confident we'd get it. But the writers' contracts were for the first thirteen episodes with an *option* for the back nine, meaning they could extend our contracts or let us go.

My thirty-third birthday fell on the same day as the back nine announcement. Despite all my worries, I was in a good mood that morning. The autumn weather was crisp and clear, and I'd gotten up early to make a big breakfast with extra bacon. When I walked into my office, I found every surface covered with funny signs the writers had made. They said things like "For your birthday, I wish you had a hot guy who turns into a doob when you're done." A gorgeous arrangement of pink roses was sitting on my desk—a gift from my agents. While my coworkers were admiring the bouquet, Marc appeared in the doorway.

His round face blanched. "Are those back nine flowers?"

"No . . . They're birthday flowers."

"Oh." He looked relieved. Then he threw in a perfunctory "happy birthday" that couldn't have sounded less sincere. His discomfort was obvious. He must've been thinking, *Patty got back nine flowers? How embarrassing, since we're about to fire her!*

Sure enough, two days later Liam poked his head into the writers' room and, like the Grim Reaper, beckoned me with an index finger— one of the few times he ever did so. The irony wasn't lost on me. I followed him into his office and sat in the same spot I was in when they told us they were firing Everett. Once again, Liam was stony-faced and silent while Marc did all the talking.

"We've decided not to pick up your option." As expected, they had fired my two coworkers minutes earlier. "If we had an unlimited budget, we'd keep all of you."

I wasn't sure why mentioning the budget was supposed to soften the blow. He was basically saying, *If we had money to waste, we wouldn't bother getting rid of dead weight like you.* The bottom line was that we were the least valuable writers to them. We were expendable. There's nothing you can say to make that sting less. Then he added, "You wanted to do development anyway, right?"

It was like dumping your girlfriend the day before the prom and saying, "You wanted to go with that other guy anyway, right?" It was much too late in the season to start developing a pilot. Besides, I never told Marc I wanted to do development again. I had soured on it after *Bridge and Tunnel*, which was one of the reasons I took a staff job that year. Solid decision that turned out to be.

Even though getting fired was no surprise, it still elicited a jumble of emotions. Part of me regressed to a child being punished; I felt ashamed and remorseful, even though I'd done my best. Another part of me saw this as one more rejection to add to the list. Yet

another part of me was incensed about the prejudice that I felt I'd
been treated with since day one. When Marc asked, "Is there anything you'd like to say?" I looked straight at Liam and said, "I just
wish I'd been given more of a chance to show you what I can do."

Liam said nothing. When you have power, you're allowed to hide
behind silence.

I spent the next hour packing up my things and saying goodbye
to my coworkers. Though I'd cried in that office before, I didn't do
it now. I knew I would miss seeing the writers and joking with them
about my hapless love life and the ridiculousness of our show. But
mostly I felt relief—euphoria, even—knowing I'd never have to
return to this hellhole again.

The other two writers who'd been fired slinked out the back door,
avoiding the walk of shame. Not me. I wanted to do it in style, like
Tom Cruise in *Jerry Maguire*, defiantly taking the office goldfish with
him. Carrying my box of personal belongings, I strode down the
main hallway, feeling like everyone's eyes were on me. I kept looking
straight ahead. I stopped by the cubicle where Nick, the hot P.A., was
stationed, and wrote my number on a sticky note.

"I just got fired. I won't be coming back. Call me if you ever want
to hang out."

He never called. But it didn't matter. I walked out the front door
with my head held high.

12

The Dating Game

Desperate Housewives had sucked my creative juices dry. But just as I became certain that no ideas would ever enter my brain again, my agent called me with an opportunity that snapped me out of my self-pity party: he told me Diane Keaton wanted to develop a series with HBO, and she had read my stuff and wanted to meet with me. I nearly lost my fudge.

First of all, Diane Keaton read my stuff? What stuff? When? I was mortified picturing an actor of her caliber reading some juvenile script of mine, which might have been mildly amusing to the average layperson but nothing on par with, say, a Woody Allen film or *The Godfather*. Why didn't Larry warn me before he sent my stuff to people like Diane Keaton?

I'd had a few meetings with Sarah Condon, the avuncular head of comedy development at HBO. She was eager for new comedies because *Sex and the City* had ended its six-year run in early 2004. Though I was still gun-shy about doing another pilot—and a comedy, no less—if I was going to do it, HBO was not a bad option. They were consistently putting out quality shows, breaking new ground, and paving the way for other networks to piggyback on their successes. They were leading the charge.

Diane Keaton didn't have a specific idea for a show. The only guideline was that she would star in it. Her latest hit at the time was *Something's Gotta Give*, a romantic comedy costarring Jack Nicholson in which she played an intelligent, gracefully aging WASP who is cynical about romance but proves to have a soft heart. Using that as a jumping-off point, I sketched out an idea for a show called *Trophy Wives*. The premise was that Diane's character gets married late in life to a rich CEO and is the only appropriately aged spouse in his social circle. At first, she's put off by these young trophy wives, but over time she realizes they're not all bad and becomes a sort of den mother to them. Seemed like the kind of show HBO would go for, and it was squarely in Diane's wheelhouse.

Usually when I had a meeting outside of the office, it would happen at a Starbucks. Diane wanted to meet at the Polo Lounge in the famously posh and pink Beverly Hills Hotel. Just figuring out what to wear was a major endeavor, and after many outfit changes, I went with a simple white top and jeans. I got there early and was seated at a table on the patio, nestled amid palm trees and bougainvillea. I ordered a pot of Earl Grey tea and a cranberry scone, and barely touched them until Diane arrived, fashionably late.

Dressed in all black, including her trademark fedora and turtleneck, she was as beautiful as I had expected—in fact, more so, because she looked so natural. Her forehead actually moved, unlike so many in Hollywood who have been immobilized by facelifts and Botox injections.

I got the awkward stuff out of the way early. As soon as Diane sat down, I told her I was a big fan. "I'm sure you hear this all the time, but *Annie Hall* is one of my favorite movies."

I knew my love of Woody Allen films was problematic. But I refuse to let cancel culture erase Diane Keaton's greatest performance from one of my most treasured movie-going experiences.

"Yeah," she said with a wry smile, "that was a good one."

Despite being a star of the highest echelon, Diane was easy to talk to. I didn't expect to have anything in common with her, but when we began to chat about dating and relationships, we were on the same page. We were both strong, successful women who were unable to find a suitable partner. Though Diane had a few years on me, I was, like her, getting to the point where I'd lived alone for so long, I was afraid I'd never be able to transition to marriage.

"If I ever get married, I'm thinking duplex," I joked. "I need my space."

Diane let out a hearty chuckle. That's right—I made Diane Keaton laugh.

She liked my *Trophy Wives* idea and agreed that accomplished men marrying young women was an area with a lot of comedic potential. We named some right off the bat: Warren Beatty, Harrison Ford, Larry King. . . .

"Woody," she muttered, rolling her eyes. I was so glad *she* said it.

I didn't have to sell the pitch very hard. Diane could see it and could see herself in the role. And I could tell that working with her would be a pleasure.

I pitched *Trophy Wives* to Sarah Condon on a conference call with Diane. Sarah didn't go for it. I was giving her everything she asked for: a specific and glamorous world the show would take place in; a timely, comedic premise; and a role that a huge star was excited to play. But Sarah felt something was missing. Her advice to me was "Try to come up with a title. Sometimes when you come up with the title, the rest falls into place."

Funny. I thought I already had one.

We could've scrapped the whole thing on the spot, but development executives rarely just make up their minds and walk away. More conference calls followed, more pitching, more vague notes. Though the project never truly got off the ground, the process dragged on for five months. I hadn't earned a cent. More and more projects were being done this way: on spec, requiring a significant amount of work from writers without paying them. Though this unfairness bothered me, I can't say I had regrets in this case. Because I got to have lunch with Diane Keaton, and she was fucking awesome.

There's another Woody Allen film, *Husbands and Wives*, in which a strong, independent woman, played by Judy Davis, divorces her husband of many years. At first, she delights when "all the festering wounds" of her marriage are "gone in one clean yank," but soon her new lifestyle loses its luster. "Now I'm single," she reflects, "and I realize I'm one of those people who needs to be married."

I had spent much of my relationship with Carl viewing it as an albatross around my neck, especially in my early twenties when I was at the peak of my horniness and steeped in a hookup culture. Now that I was free to partake, I was coming to the same conclusion as Judy Davis: I needed to be in a relationship to be my best self.

The idea was anathema to me because I'd always championed independence. *I shouldn't need a man to be complete.* But it wasn't that I needed a man to define my self-worth. Rather, I enjoyed intimacy and companionship, the feeling of being in it together. Though I could eke out only a fraction of that with a recalcitrant partner like Carl, I had a sense that with the right partner, those aspects of a relationship would bring me so much joy.

So I started dating like crazy, casting a wide net. Friends set me up on disastrous blind dates. One was a guy who worked for the L.A.

branch of the FBI, a job that I thought was cooler than anything in showbiz. But he was no Fox Mulder. He turned out to be deathly boring. Maybe he wasn't allowed to talk about his job, but how about hobbies? Books? Food? His favorite pair of socks? *Anything* that might contribute to a conversation?

I went on another blind date with a manager of the now-defunct music store Sam Goody. He brought me to his apartment after dinner, and it was crammed with garbage—not just junk you might sell on eBay but actual trash, like empty hot dog packages and smelly, black banana peels. It looked like something out of *Hoarders*.

I also got set up with a development assistant who took me on a romantic getaway to New York and then got cold feet, revealing that he really wanted to be a writer (big surprise) and would no longer have time for dating because he had to buckle down and work on his screenplay. On top of that, he was awful in bed. But that didn't stop me from feeling bad when he blew me off.

Eventually, I considered signing up for Match or eHarmony—two of the few dating sites that existed in those days—but every time I was about to pull the trigger, I would meet someone the old-fashioned way, or, as the kids call it, "IRL." That went just as badly as the setups.

One night at a restaurant, I started flirting with the waiter, a cute, friendly dude from New Zealand with blond dreadlocks in a topknot. I pulled the cheesy move of writing my phone number on the check, and he called the next day. We went out for drinks at a hookah bar and made out in the cab back to my place. I was fully prepared to close the deal until he asked me what shows I'd worked on and I drunkenly dropped the F-bomb, thinking, *What's the worst that can happen?* His eyes bugged out and he said, "My roommates and I used to pretend we were the Friends!" There was my answer.

At a coffee shop's open-mic night, I met an aspiring musician with whom I had a strong physical attraction. This guy turned out to be a champ in bed. That was pretty much all he had going for him. He had to take the bus to his part-time barista job because he didn't own a car, and since he was too broke to rent an apartment, he squatted at a friend's place, sleeping in a corner that was curtained off with a batik sheet. But this wasn't the problem; it was the fact that he was a total flake and treated me like shit.

There were also guys I never actually went out with because they scared me off. Like a handsome man with chiseled features and a gleaming smile whom I met in the checkout line at Gelson's. We had, as they say in the rom-com business, a "meet cute." As I unloaded my cart onto the conveyor belt, he surveyed the large assortment of produce.

"What are you making?" he asked.

"Vegetable curry." I pointed to the one item he was buying, a four-pack of Boddington's. "What are *you* making?"

He laughed and said, "A hangover."

Then I could've sworn he said something about his British husband. Therefore, I was confused when he asked for my number so he could "see how the vegetable curry turns out." I acquiesced, mostly because I was curious. Why would a gay man ask for my number?

Over the next few weeks, he left me a series of rambling messages, never quite asking me out, and each time addressing me as "Vegetable Curry Patty" and signing off with a continental "ciao!" I remained unsure of his intentions and didn't call back. On his last message he let loose.

"I'm just saying thank you to all the women who have broken my heart in this city!" he spat, his voice dripping with sarcasm. "If a nice guy calls you, just fucking call him back. You have everything to gain and nothing to lose. Don't give your number out if you're not willing to take a chance. Sorry, but I think it's lame. Ciao."

I learned three things from this experience. First, it's okay to tell someone, "No, you cannot have my number." Second, even if a guy says he's gay, that doesn't mean he won't stalk you. And third, there are nutjobs everywhere, but in L.A., a lot of them are good-looking.

Ever since Carl and I had broken up, I'd been having recurring dreams in which he would walk in on me having sex with another guy and go ballistic. At first, I figured the dreams sprang from some sort of vestigial loyalty. But then I realized they were like the ones I had in high school, in which my parents would walk in on me and my boyfriend having sex and lose their minds; they didn't even know I was sexually active. I talked about these dreams in therapy, pointing out the obvious connection.

"Carl was always a parental figure in my life," I told Bonnie.

Then I started to talk about something else, but she interrupted me. "Wait, this is important."

She never did that. That was when I knew I'd uncovered something deep. Carl's role in my life had been very similar to my parents' in many ways: the condescending advice, the overprotectiveness, the way he had pushed me to achieve. I had looked to Carl for the approval that I couldn't get from them. I'd work at it and work at it until I won him over, and this would make me feel good about myself until he'd inevitably pull away, withdrawing his approval, which would set the whole cycle back in motion. I was, essentially, reliving my relationship with my parents over and over.

But my *actual* relationship with them had been changing. My fears about them smothering me when they moved to L.A. had not come to pass. Now that they were both retired, they had each other for company and kept themselves busy, babysitting my nephew and nesting in their new home. Our visits used to be fraught with pressure to cram as much interaction as possible into a short window of time. But that pressure had dissipated now that we saw each other more often. Even though we still had our differences, I felt more comfortable with them now because—thanks to therapy—I was no longer projecting that they were judging and criticizing me. And the better things got with them, the less I had needed Carl to play that parental role in my life.

This breakthrough deepened when I read the self-help book *He's Scared, She's Scared: Understanding the Hidden Fears that Sabotage Your Relationships.* It described to a T every romance I'd had since the fifth grade. I feverishly underlined passages and scrawled the names of my ex-boyfriends in the margins. I took quizzes to determine if I had a "commitment conflict." Though I was already aware of my penchant for commitment-phobic men, the book opened my eyes to an important piece of the puzzle: it takes two to tango. *Both* partners are afraid of commitment. It's just that one actively avoids it while the other does it passively.

In most cases, I had been the passive avoider, choosing men who (a) didn't like me back, (b) were clearly wrong for me, or (c) had "serious, obvious commitment problems" and ran like crazy so I didn't have to. Carl was, of course, in the latter category. Now I was asking myself: Why did I stay in that relationship for ten years? Many women would've left much sooner. I stayed. I used to think it was because I loved him, but that wasn't the whole truth. I stayed because the relationship served me: it kept me from having to commit to *him*.

With this new perspective, I felt ready to respond to the long, plaintive letter that Carl had sent me that day at *Desperate Housewives*. I didn't want to talk to him face-to-face because he was a master at manipulating me, another hallmark of a commitment-phobe. So I wrote back instead, resisting the urge to lay out a laundry list of what went wrong between us. I didn't want to give him the impression that they were things we could fix.

"I'm not angry or bitter about the past," I wrote. "I just want to move on." I also took responsibility for my own commitment issues and thanked him for going to therapy at my behest. "The end of our relationship was what prompted you to do that work—so hopefully you can see it as the start of your spiritual journey instead of just a sad ending." I had grown a lot since we'd split up, and I wished the same for him.

One night after I wrote the letter, I was lying on my couch, watching a special about the making of *Seinfeld*. I kept thinking, *This is something we would've watched together*. We would've had fun talking inside baseball, bonding over our shared experience. I had to admit the truth: I did miss Carl once in a while. Mostly I missed the laughs. Regardless of whatever neuroses fueled his need to be funny, Carl had been my court jester, my personal Joe Pesci. ("I'm here to fucking amuse you?") Being able to think about the good times proved to me that I was ready to close that chapter of my life.

That didn't mean Carl was ready. Over the next few years, he would try to contact me several times, begging for *closure*—a word so often abused in the aftermath of a breakup. He would bait me with emails that were either ingratiating or outlandishly accusatory. Though it was hard to resist defending myself, I did not engage. I knew he was just trying to get me back in his orbit and keep the drama going. One thing I'd read in *He's Scared, She's Scared* that stuck with me was this: a commitment-phobe can't commit to yes, but he can't commit to no, either. He always leaves the door open.

In December 2005, my best friend from middle school, an eccentric singer named Jill, came to town for a gig with the jazz band she sang in. Jill was the first friend I made when I moved to New Jersey; we had geeked out over Culture Club and bonded in choir. During her visit, we got together for dinner with some friends of hers who lived in L.A. That's when I met someone who would eventually make my heart beat faster without making a mess of my life. In fact, he did the opposite.

His name was Mike, and he was tall and thin, with sandy-blond hair and pale blue eyes behind wire-rimmed glasses. He wasn't my type— that is, emotionally unavailable comedians who live in their heads. He was funny and smart, but also kind—and very geeky. I wasn't interested and left the dinner assuming I'd never see him again.

But a few weeks later, I was invited to a Christmas party at the famed recording studio where David Bowie, Rod Stewart, and many other music legends had recorded hit albums. I was hoping to meet a rock star, or at least ogle one from across the room. The last person I expected to see was Jill's geeky friend Mike.

One of my friends caught me staring. "Do you know that guy?"

"I think I've met him before," I said, surprised to see him kissing a tall, spiky-haired woman. "But the guy I met wouldn't be making out with that chick."

The curiosity was killing me. I waited for an appropriate moment to approach, then walked up to him and tapped him on the shoulder. "Mike? Is that you?"

"Oh, hi!" he said, his face lighting up.

He left his incongruous companion at the bar while we headed off to a quieter spot to chat. Even though he was on a date, he seemed excited to see me. I still wasn't sure how I felt about him. My eyes kept going to his outfit: a velvet tux jacket with grosgrain peak lapels and a button-up shirt printed with sheet music. That shirt was as dorky as a piano-key necktie. But when Mike told me the music was from

Jerry Springer: The Opera, I laughed and gave him a pass. We talked about going to a movie together and he gave me his card. Under his name it said PLANETARY AIRSHIP.

"Why 'Planetary Airship'?" I asked.

He smiled and replied, "I like blimps."

As the Vegetable Curry Guy would say, I had nothing to lose. The next day I emailed Mike. When I didn't hear back, I was a little miffed, and thought about sending another that said, "Don't give your card to a girl if you're not willing to take a chance. Ciao." But believe it or not, I still had some dignity left.

He replied two weeks later, after he found my email in his spam folder. We made plans to go to a Writers Guild screening of *The 40-Year-Old Virgin*, written and directed by my old boss Judd Apatow. But it wasn't a date. Mike was still seeing the woman from the party, and in the meantime, I had met someone on New Year's Eve, an architect named Travis.

To be honest, I hooked up with Travis only because it was midnight and he was willing. He had bad teeth and unwashed hair that was alarmingly close to a mullet, and as we began to date, I discovered he was not the cosmopolitan hipster he pretended to be. He joked that he was really a "hillbilly"—but he wasn't the endearing sort like Jed Clampett. He said things that were sexist, racist, or just plain crass. When I pointed that out to him, he replied, "If I were a racist, I wouldn't be going out with *you*."

My gut was screaming at me to get away from this douchebag.

But going out with Mike was what really lit a fire under my ass to end it with Travis. When we went to the movie screening, I noticed for the first time that Mike was pretty cute, and we were both laughing at the odd, subtle jokes that most of the audience didn't get. One of my teachers used to say, "When you think someone has a good sense

of humor, that's because they have the same sense of humor as you."
Guilty as charged.

After, we went across the street to an upscale diner to get some
food. We settled into a high-backed wooden booth by the window
and ordered a few plates to share. Our conversation was easy and
fluid, but it might have remained superficial if the following had not
occurred: halfway through the meal, Travis walked up to our table.

My first thought was that he was checking up on me. But there was
no way he could've known I'd be there; it was a spur-of-the-moment
decision. Running into him was purely a coincidence, and I've come
to see it as the universe doing me a big favor. Because my reaction to
seeing Travis was a sick, sinking feeling in the pit of my stomach, which
made it clear how I felt about him—plus guilt, which made it clear how
I felt about Mike. We weren't on a date, but it sure felt like one.

I made introductions, knowing that the polite thing to do was
invite Travis and his dinner companion to join us. But that was the
last thing I wanted. Instead, I told Travis I'd call him later, and he
walked awkwardly back to their table. When he was out of earshot,
Mike whispered, "What was that all about?"

I told him everything. I explained who Travis was and why I
wanted to ditch him. Mike understood. He shared his own doubts
about the woman he was seeing, whom he had met on eHarmony
and, despite their algorithm-computed compatibility, felt only tepid
about. I could see that Mike was a deep, sensitive, mature person
with an emotional intuitiveness that matched his prodigious intel-
lect. We talked until the restaurant closed at two a.m. and the staff
kicked us out. By the time we said goodnight in the parking garage, I
no longer had any doubts about whether I was interested. I was all in.

The next day I called Travis while having lunch at a vegan café in
my neighborhood. The first thing he said was, "Were you on a *date*

last night?" I hadn't intended to break it off with him until we could talk in person, but he flew into a rage, and before I knew it, I was having the Breakup Conversation on my cellphone in a room full of annoyed vegans.

"I'm just not politically correct enough for you," he sneered, before veering off into a barrage of unrelated, childish insults. So intense was his hatred that I expected to never hear from him again, but he called me back that night and left a message. "I've got a temper, darlin'," he explained, by way of apology. "Can we be friends?" I deleted the message with extreme prejudice and blocked his number from my phone.

Later, Mike would joke that Travis—and all those other douche bags I'd dated—had done him a big favor by "lowering the bar." True, but even if the bar had been high, Mike would've exceeded it.

As soon as he broke off his current relationship, we started officially dating and getting to know each other. Originally from the Bay Area, Mike had moved to L.A. in the early aughts to work in film and wrote two screenplays. But his writing career stalled, mostly because he didn't have the kind of ruthless ambition that it takes to make it in Hollywood. My days of being impressed by such ambition were decidedly over.

In fact, one of the things I liked most about Mike was that he prioritized his personal relationships over getting ahead. While writing, he had traveled to San Francisco almost every weekend to be with his sick grandfather. I couldn't imagine Carl taking that much time away from work to be with anyone. It didn't matter to me that Mike wasn't a bigshot screenwriter. I admired his values.

The morning after our first sleepover date, I kept waiting for Mike to run away, but he didn't and it confused me. *You mean intimacy isn't always followed by frantic fear?* Instead, we lounged in bed, drinking tea and doing the *New York Times* Sunday crossword puzzle, the hardest of the week. With Mike's help, I was able to finish it for the first time ever. We filled in each other's blanks—literally.

Not only did we click on a deep emotional level, but we also had a lot of silliness in common. We were both into the Muppets and got teary-eyed every time we heard "Rainbow Connection." We were both *Star Wars* nerds who revered Yoda but didn't care much for Ewoks, despite their catchy "Yub Nub" song. We both loved stuffed animals and still cuddled with our favorite ones, including an A. A. Milne–style Winnie the Pooh we bought together at Target. One day, early in our courtship, we got pedicures on Sunset Boulevard and wandered over to a thrift shop while our toenails were drying. A half-hour later we walked out with a tandem bike.

People who are afraid of being in a couple do not buy tandem bikes.

Don't get me wrong, our romance wasn't smooth sailing from the get-go. We both had baggage, and we had our share of misunderstandings and stupid fights. When Mike did or said anything that reminded me of Carl—especially when he seemed to be choosing work over me—I'd get scared and shut down. Mike called this "turtling up." In response, he just showed me that he cared and he was there for me no matter what. Holding me in his arms while I cried, he would keep saying "I love you" over and over.

"Why?" I croaked.

Because deep down I still believed I was unlovable. I would eventually overcome this lack of self-compassion with the help of therapy and spirituality, but an equally important part of my journey was finding an unconditionally loving partner, someone who would mirror what was lovable in me until I could see it myself.

And I did the same for him. Mike had a history of depression, and though he tried to keep it hidden from me at first, he couldn't stave it off forever. One day when he was feeling down, I went to a yoga class and, on my way home, passed a newsstand where I saw a *Popular Mechanics* magazine with a blimp on the cover. It made me think of that night at the party and Mike's calling card, Planetary Airship. When I got home, I found him facedown on my bed, sobbing into a pillow.

"You okay, sweetie?" I asked, rubbing his back.

"I'm just so sad" was all he could get out.

I pulled the magazine out of my bag and laid it next to his head. "Here . . . I got you this."

He lifted his face, looked at the cover, and burst into tears again, pulling me close. I held him like that, again and again, until the cloud lifted, as it always does. He has kept the blimp magazine to this day.

We'd been dating about three months when Mike met my family. I wasn't worried because I knew they'd love him. Still, it probably would've been a good idea to arrange something more casual than meeting my parents, brother, sister-in-law, and sister-in-law's parents all at once, at a fancy Mother's Day brunch at the Biltmore Hotel.

Mike braved this gauntlet unafraid—the first of many instances where he showed grace under pressure. My whole family loved him, including my toddler nephew; Mike was a natural with him. And even though Mike was busy making a good impression that day, he wasn't too busy to playfully grab my ass while we were alone at the dessert bar.

Five months later, Mike was at my apartment one day, using my computer, when I caught him looking at rental house listings on Craigslist. He was trying to find a place where we could live together. I was surprised but happy, and it didn't take much for him to talk me into it.

We looked at three or four houses before we found one in Burbank with blue shutters and gingerbread trim. It had a fireplace and a couple of added-on rooms that were weird but cool. In the backyard there was a patio shaded by a trellis covered in dangling wisteria blooms, and the lawn was dotted with flagstones and bordered by bamboo plants. After the landlord gave us a tour, Mike and I went out to the front yard and hugged under an enormous evergreen.

"What do you think?" I asked.

Mike started to well up. "I think we should do it."

Soon we were signing the lease and packing up our apartments. With Carl, I had spent ten years coming up with rationalizations for why we didn't live together. And now, nine months after meeting Mike, we were consolidating our kitchen appliances and buying sheets for our bed.

I never would've thought this was possible. But becoming aware of my "commitment conflict," watching it play out in the poor choices I was making, and, of course, working through it all in therapy were the keys to overcoming my hidden fears. I was finally able to share myself fully and enter a true partnership. Turned out I didn't need that duplex after all.

13

The Velvet Rope

After the nightmare of *Desperate Housewives*, I was still wrestling with the idea of quitting television. But over the past year, I had spent so much energy getting my love life back on track that I didn't put any into figuring out what I would do if I quit. Plus, I'd been living on savings and needed a job. So, for lack of a better option, I decided to pursue another blind script deal in the fall of 2006. I told myself that the lessons I'd learned and the equanimity I'd gained since *Bridge and Tunnel* would make for a better experience this time around.

You know what they say about that river in Egypt.

Larry put the word out and got me a bunch of meetings with development executives, including Peter Traugott from Brillstein-Grey. Despite my frustrating experience on *Bridge and Tunnel*, my respect for Traugott remained intact and he offered me another deal. But I also got one from CBS Studios, whose head of drama development was an intelligent, personable woman named Julie, whom I remembered from a general meeting years before. I had a good feeling about her and thought that working with someone new would broaden my horizons, so I turned down Traugott's offer, apologizing to him personally.

Once my deal was in place, Julie proposed a project that was already in development at CBS: an adaptation of a novel called ¡Yo! by Julia Alvarez. The president of CBS Entertainment, Nina Tassler, was reportedly passionate about the book, and Salma Hayek was attached as a producer. I knew of Salma only as an actress, but her producing career was off to a successful start with the ABC dramedy *Ugly Betty*, a remake of a Colombian telenovela.

The executive responsible for bringing *Ugly Betty* to America was Ben Silverman, a young hotshot who had also co-opted the British series *The Office* and turned it into NBC's number-one comedy. With these two shows, Silverman's production company, Reveille, was on fire. I had no idea how I was getting involved with these high-profile people. It was like stumbling into the Land of Oz.

The author of ¡Yo! had Dominican roots, and, in retrospect, they really should've hired a Latina writer to adapt it. But I loved the book and related to the main character, Yo (short for Yolanda), because she's a writer. I met with Reveille's development executive, a lean, energetic woman named Teri, and Salma Hayek's producing partner, Pepe. They asked me about the shows I'd worked on and did a lot of sympathetic head shaking as I regaled them with tales of long hours and demanding bosses—though I had a feeling that Teri, with her Type A, get-er-done personality, might've been faking that sympathy a tad. But it didn't matter. I had, as they say, passed the audition.

The next week I went to Raleigh Studios to meet Salma, while she was on a smoke break from playing a guest-starring role on *Ugly Betty*. Like most movie stars, Salma was even more stunning in real life than she was onscreen. She had smooth skin, lustrous hair, and a curvy figure that was a welcome departure from the typical emaciated actress. Her costume, a clingy red dress with a plunging neckline, showed off her canonical bosom. When we met, she seemed either preoccupied or unfriendly, and this attitude—along with her heavy makeup and cigarette—reminded me of the cool, slutty girls from my high school.

I blathered like an idiot. Salma barely said a word. Then the stage bell buzzed, indicating her break was over, and she went back inside.

I was already spent and my work was not yet done—or even started. After Salma finished shooting, we gathered in Teri's office to talk about ¡Yo! Salma said she wanted us all to go to the Dominican Republic to do research. I didn't expect this to happen anytime soon. It was now the beginning of November, when *Ugly Betty* was at the height of production. These folks had their hands full.

So imagine my surprise when, a few days later, Salma's assistant called and asked me to fax her my passport. Mike and I were in the process of moving into our house; I started frantically ripping open boxes to find it. Salma was friends with Sammy Sosa, the Dominican baseball player who'd been a star hitter for the Cubs and the Orioles. When he invited her to his birthday party, to be held at his swanky island estate, she decided to bring the ¡Yo! team along as our "research trip."

Suddenly I was packing a suitcase in a total panic. I had to spend an entire weekend with people I had just met, one of whom was a gorgeous movie star. What the hell was I going to wear? My wardrobe consisted of jeans and T-shirts that said things like JERSEY GIRLS AIN'T TRASH—TRASH GETS PICKED UP. And there was no time to go shopping!

Early on Friday morning, I reported to a private airport in Van Nuys to board one of Sammy Sosa's Gulfstream jets. I showed up on time and not a soul was there yet except for a couple of flight crew guys. Soon Teri arrived with her boyfriend, a writer who bore a disturbing resemblance to Carl. Then Ben Silverman showed up. This was the president of the hottest production company in town—a busy man, but not too busy to party in a tropical locale with Salma Hayek. That's when it started to dawn on me that this trip might be more about pleasure than business.

We all waited in the lounge for Salma to arrive. Teri paced back and forth, checking her watch, while Ben and I sat on the couch, getting to know each other. Ben acted like we were old friends. He was effortlessly likable and cool. With his handsome Sephardic looks, he reminded me of Sacha Baron Cohen, whom I had a crush on after seeing *Borat*, a movie in which he carries a bag of his own feces to the dinner table. If Ben was half as charming as Borat, I was fucked.

When Salma and Pepe finally showed up an hour late, Salma was unapologetic. She'd brought along her dad, a sweet old man who spoke little English, and a cheerful young friend of hers who worked as a Spanish translator on film sets. The crew whisked our luggage away and we climbed a flight of steps straight from the tarmac onto the plane. I looked around the cabin, hoping that no one noticed my eyes popping out of my head.

I had never been on a private jet before. Even first class on a commercial plane was like a sardine can compared to the Gulfstream. The seats, upholstered in buttery leather, were as big and cushy as La-Z-Boy recliners. The walls were paneled with dark, glossy wood. In the lavatory there were plush burgundy hand towels with SOSA embroidered on them in cursive. Part of me wanted to soak in every minute of luxury, but having popped a preflight Xanax, I passed right out and missed the entire takeoff and ascent. When I awoke, a smiling flight attendant brought me a glass of orange juice, a fruit salad, and the freshest croissant I'd ever tasted. I wouldn't have been surprised if the plane came with its own pastry chef.

Ben was in the middle of telling Salma how he came up in the business. It was one of those "from mailroom to president in thirty days" success stories that people love. No one wants to hear that you became a star because your uncle owns the studio or, conversely, that you worked your ass off for twenty years eating shit. Fairy tales— that's what everyone wants. Ben was a go-getter who was in the right place at the right time and had the self-confidence to seize the opportunity. Even though I wouldn't want to trade places with him, I admired his chutzpah.

The whole reason for us coming on the trip was to see how people in the Dominican Republic lived. But the closest we got to seeing "the people" was when we flew over some towns on our way in, pointed out the window, and said, "Hey, look at those little shacks." Once we got to Sammy Sosa's compound, we barely left.

Sosa was a gracious host. He had planned lots of activities for us: a cocktail party, a chartered boat ride, and, of course, the massive birthday bash at his mansion, next door to the guesthouse where we were staying. To be clear, when I say "guesthouse," I mean a sprawling beachfront resort surrounded by palm trees and birds of paradise. Sosa's own house was grand and a little garish, but his guesthouse was perfection.

After the cocktail party on Friday, we hung out in the open-air lounge, chatting late into the night. I mostly just listened as Salma held court and chain-smoked. She explained, in her husky Mexican accent, that she'd picked up the habit on the set of *Frida*.

"Now I'm afraid if I ever quit smoking, I might never be able to shit again."

The woman was a riot once she let her guard down. My first impression of her as a snobby bitch had been way off base; she was warm and high-spirited. She started drawing me into the conversation, asking for my opinion on things, even about a biopic she was planning to make about Sosa. I didn't know anything about the guy, but I did know how to tell a story, so I just responded honestly to Salma's ideas and she actually seemed to care.

The next morning, we had some time to kill after breakfast and before the boat ride, so we took turns jumping on a trampoline in the yard, and then decided to go for a swim in the ocean. As we strolled down toward a crescent of sandy beach, Salma noticed the bikini straps peeking out of my top.

"Look, Patty has skulls on her bathing suit," she called out to the group. "It's so punk."

Salma admitted that before she met me, she had expected someone older and more matronly. "Then this hot girl walks up to me wearing a miniskirt and motorcycle boots!"

She'd been so aloof that day at the soundstage, I couldn't believe she noticed what I was wearing. I had, in fact, chosen my clothes carefully—one of the few outfits I owned besides jeans and ironic T-shirts. I wanted to make a good first impression. But upon the sight of her in that tight red dress and stiletto heels, my attempt to look cool had seemed sad, and I'd wilted like a plucked dandelion.

Wilted or no, Ben Silverman was now openly flirting with me.

Earlier that morning he asked me what my boyfriend did for a living. I told him that Mike had given up screenwriting and, since he had an engineering degree, was doing coding jobs to make ends meet. Now, as I undressed on the beach, unveiling my punk bikini and pale November thighs, I caught Ben checking me out in a way that would've been creepy if I didn't like it so much.

"That is one lucky computer programmer," he muttered.

Salma let out a throaty laugh. She'd heard us talking about Mike earlier. "How long have you been seeing each other?" she asked.

"Nine months."

"And you already moved in together? That fast?" Her sultry brown eyes went wide. "Wow . . . The sex must be great!"

Ben smirked. "It'll never last."

But it wasn't until the boat ride that he really started pouring it on thick, and I realized what a test this weekend would be. Ben's magnetism was hard to resist. Steeped in his attention, I started to feel the way I did with Jason Segel: smitten and guilty. On the deck of the boat, someone took a snapshot of Ben and me huddling together against the wind. Tilting his head toward mine, he chuckled and said, "This is the kind of picture that'll get you in trouble."

I think he liked that idea.

Sosa's birthday party was clearly going to be more like an awards ceremony. All day his estate was buzzing with activity as workers erected the stage and sound system, set up dinner tables and bars, and laid down a massive dance floor. Salma even had to attend a rehearsal for her part in the show.

The party was a black tie event, so I put on the same little black dress I'd had for years and my one expensive pair of heels, strappy Manolo Blahniks that I'd bought during my reckless post-Carl-breakup period. When I realized I'd forgotten to pack my hairdryer, Salma offered to pay the on-site stylist to do my hair.

We could've cut across the back lawn to get to the party, but then we would've missed the red carpet. Yup, there was an actual red carpet rolled out on the porte cochere of Sosa's mansion, complete with paparazzi. Salma, radiant in an indigo evening gown, led us through the gauntlet of blinding flashbulbs, pausing to smile for the cameras and do some quick interviews.

By now most of us had concluded that Sosa was in love with her. The way he treated her that weekend seemed a lot like wooing. Sosa's wife, a busty Amazon with gigantic coiffed hair, did not seem pleased to see Salma sashaying up the front steps of her house. The woman looked like she could topple Salma with a single hip check. But it was clear to me that Sosa's feelings were unrequited. Salma didn't go to that party to flirt with him. She went there to work.

And she worked hard. While the rest of us enjoyed a lavish dinner, champagne, and Cuban cigars, Salma had to go onstage and be part of the entertainment, a series of exuberant bits akin to a variety show you'd see on Univision. The big finale was a concert by a high-energy rock band called Bacilos, whom Pepe described as "the Latino U2." Everyone went apeshit for them. And then, as if I weren't already spoiled by the private plane, beach resort, and limitless supply of tropical fruit, I got to meet the band after the show.

While I was chatting with the drummer, Ben swooped in and whisked me away to go find pot. Seemed like a reasonable errand. Some arty friends of his were in town for a film festival and he suspected they would be hooked up, so we took a cab to their hotel. I felt like I was on spring break, sharing a fat joint with them by the pool and lounging in the balmy nighttime air.

Brilliant ideas began to flow. Not about ¡Yo! but about a porno movie that would parody The Office, the show that made Ben's career. The porno would be called The Orifice. That title alone would be enough to sell it! The characters would be sexier versions of Pam, Jim, and the other office drones. They'd fuck on the Xerox machine, inadvertently photocopying their bare butt cheeks, or they'd have an orgy on the conference table while on speakerphone with an important client. (To whatever adult film company is poaching this idea right now: I want royalties.)

After a while Ben got paranoid that our group would be wondering where we'd gone, so we headed back to the party. In the back seat of the taxi, he slid over toward me until our thighs were touching. An electric current zinged through my body. Then he turned to me in the darkness and planted a kiss on my cheek. I'm pretty sure it would've landed on my mouth if I'd wanted it to.

Let me be clear: this was not a #MeToo moment. The attraction was mutual, and all weekend Ben had been making me feel wanted and special. If circumstances had been different, that cabdriver might've gotten quite a show. But I had *just* moved in with my boyfriend. When I came close to messing around with Jason Segel, I had a neglectful boyfriend who pushed me away. My relationship with Mike was entirely different; cheating on him would be nothing but self-sabotage. Infidelity is the ultimate way of creating distance, so if I wanted a way out, this would've been it.

But there was no time to think about all this—I had to act on instinct. And my instinct was to give Ben the cheek. We were both stoned out of our gourds, which somehow obscured the awkwardness and exacerbated it at the same time. Thankfully, when we got back to Sosa's, no one even noticed we'd been gone. The party was now in full swing. A floppy-haired deejay was pumping out a buoyant beat, and sweaty partygoers were tearing up the dance floor.

I was dying to join in, but my feet were screaming in pain, so I dashed back to the guesthouse to ditch my spindly heels. I threw on a pair of faded jeans, a black tank top, and flip-flops, not bothering to fix my smudgy makeup. Too baked. Too eager to get back to the fun.

When I returned to the dance floor, Ben kept ogling me and telling me how "hot and punk" I looked. But I kept a safe distance between us, hoping to defuse the sexual tension. And then Salma found me. She, too, had changed into jeans and appeared to have made up for lost time at the bar. She wrapped her arms around me in the kind of hug you'd get from your BFF, and over the thumping music she yelled into my ear, "Patty, I *loooove* you! I want to be friends with you, I want to work with you. . . ."

My chest swelled with affection. "I love you, too!"

Okay, so I was high and she was hammered, but it still felt amazing to be accepted into Salma's inner circle, which was, like all celebrity entourages, an intensely vetted clique. The best part was that I hadn't done anything to get there except be myself.

We danced until dawn. As the sky grew light, Sosa's staff emerged from the mansion carrying dozens of steaming bowls and began handing them out to the bleary-eyed guests. When I accepted one, baffled, Salma explained, "In Latin America, it's a tradition to eat hot chicken soup after a long night of partying." Soup! That was the most genius thing I'd ever heard. Watching the sun rise over the ocean as the warm broth filled my belly, I felt deliriously happy. The whole weekend had been like a fantastic dream.

After we flew back to L.A., Ben offered to drive me home from the airport. In the car, I could still feel his attempted kiss lingering on my skin, and I wondered if we were going to talk about it. But no, he was already in work mode, checking his email and gearing up for Monday morning. I watched him typing on his BlackBerry with his thumbs and steering the car with his knees, and I knew this was the *real* Ben Silverman—not vacation Ben, not flirty Ben, but the Ben who would've driven me insane.

When we got to my house, I invited him inside to meet Mike. I never would've done this with Carl, knowing he'd be jealous and suspicious. But Mike greeted Ben as he would any friend, offering him our finest beverages and snacks, and looking genuinely disappointed when Ben took off.

After he left, I told Mike everything that happened on the trip. He listened with no insecurity or possessiveness whatsoever. I was floored. Could I really be this honest with my boyfriend? Was this what a mature relationship was like, where such a confession could bring you *closer*? When I was younger, I used to think that a good relationship meant never being attracted to other people. But now I realized how naïve that was—it's what you *do* with the attraction that matters. Telling Mike about my crush on Ben defused it, probably because the secrecy had been part of the draw.

From then on, I would tell Mike any time I developed a crush and watch in awe as the juice drained from it, like magic. In fact, these crushes became fodder for our sex life. When I told him I'd once masturbated while watching *Point Break*, he made me a playlist of Keanu Reeves sex scenes. That's love.

The weekend at Sosa's turned out to be the last face time I would have with anyone on the project. Thereafter, all our communication was done by phone and email. Of everyone involved, Salma was the busiest and hardest to pin down, but when she showed up, she was truly present and full of inventive suggestions that she pitched in an animated manner. Ben, having bigger fish to fry, joined only one call, which took place at nine a.m. He said nothing but a raspy hello and "I like waking up to Patty Lin."

Our first pitch, to Julie at the studio, went well. But when it was time to pitch to the network, Nina Tassler wasn't on the call, only her underlings. These two junior execs made Peaches and the android at Fox look like geniuses—nothing they said made sense. Then Julie started making me mess with the outline ad nauseam, each time requiring a "beat sheet" laying out the story points in their new sequence, which she would then nitpick to death. It was busywork, a huge waste of time when I could've been writing the damn script. All the red tape drove me nuts.

I was finally given the green light to write a script just before Christmas, and my deadline was January 2—meaning I'd have to spend my entire holiday working. Trying to console me, Teri told me that she and her boyfriend had to cancel their New York vacation because they were both swamped. She sighed and said, without a trace of irony, "But, you know, we're just so blessed to be able to do this kind of work."

Blessed? Really? I no longer had any illusion that my job had a lofty purpose. Sure, it paid well, you didn't need a PhD to do it, and if you were lucky, you might get to fly on a private jet and party with some famous people. Glamorous, maybe, but I wouldn't call it *blessed*. It was more like being in the Mafia.

I barreled through the holiday and wrote ¡*Yo!* faster than I'd ever written anything. Under normal circumstances, I'd write maybe three or four pages of a script before hitting the wall. But with this script, I was averaging *fifteen to twenty*. For days on end, I did nothing but write, ignoring basic needs like eating, sleeping, and showering. Now writers are starting to be replaced by robots—but most of us are still animals that need care and feeding and rest. Working at such a pace wasn't kind or sustainable. I knew that as soon as the project was over, I would collapse into a heap and never want to write again.

Fortunately, I was getting mostly green lights from Teri, Pepe, and Salma. But Salma was the only one who seemed to understand the importance of sincere praise. Once, after I wrote a bitch of a scene—the kind that feels like you had to make magic happen—everyone started diving straight into notes, business as usual. Not Salma. She blurted, "Patty, that scene made me cry!" I was so grateful that I almost cried, too.

Meanwhile, Julie continued to get hung up on trivial details. Things got even more fraught when she began emailing me notes directly, leaving everyone else out of the loop. This put me in a difficult position: I couldn't change the script without making sure the rest of the team was on board.

When I told Teri about the emails, she asked, "Are you okay with that?"

"Uh, yeah . . . I guess. . . ."

"It's just that I'm very protective of my writers."

I've always hated it when producers or showrunners say "my writers" the way a pimp says "my bitches." But soon I was running to my pimp for protection. After opening the door to Julie, I got bombarded with notes from all directions, and fielding these disparate requests was a huge time and energy suck. Teri had to shoo everyone away so I could get back to writing.

The reason for the big rush on ¡Yo! was that Nina Tassler couldn't wait to see the script. I heard she was going around telling people, "This show is exactly what CBS needs." In fact, everyone was talking about ¡Yo! as if it were a done deal. But here's what I've learned: *nothing is a done deal.* After I handed in my final draft, the CBS execs told us they had decided to shoot some of their pilots, including ours, as "presentations."

A presentation is a shortened version of a pilot. It's a network's way of reducing its financial commitment. And it's totally stupid. The way I see it, once you put in the effort and expense of casting actors and hiring a staff and crew, you might as well shoot the whole thing. I took this as a sign that our pilot wasn't as important to CBS as their full-length ones. As for me, I had to figure out how to shrink a sixty-page script down to twenty pages and still get the idea across.

Minutes after I hung up with CBS, Larry called and said, "I just heard." For years I'd had a sneaking suspicion that he always received news about my career before I did and waited to call me only out of propriety. "How are you doing?" he asked delicately. "When they told me about the presentation, I thought, *Patty must be spinning out*."

I *should've* been spinning out. But I was numb. I was so used to being subjected to preposterous tasks that I felt like a contestant on *Fear Factor*. "Here, eat this live cockroach dipped in wasabi oil," and I go, "How much time do I have to swallow it?"

Well, I did it. I condensed the script down to twenty pages, cutting out a lot of funny, character-building material that I told myself we'd put back in when we shot the full pilot. Though no doubt a compromise, I was reasonably satisfied and so was the rest of the team. Now we just had to wait for Nina to put her money where her mouth was.

The Golden Globe Awards were given out at the end of January, and Teri invited me to an after-party that Reveille was hosting at a hipster club called Les Deux. *Ugly Betty* and *The Office* had both won multiple awards that night, and my *¡Yo!* teammates were the belles of the ball. They were the only people I knew at the party, but I didn't see them for most of the night. Mike and I sat at a table, eating lamb lollipops by ourselves. When I finally spotted the *¡Yo!* folks, they were secluded in a roped-off VIP section guarded by security. Was that necessary?

Withering under the stink-eye of a guard, I waved and called out to Ben Silverman until he noticed me crushed against a stanchion. His dapper tuxedo was offset by his sloppy drunkenness. He staggered over to me and kissed my cheek—a superficial showbiz kiss, not the kind he had given me in the Dominican taxi. Then, without so much as a "Hi, how are you?" he turned on his heel and lurched back to the far corner where Salma was relaxing on a divan, sipping insouciantly from a champagne flute. These were the people I had bonded and partied with, got high and slurped soup with—not to mention worked closely with for the past three months. And now I was looking at them across a velvet fucking rope.

My feeling of isolation grew worse as weeks went by without any word on the pilot. Sometime in February, Teri and Pepe called to say they hadn't heard anything yet, adding, "We just wanted you to know how much we enjoyed working with you." Call me paranoid, but that sounded like a goodbye. They clearly weren't expecting the show to get ordered, and after the lengthy radio silence, neither was I.

A few weeks later CBS made a decision—kind of. They were rolling the pilot to midseason. That didn't mean it was a sure thing, though, because ¡Yo! would then have to compete with other mid-season pilots and still might not get ordered. Two more months went by, with my life on hold, before I got the call from Julie. She told me that Nina Tassler had ordered a drama called *Cane* about a Cuban American family starring Jimmy Smits.

"She passed on ¡Yo! Not that there isn't room for two shows about Latino families. . . ."

But that's exactly what she was saying: the quota was filled. It's tough when you're competing to be the token minority. CBS wasn't giving up on ¡Yo! for good, but as far as this season was concerned, the pilot was dead.

I greeted the now-familiar mix of disappointment, relief, and anger like an old enemy. Months of hard work and personal investment down the drain. I felt like a failure and dreaded telling people my pilot didn't go, especially after Nina Tassler had blabbed to everyone and their mother about how CBS "needed a show like this." Apparently, the "show like this" turned out to be *Cane*. The irony was that Julie, the person who had given me the most agita, was the only one who called me when it was over.

But that wasn't the final blow. There's an epilogue to this story.

After a few months, CBS decided to redevelop ¡Yo! with a new writer. This is a common practice when adapting source material, but it was still a shock. Larry assured me, "This decision has nothing to do with anyone being unhappy with your work." I found this hard to believe. Frankly, I didn't care if the network didn't like me, because the feeling was mutual. But I did care about Salma Hayek.

My bruised ego kept trying to figure out why she didn't fight to keep me on the project. I started questioning our whole relationship, starting with our weekend of bonding in the Dominican Republic. Was it all fake? Was Salma even more wasted than I thought when she told me she *looooved* me? Was she just bullshitting me when one day she gushed, "Thank you for being so talented and sharing your talent with us"?

That's when it hit me, though not for the first time: *this business is so fucking weird.* The feeling of instant friendship was the thing that hooked me when I interviewed for the *Letterman* internship oh so many years ago. But the sunshiny, buddy-buddy attitude that was so ingrained in showbiz did not represent actual intimacy or, in many cases, even basic respect. People acted like they were in love with you and then never talked to you again.

As far as I know, ¡Yo! was eventually shelved and never got made. But a year or so later, Larry told me that Salma and Pepe wanted to hire me to write another pilot, a drama for the ABC Family network about a young mother and her daughter both attending the same college—a sort of Latina *Gilmore Girls*. I told Larry to thank them for thinking of me and to give them my regards. And then I turned down the job.

14

Thirty Days in the ABQ

Six years had passed since I first thought about quitting TV. With each job, I had more cumulative trauma, more evidence that the business was exploitative, unsatisfying, beyond hope. But even though my career was miserable, it was a *familiar* misery. Anyone who's ever stuck it out too long in a bad marriage knows what I mean. Just like in my relationship with Carl, there was a level of investment that was hard to let go of. It's the "wait/walk dilemma." The longer you wait at a bus stop, the more unthinkable it becomes to give up, cut your losses, and walk to your destination instead.

Getting off a glide path and changing course is scary. The fantasies I once had of going to art school or cooking school seemed even more foolish to me now, given my advancing age, and no new fantasies had taken their place. To my mind, none of the things I enjoyed doing were feasible career options. Yoga teacher? I couldn't even do a handstand! Short story writer? Did anyone make a living doing that? Looking back, I want to tell myself, "You'll be fine. You'll figure something out. Just take the leap." But I didn't yet have that kind of faith. I was still driven by the need for safety and security and the illusion of control.

So when a remarkable script landed on my doorstep in the spring of 2007, I broke my vow to stay away from staff jobs and agreed to take a meeting. I was like Charlie Brown running for Lucy's football, thinking, "This time I'm gonna make it work!"

The script was *Breaking Bad*. It was for AMC, the network that had produced *Mad Men*. At this point no one had heard of *Breaking Bad*, which would go on to become one of the most-watched cable shows on American TV and, in 2012, enter the *Guinness World Records* as the most critically acclaimed show of all time. It was about a milquetoast high school chemistry teacher named Walter White, who finds out he's dying of lung cancer and tries to create a nest egg for his family by making high-quality crystal meth. His partner in crime is a former student and small-time drug dealer named Jesse. A pushover his whole life, Walt is finally "breaking bad."

The pilot was twisted and funny. In my favorite scene, Walt's wife, Skyler—a loving, well-meaning ballbreaker—gives him a perfunctory hand job under the covers while nagging him about chores and monitoring the auction of an item on eBay.

I had no idea why the creator and showrunner, Vince Gilligan, was interested in meeting me, since my scripts were quite different from *Breaking Bad*. Then I found out my agent sent him a short story I wrote based on the caretaker of Paul McCartney's childhood home in Liverpool, which I had visited on a trip to England. The middle-aged caretaker, with his abandoned dreams and wistful existence, was a lot like Walter White.

Vince was primarily a feature writer. Though *Breaking Bad* would be his first time running a show, earlier in his career he had written for *The X-Files*, which was why I was in awe of him. An introverted forty-year-old with a boyish face and a cowlick, he was polite and spoke in a soft Virginia accent. Seemed like a nice guy.

I was hired on the show as a supervising producer and had the shameful feeling of having done nothing to deserve this title other than get fired from a bunch of shows. During my first few weeks in the writers' room, I often felt insecure and competitive—scar tissue from my former jobs. I'd had three years to recover from *Desperate Housewives,* but the memories were as vivid as a 'Nam flashback. Luckily, the other writers were decent people, and I began to relax when I realized the vibe was cooperative and jovial.

There were four of us besides Vince. I was the most senior writer. The others were all male. One of them, a Black man who had been Vince's assistant on the pilot, would confess to me later, "That first day when I saw you walk into the room, I was so relieved." He was afraid all the writers would be white. I was so used to being the only person of color, it never even occurred to me that I might not be.

Our headquarters were in a brick office building in Burbank, a mere seven blocks from my house. I often rode my bike to work, smiling as the sun warmed my face and the breeze tousled my hair. One morning, one of the writers saw me pedaling my beach cruiser up the sidewalk and said, "You must feel like a schoolgirl." During preproduction, we worked from ten to six, taking a midday break for lunch. It was a humane schedule, and we got a lot done even though there was enough goofing around to keep things light.

Like Marc Cherry, Vince eschewed whiteboards and broke stories using a corkboard with index cards tacked to it. He believed that the ritual of distilling each scene down to a logline that fit on a three-by-five card would lead to story breakthroughs. Therefore, he insisted everyone write their own cards. What a relief. Still, Vince's perfectionism with the cards was irksome. Whenever he was writing one, slowly and meticulously forming each block letter with a Sharpie, he reminded me of Rain Man hunched over his spiral notebook with his cup of pens and his cheese puffs. Vince was obsessive about those cards. Stacks of them were thrown out for the tiniest mistakes. Many trees sacrificed.

Vince was about halfway done breaking the second episode when the rest of us joined the staff, but he was having trouble with the structure. I'd come a long way since my first few shows, when story breaking had been a mystery to me. Now I could take one look at the board and diagnose a story problem. I'd shuffle some cards around and—boom! Problem solved.

The problem with episode two was that it didn't exploit the concept of a double life. There were no scenes of Walt juggling his meth-related activities and his job as a teacher. In fact, the story took place over a weekend, so we never even saw him at school. Where's the fun in that? How interesting would Superman be if he never had to be Clark Kent? Baffled by the missed opportunity, I lobbied for the episode to take place during the week so that Walt would have to report to school while figuring out how to murder the drug dealer he's holding prisoner in Jesse's basement. Vince took my suggestion and the story sprang to life.

Though an interesting writer, Vince had a storytelling weakness: he would get his characters into complicated binds and get them out with a deus ex machina, usually some coincidence that was impossible to swallow. Me, I was a stickler for plots that made sense. But Vince didn't care as long as it was cool. If any of us pointed out a logic loophole, he would brush it off, confident that viewers would be too dazzled to notice.

Breaking Bad was being shot in Albuquerque—known as "the ABQ"—since it was cheaper than L.A., thanks to New Mexico's film incentive program. Vince also felt the location was more authentic to the world of crystal meth. But shooting in Albuquerque while much of the staff was in Burbank was like having a long-distance relationship. I don't think Vince foresaw how challenging it would be. Once shooting began, he often got pulled out of the writers' room to deal with production crises, leaving us to our own devices.

Meanwhile, Vince was supposed to be writing the first three episodes after the pilot. But he was an incorrigible procrastinator. Mounted on the wall of the writers' room was a huge calendar with important production dates on it, and Vince would simply ignore the information that applied to his own episodes. The tactic puzzled me. Pretending you don't see the deadline doesn't make it go away.

As the most senior writer under Vince, I was assigned to write the fourth episode, titled "Gray Matter." We had all been researching crystal meth, reading books and articles and learning the terminology—pretty depressing homework. I was relieved when my episode turned out to be about Walt's backstory as a failed scientific genius and his decision to forgo cancer treatment. That kind of character stuff was far more interesting to me than any criminal plot.

When I turned in my script, Vince was in Albuquerque. He sent me a brief email with a few general thoughts and promised we'd have a more in-depth notes session soon. The most positive thing he had to say was "Your script hewed to the outline really well," which wasn't really a compliment. Now I realized that sticking to the outline wasn't what he wanted. He wanted us to play jazz.

But even the best jazz musician needs direction, and Vince gave me none for my next draft. He didn't know what the show was yet, so how could anyone else? My stomach dropped when it dawned on me: this was what happened to Everett at *Desperate Housewives*. Only this time I was Everett. I was the guinea pig.

Even before I turned in my script, I'd started to get a creeping sense that Vince was excluding me. His favoritism wasn't as blatant as Liam picking teams and saying, "You, you, and you," but I saw it. To assist our research on lung cancer, I arranged a conference call with my cousin, who was a pulmonologist. Vince didn't bother to show up for it. Later, one of the writers, a quiet ex-lawyer named George, arranged a similar call with his brother, who was an oncologist. Not only did Vince show up, but he hung on the guy's every word and even sent him a thank-you card that he'd made us all sign.

Even more troubling was what happened the day after George turned in his script, the episode after mine. I was heading to the office kitchen to grab an instant ramen when I heard Vince talking to George in there, fawning over his script with the unbridled adulation of a fanboy. George was an imaginative, skillful writer, and his script was indeed excellent, but to hear Vince gushing over it, compared to the limp email he'd written about mine, was a slap in the face.

The worst thing I could imagine was reliving what happened to me at *Desperate Housewives*. I saw the signs, but I was in denial. I had to justify to myself why I went back to staff writing. I had to make this work, like Charlie Brown and that fucking football. So I kept pouring my heart and soul into the job, ignoring the signs the way Vince ignored the dates on the production calendar.

By September, Vince had been summoned to Albuquerque to oversee production full-time, leaving the rest of us on our own. He ordered our writers' assistant to set up a Skype connection (not very common at the time) so we could do video conferences—a sort of virtual writers' room. We used it only once. Vince complained that the picture was "too jerky." But there was still the good old-fashioned phone. We called him on it every day for two weeks straight, leaving messages with his assistant. He never called us back.

When preproduction on my episode began, I, too, was called out to Albuquerque for an indeterminate length of time. I packed a smallish bag, hoping it wouldn't be long. I arrived on a Sunday, the last day of September, and the purported charm of the place was lost on me. The Residence Inn Marriott, official hotel of the *Breaking Bad* staff, was in a sprawling business park with nothing around but office buildings and strip malls. The only restaurants in walking distance were P.F. Chang's—which, thanks to *South Park*, I always think of as "P.F. Chunks"—and another chain called Twin Peaks, a sports bar akin to Hooters. A regional fast-food chain called Whataburger was a short drive away, but I would find out it was no better than McDonald's, despite having a cuter name.

After getting settled at the hotel, I went to Vince's suite to talk about my script: our long-awaited notes session. He still wasn't ready. But with me sitting across from him, staring him in the face, he couldn't drag his heels any longer.

Basically, all he said was "Walt should talk less." Okay, that was a fair note. When I wrote the first draft, I hadn't seen much of Bryan Cranston, the actor who played Walt, inhabiting the character. Now, having watched dailies, I could see that Cranston was playing him as more introverted. Vince pointed out a few places to pare down Walt's dialogue—finally, some specific feedback! But he was having such a hard time explaining what he wanted that soon he gave up and said, "You hungry? Let's go to lunch."

He took me to Cracker Barrel, yet another chain restaurant, which we writers would later nickname "Crapper Barrel." Instead of discussing my script, we made small talk over giant plates of mediocre comfort food. I always felt a little uncomfortable with Vince one-on-one. Even though he was nice, he was intensely guarded—someone who doesn't tell you what he's thinking. On a personal level, that was off-putting. On a professional one, it was beyond frustrating. He was the most insular writer I had ever worked with.

We never finished our notes session. After lunch, Vince handed me a few pages of my script that he had scribbled some notes on and promised to give me the rest shortly. His notes were simple line changes that took me fifteen minutes to type into the script. *This* was why he flew me out to Albuquerque?

And that was how the rest of the rewrite went. Rather than letting me take another crack at the script, Vince rewrote the lines himself—a shortsighted approach that ultimately made his life harder. Judd Apatow could be blunt with his notes sometimes, but at least he had given us a chance to learn from our mistakes. He had invested in us. Vince never gave me a chance.

I typed up these revisions in our Albuquerque headquarters, a modern open-plan building located at the end of a long, desolate road. I wasn't given my own office, so I borrowed the director of photography's, a tiny windowless room he rarely used. I had never felt so lonely.

Vince told me that I should plan on staying in Albuquerque for the rest of October. The other writers were coming to join us in a few days and we would reestablish our writers' room. He also wanted me to be on set for my episode, scheduled to wrap just before Halloween. Part of me was thinking, *P.F. Chunks for another three weeks?* But another part of me was relieved that I wasn't getting sent home to burn off the rest of my contract. I figured that if Vince still wanted me around, I couldn't be fucking up that badly.

Things started to look up when the other writers arrived. I had asked Mike to send some of my clothes and personal items along

with them on the flight. They walked into the office and handed me
a huge duffel bag bursting at the seams. When I opened it, I found
heart-shaped sticky notes stuck to all my stuff. A box of tampons had
one that said "These get to go somewhere nice." Knowing about my
cupcake fixation, Mike had also sent a chocolate cupcake from my
favorite bakery, packed with such care that it arrived perfectly intact.
George, who was married with two kids, saw it and shook his head.
"This guy's courting you *hard.*"

The promise of a writers' room in Albuquerque went unfulfilled.
We spent most of our time chasing Vince to various shoot locations,
trying to steal a few minutes with him to break stories. Onlookers
probably wondered why we were walking around the neighborhood carrying a big corkboard—the Traveling Board, as we called
it. But it was impossible to get any work done with Vince's attention
so scattered.

He didn't always *need* to be on set. Sometimes he went just to
watch stuff blow up. We once wasted half a day at a gas station,
waiting for Walt to blow up some guy's car. I dig explosions as much
as the next pyromaniac, but come on . . . we had work to do.

We worked every day that month, including weekends. But we
were more *on call* than actually working—worse in some ways. The
stress started getting to me. At night, too wound up to sleep, I'd turn
on the TV and watch a public access show where a shirtless hippie
with long gray hair and wild eyes was ranting into the camera. A raw
food fanatic, he asserted that cooked food was poison. "Don't eat dead
food!" he kept yelling. I'd find myself riveted to this sermon while
chomping on a soggy Whataburger. Pretty soon I started to believe him:
dead food bad. That was when I knew I'd been in Albuquerque too long.

All my self-care routines fell by the wayside. I didn't meditate at
all that month. My first week in town, I looked up yoga studios in the

area and printed out a schedule, but I was always working during the class times. I suppose that in the evenings I could've rolled out my yoga mat in my hotel room and done some gentle poses, followed by a warm bath infused with essential oils and a few minutes of breathing exercises before bed. Instead, I'd go fetch the other writers and head over to Twin Peaks for hot wings and beer.

Thank God the four of us liked one another. Sony was too cheap to get us each a rental car, so we had to share one, an unsexy blue sedan that smelled like stale cigarette smoke. We went everywhere together. If it weren't for these guys, I would've lost my mind for sure.

In my episode, "Gray Matter," Jesse decides to turn over a new leaf: stop cooking meth and get a regular job. But after botching a job interview at a bank, he runs into a sign spinner on the sidewalk who turns out to be his old drug buddy, Badger—and he falls right off the wagon. Badger briefly becomes his new meth cooking partner.

We hired a guy named Matt Jones to play Badger. In my original draft, Jesse's job interview is at a children's pizza restaurant where his friend is in a badger costume, like the mouse at Chuck E. Cheese. The pizza restaurant turned out to be too expensive to shoot, so we changed the location, but the name Badger remained. A comic actor who did mostly stage improv and commercials, Matt was tall and goofy, with bushy black hair and a raspy voice. On his first day, we were the only two passengers on the early-morning shuttle and started chatting like kids on a school bus. We became buddies on set and off.

Matt was originally hired to be in two consecutive episodes, mine and George's. In George's episode, Walt was going to enlist Badger to get him a meeting with the meth kingpin. But after we saw how sweet and funny Matt was, Vince decided we needed someone scarier to play the liaison. We replaced Badger with a dealer who had appeared in an earlier episode and whom we all agreed looked like a real scumbag.

Matt was shooting his last few scenes in "Gray Matter" when George's script was scheduled to come out, sans Badger. Vince, true to form, was putting off breaking the news to Matt. Several times that day, I stepped away from the set and called Vince to remind him about it, getting his voicemail every time. "I'm seeing Matt Jones on the set today," I said. "The script is coming out, and it's gonna be really awkward if he doesn't know he's not in it."

Vince didn't call me back. He did nothing.

I was sitting next to Matt in video village when he received a copy of George's script. I'll never forget the confused, dejected look on his face as he flipped through its pages, searching in vain for his character's name. You know how the former FBI director James Comey found out he'd been fired by Donald Trump when he saw it on TV? I imagine he had that same expression. As gently as I could, I explained our decision to Matt and insisted it had nothing to do with his performance. He was crushing it in my episode, and everyone loved him.

Matt would later reprise his role in season two, but no one knew that at the time. He handled the whole thing with grace and professionalism, which was more than I could say for Vince. I was furious that I had to deliver bad news that should've come from Vince— and, more important, that his cowardice led to a good guy getting humiliated.

Shockingly, the Matt Jones incident wasn't my worst day on the job. One early morning when I walked onto the soundstage, a producer descended on me in a panic. Some of the crew had gotten revised pages of my script the night before and some hadn't. Those who hadn't were now scrambling to make the changes, and the intricate dance that normally took place behind the scenes had devolved into chaos.

The producer bit my head off, demanding to know how this mistake had occurred.

"I didn't know there *was* a revision," I stammered.

Vince must have rewritten the scene without telling me. To defuse the blame wave coming at me, I explained this to the producer, who then made me get Vince on the horn. I rang him in his hotel room at this ungodly hour and fortunately he picked up. He confirmed that he had indeed put out a revision in the middle of the night. Because, of course, everything he did was last minute.

All shows have a standardized procedure for distributing revised script pages that involves specific colors of paper, notations in the margins, and a long list of recipients. The script coordinator handles all this. Problem was, the show didn't bother to fly him out to Albuquerque. So an assistant had distributed the pages, without proper training—*I* didn't even get them and my name was on the cover.

Once the confusion had abated, I collapsed into my chair at video village and told the director what was going on. She was a middle-aged Southern woman who had seen plenty of awful things happen to writers. She used to be one.

"That is so embarrassing," she said, with a pitying look.

I'd been so busy doing damage control that I didn't even register how I was feeling until that moment. And then it hit me hard: I *was* mortified. And livid. It was bad enough that Vince didn't let me write a second draft, but this was taking it to a whole new level. When a showrunner does a rewrite, they should at least give the writer the courtesy of keeping them in the loop. By not alerting me to the revision, Vince was sending a message that I didn't matter. He made me look like an idiot in front of everyone.

This was a man who didn't seem to think about how his actions might make people feel.

Vince came by the set later, looking repentant, and told me he was sorry. But the damage was done. To me the worst thing in the world was to feel useless, and I'd never felt more useless than when those pages came out and I had nothing to do with them. Here I was, with nine years of experience, going through the exact same thing I had on the first show I worked on. Not what I would call progress.

I'd been through some harrowing shit in my career and thought I'd seen the worst. But that day on *Breaking Bad*, I hit a new low. The incident was so painful that my subconscious blocked it from my memory, and the recollection didn't resurface until years later when I started writing this book. Amazing what the mind does to allow us to survive.

A few days before we wrapped on "Gray Matter," I loaded up my lunch tray in the catering tent and sat down to eat with Bryan Cranston and some other cast members. They were talking about the possibility of a writers' strike. The Writers Guild of America (WGA) contract was about to expire. Patric Verrone, then president of the union, was threatening to call a strike to force the studios, networks, and producers to give us better deals on New Media, i.e., streaming. Television and film were rapidly making their way into this uncharted territory, and we needed to make sure we were getting our due.

"What do you think, Patty?" Cranston asked. "Is it gonna happen?"

I'd been too preoccupied with work to think much about a writers' strike. Since I had ignored most of the WGA's emails, didn't read the trades, and had no insider sources, I basically knew nothing. There hadn't been a writers' strike since 1988, almost twenty years ago. I figured Verrone was just bluffing.

"Nah," I told Cranston. "Not gonna happen."

Soon we were done shooting my episode and—hallelujah!—I was packing to go home. I couldn't wait to get out of that town. I was burned out, fried like an egg in that old "this is your brain on drugs" public service announcement. I needed to sleep in my own bed and eat a home-cooked meal that didn't involve hot wings. I needed a haircut. I needed to do yoga and meditate. And I needed to see my therapist and get some of my marbles back.

I'd been home for less than twenty-four hours when Verrone called a strike. All WGA members were instructed to clear out our offices, collect our personal belongings, and go home until further notice. Starting at midnight, we were forbidden to write anything for film or television, even revisions that were already in progress. Even spec scripts.

Stunned, I followed our commandant's orders and reported to the *Breaking Bad* office in Burbank to gather my things. I was happy to see the L.A.-based staff after my long absence. But with a few exceptions, that loving feeling wasn't mutual. The editors were mighty pissed about how the strike would affect their own jobs. They started to take it out on me, asking hard questions I didn't know how to answer.

After trying my best to impart what I did know, I crawled away to my office and packed up my posters and fake plants, marveling at how little time I'd spent in this building so close to home. There was only one thing left to do: call Vince in Albuquerque. He probably had no clue how his employees were reacting to the strike. I phoned him and suggested he call a meeting with the staff, cast, and crew to answer their questions.

"People are confused and upset," I told him. "You should talk to them."

If there were ever a time the show needed a strong leader, this was it. But all Vince wanted to talk about were the rules of the strike.

"How long am I allowed to do rewrites before the strike technically kicks in?"

"I think they said midnight"

"Midnight tonight? Or midnight last night?"

I wasn't sure why he was so worried about getting in trouble with the Writers Guild, since I doubted they would hold someone in his position accountable. And it didn't surprise me that he never called a meeting with the staff, because from what I could see, all he cared about was his show. Not the people who worked on it.

15

Chasing the Dragon

Even though I would be standing around picketing outside studios for months, being on strike felt like summer vacation. A sabbatical without the guilt. I had spent four months at *Breaking Bad*, and though that may sound like a short time, one-third of a year on a TV show is like ten in human years.

In January 2008, *Breaking Bad* had a premiere party on the Sony lot to kick off its debut on AMC. I accepted the invitation with mixed feelings. On one hand, I wanted to see the other writers again. During the strike I had run into them on only a few occasions—an abrupt separation after our intensive time together in Albuquerque. But otherwise I dreaded the party. It was bound to be full of uncomfortable exchanges due to the strike.

When Mike and I arrived, the screening of the final-cut, ready-for-broadcast pilot had already started. Other latecomers were clogging the ornate lobby, chatting as they filed through the gilded double doors that led into the theater. Before we could find Vince to say hello, a production executive intercepted us and brusquely pointed us toward the balcony—the nosebleed seats. She had always been friendly to me before. That was when I realized the party was going to be even worse than I'd feared.

After the screening, everyone moved into a beautifully decked-out room with a fancy catered spread. To go with the chemistry theme of the show, neon-tinted drinks were served in oversized test tubes with dry ice mist billowing from them. But I was too anxious to enjoy myself. All I could think about was the strike, even though no one was talking about it. A few times I brought it up just because it seemed absurd not to. The topic elicited either avoidance or cold stares. Our industry was in the middle of a crisis, and everyone was laughing and sipping cocktails, pretending everything was fine—like the willfully ignorant passengers partying on the *Titanic* as it sank.

A month later the strike ended with a whimper, resulting in a deal that could hardly be called a triumph. The Guild sent out an email instructing us to notify our employers that we were ready to return to work. We still had several episodes to finish for season one of *Breaking Bad*. I was gearing up to go back, feeling a mixture of resignation and low-level dread, when I got a phone call from Vince that threw me for a loop. He wasn't picking up my option.

"It's obvious from your writing samples that you're a good writer. And you're good in the room. But for the amount we're paying you . . . I just had to do too much rewriting on your script."

For the amount we're paying you? Jesus. That was harsh and more than a little insulting. It wasn't until later that I remembered Vince had a fixation on "earning one's pay." When someone pitched a great idea in the room, Vince would often say, "You really earned your pay today." Apparently, I didn't earn mine. But I do wonder: If I were a white man, would my salary even be an issue?

I sat at my desk with my phone in a death grip. Now I understood why I was treated like a leper at the premiere party. It infuriated me that Vince—and obviously others—must've known he was going to fire me, but he waited until now to tell me. I was too shaken to defend myself, let alone air my grievances about the way Vince ran the show. It wouldn't have made a difference anyway.

But I did say, "I'm heartbroken." It was true: I *was* heartbroken, not about leaving the job, but about my tremendous effort not being appreciated. "I worked so hard on this show. I put everything I had into it. Can you at least tell me what I could've done differently?"

Vince said there was nothing I could've done, though I knew one answer was "You could've written more like me." That's what it boils down to on every show. Getting the voice of the show means writing like the showrunner. That is the peculiar gift of a television writer. Ever since that high school English assignment in which I channeled Holden Caulfield, I had always thought I was good at taking on someone else's voice. But perhaps I wasn't.

Then there were my other sins and crimes: I bugged Vince to give Matt Jones the bad news. I called him out for revising my script without telling me. I insisted he talk to the cast and crew about the strike. Time after time, I pressured Vince to step up and do the right thing—and that must've made me super annoying.

After we hung up, I called Larry. "Guess what? Vince just fired me."

For once he seemed genuinely surprised, and my lighthearted façade crumbled. Crying to my agent was never my thing; I wanted him to see me as strong and capable. But now I felt a lump forming in my throat, my eyes stinging with impending tears. Before Larry could offer me a pep talk, I stammered an abrupt goodbye and hung up. Then I ran to the bedroom, flopped down on the mattress, and sobbed.

As I lay there convulsing in a fetal position, I kept thinking, *Why am I so upset?* This wasn't the first time I'd gotten canned, and I wouldn't miss anything about the job except for a handful of people.

But I couldn't stop crying, no matter how irrational it was. Maybe because on some level, I knew I was nearing the end of my rope. There were only so many times I could keep throwing myself into something I knew was killing me.

When my episode aired a few weeks later, no one called except my mom. She didn't have much to say about it, but she did ask whether I was going back to the show for season two. I had to tell her that I was fired, something that never got any easier. Though we talked a lot more now, the ins and outs of my writing career remained a touchy subject. Getting fired might be commonplace in the TV business, but to my parents it was still a failure. *This* was why they sent me to an Ivy League school? I could feel the old frustration arising in me, the disappointment that my parents didn't understand me or my life.

At times like this, the terrible phone conversation we'd had when I first moved to L.A. loomed in my mind—the one where she'd talked about her friends' kids being doctors and lawyers, "and we have to tell them what *you're* doing?" That's the kind of hurtful comment you can never take back. Deep down I still believed my mother was ashamed of me. Now, as I confronted her about it, she insisted that she and my dad had always been proud of me, even if they didn't make a habit of saying it out loud.

"We're not like American parents who are always telling their kids how great they are, spoiling them with praise. That's just not how we are."

I felt a despair that left me at an uncharacteristic loss for words. "Well, I don't like that" was all I could squeak out.

She had no reply, and we seemed to be at an impasse. But the next day, she sent me a long email in which she wrote, "If I have been hard on you, it was because I feared for you, not because I was ashamed of you. It has nothing to do with whether I have confidence in you."

When I thought about the hardships my mom had faced—leaving her family and country behind, starting over in an unfamiliar and often unfriendly place—I began to see why this might be true. "You are such an intelligent, sophisticated, artistic, hardworking, humorous, and sensitive person that a mother cannot ask for more in a daughter."

Like me, my mom was better at expressing herself in writing.

For months after leaving *Breaking Bad*, I dealt with the psychological and emotional fallout in therapy. The worst part was feeling like there was something wrong with me for not being able to just suck it up like most TV writers managed to do. I was sure that any writer with longevity in this business, especially women and people of color, had plenty of experiences like mine, yet they didn't let it stop them. Why was *I* so damn sensitive?

But my inability to grow a thick skin was a blessing in disguise. It allowed me to see the insanity of what I'd been through. I had a breakthrough when I realized that I still thought of Vince as a "nice guy" and was twisting myself into knots trying to reconcile his benevolent image with the insensitive, unkind things he had said and done. I'd been trying not to "overreact" to what happened to me at *Breaking Bad*, hoping that if I didn't make a big deal out of it, the pain would go away. It didn't work.

And then I stopped being in denial. I called this phase "getting in touch with my anger."

I had no desire to talk to Vince again. But during the show's second season, his assistant contacted me. Vince wanted me to submit my *Breaking Bad* script for a Writers Guild Award. I couldn't understand why. I mean, obviously, it would be good publicity for the show to have as many nominated scripts as possible. But why mine? I thought he hated it. I was perplexed but figured what the hell. I submitted the script to the WGA—my original draft, not the version Vince had rewritten—and it was nominated for Outstanding Script of 2008 in the Episodic Drama category. Vince's pilot script was nominated for the same award. The series itself was nominated for Best New Drama.

When the nominations were announced, Vince sent me a congratulatory email that said "You wrote a great script." This was the script, mind you, that he cited as the reason for firing me. Though flattered by the nomination, I declined the invitation to attend the awards ceremony. Vince called me and tried to coax me into going. "We'll all have a good time," he urged. You think so? Sitting at a table with the writers I no longer work with—all of whom were hired back—plus the boss who fired me? I would've had more fun getting a colonoscopy.

All I wanted was to be left alone. But Vince seemed to need something from me that I wasn't willing to give. Did he feel guilty about the way he treated me? Had he realized I was a better writer than he'd thought? I would never find out why he was being so magnanimous, but my strong hunch was that he did it to prove he was the "nice guy" he considered himself to be. Seen that way, his bizarre behavior made perfect sense.

Vince's pilot script won the award, as I had expected. It deserved to win. Out of courtesy, I emailed him to say congratulations. He thanked me, and that was our last communication. He could finally close the book on me with a clear conscience.

Could I do it? Could I quit the business? I felt torn as I went back and forth trying to make up my mind. This was not just my livelihood, but my identity. I thought back to my "*Shawshank Redemption* moment," when I quit *Letterman* and announced that I was going to be a writer. It felt like coming out of the closet, embracing who I really was. Was I willing to give that up? To admit that my dream had turned into a nightmare?

Over the years, my interest in spirituality had deepened and I had dabbled in different traditions, seeking something that would help me find answers to these questions. I read some books, written by a Zen teacher, that focused on the practical application of Buddhist principles in a Western society. Her no-nonsense advice, "Don't take anything personally," became my mantra. She emphasized the difference between "content" and "process"—for instance, if you're angry about what's happening in the White House, the content is politics, but the process is being angry. Though most of us try to fix the content, examining the process is more fruitful. Because if your process is anger, you'll always find something to be angry about.

The Zen teacher hosted an internet call-in show where she gave spiritual advice to people about any aspect of their lives. These calls often revolved around banal topics, but somehow she always made a teachable moment out of them. I learned a lot from listening to the show and even started calling in myself, and the guidance I received was always eye-opening. So, naturally, this was where I turned at the height of my career angst. Of course, I'd talked about this issue in therapy many times, but here was an opportunity to hear a fresh perspective from someone who didn't know me and my whole life story.

I called the teacher to ask for advice about my dilemma.

"I'm struggling with making a decision," I began, my voice trembling. "I'm kind of on the verge of leaving my career." I felt too self-conscious to say what the career was, and I knew no one was expecting me to. Because of the focus on process rather than content, nobody ever talked about specifics.

"For the last few years, I've been slowly, gradually extricating myself from it," I went on. "But I still have a toe in it—and I'm contemplating taking that last toe out. The culture of the business I work in doesn't reflect my values and priorities anymore. So I feel pretty sure about that, but what happens is I start to second-guess that. I start to wonder, is this just a relationship that doesn't work for me anymore, or am I going to bring the same process to my next job?"

"And what if you did bring the same process to your next job?" she asked.

I was stumped. It was so Zen of her to ask a simple question that blew apart my whole reality. I had expected her to say something like, "You might as well stay in your job because if you go do something else, you'll end up just as miserable." Now I realized how pessimistic and punitive that would've sounded. It was the voice in my head.

"Either way," she continued, "you have the process you have, right? And the content of our lives always provides us with the opportunity to look at the processes we do that cause us suffering. In my experience, that's a project over time. But you're supposed to suddenly have clarity so you can make this decision about whether to pull your toe out or not."

"There's just a lot of fear about leaving this career that I've worked so hard to achieve. The voice in my head says, 'If you left and tried something else, if that became a disaster . . . then you threw away all of this hard work.'"

She asked me what would be worth giving up all the hard work for. In other words: What was I looking for that I didn't have now?

"I have a creative job, and it doesn't feel like the creative person in me is getting nurtured. There's a lot of rejection involved, and my self-esteem takes beatings constantly. It's very abusive. There's a part of me that just wants to find creative outlets other than my job."

I had, in fact, already found some of these outlets, like sewing, which was fun and fulfilling. Why couldn't I bring that same excitement to my job? Why was writing a TV show so different from making a dress?

"So, you're just going along, kind of feeling your way through," she said. "There are these parts of you that have needs, and you're wondering how you might meet those needs. And asking yourself: Is the job an overall plus to your life or an overall negative? To approach one's life in that way is going to end in happiness. It just is. Because we begin to bring a spirit of adventure to life, and of experimentation . . . and everything starts working. Regardless of the *content* of our lives, we start to enjoy the *process*."

The thought of living in this curious, openhearted way gave me goosebumps. What she was describing was freedom. Freedom from the self-imposed standards, the idea of who I was supposed to be. I told her I had fantasies of leaving my career and just doing a "regular" job. Sometimes I really thought I could be happy flipping burgers at In-N-Out—clock in, clock out, and you don't take your work home with you. Plus, no one's giving you notes on the Double-Double you just made. But did I really have the stones to do something like that? What would I tell my parents? What would people think? How would I support myself?

Once again, she steered me away from the content. "So, it feels like the project is: Do I stay in my job or not? But the *real* project is how to care for this person who has all this creativity inside of her. There's a part of you who wants to be nurtured, who's looking to the job to meet that need where it will never be met."

I was shocked to hear the truth stated so plainly. For years I had lamented the cruelty and dysfunction of the television business, an unhealthy culture filled with damaged people who both perpetrated abuse and accepted it, believing it was all they deserved. But here was another take on it: the job simply wasn't meeting my needs *and it never would.*

I'd been clinging to the hope that one day I would recapture the glory of my time at *Freaks and Geeks.* But now, looking back, I could see it wasn't even that glorious. There was the sleepless night after telling Judd I didn't want to write a script based on someone else's idea . . . the mortifying clashes with directors . . . the constant anxiety about the show getting canceled. When I took a good hard look at the so-called Best Job I Ever Had, I realized I was chasing a dragon that wasn't worth chasing.

"It just occurred to me that maybe the person I've been sending to my job is this very young person, sort of a third-grader, who used to have all this enthusiasm for creativity." I thought about how much I had thrived with Mrs. Aschauer's encouragement, and what happened when Ms. Merck didn't give me the same support. "And then, slowly over time, that joy got beaten out of her. But that third-grader is still going to the job, feeling hurt."

"Exactly. Because she just wants to go color, just have at it with the paints and the crayons and the whole thing. But now she's got someone looking over her shoulder, critiquing what she's doing. Which might work for an adult in the art world, but it really doesn't work for a third-grader. I mean, you'll never find a third-grade teacher who'll stand over her and say, 'That really doesn't look like a horse.'"

A bitter laugh escaped from my lips. "In my job, that's what a lot of people do. They tell you, 'That doesn't look like a horse.' And they do it in a really mean way."

"It's not helpful, is it?"

My shoulders melted with relief. I felt like I was finally talking to someone sane after being trapped in the loony bin for years.

Everything made sense now, and I understood why I cried when I got canned from *Breaking Bad*. The person who felt inadequate at all those jobs—the one who was crushed when she got yelled at or rewritten or fired—was just a kid. Though I had always balked at "inner child" clichés, I now saw that a part of me remained stuck in a kind of arrested development. The thought of that inner third-grader being put through all the pressures and humiliations of my career filled me with compassion. I would never let that happen to her again.

The decision to quit had been forming for years, gaining mass like a snowball rolling down a mountain. I had been working as a television writer for ten years, and for at least five of them—half of my career—I wanted to quit. The experiences I've shared in this book are only a fraction of what happened to me, a representative sampler plate that leaves out so many similar stories with similar characters. How many times did I relive the same script? Step optimistically into a new writers' room only to get kicked in the face by the same hurtful habits? Be berated for someone else's bad day? One of the things the Zen teacher often said was, "When are we ready to make a change in our lives? When we've suffered enough."

That night I had a long conversation with Mike in my office. He was sitting in the overpriced ergonomic chair I'd bought to relieve the chronic tension in my shoulders, and I was cross-legged on the shag rug, my hands shaking. He was supportive of my decision to quit, even though it meant we'd have to depend heavily on savings and residuals. Financial insecurity scared me, especially as we were now in a full-blown recession, but I had survived many stretches of unemployment before. Having spent my whole adult life working in television, I didn't know how to do anything else. But I was going to have to learn.

Knowing that I had waffled many times before, I begged Mike, "If I wake up tomorrow and I've changed my mind, please remind me of this conversation." But when I opened my eyes the next morning, I felt the same. In fact, I had even more clarity and resolve. There was no more waffling. I was taking that last toe out.

Still in my bathrobe, without even brushing my teeth first, I went straight to my office and called my agent.

"It's over, Larry. I'm quitting the business—for good."

It wasn't the first time I'd talked to him about this, and if there was anyone who didn't need an explanation, it was Larry. He'd been with me from the beginning, and even though I didn't share every grisly detail with him, he knew enough. He had worked intimately, for more than a decade, in a business that he himself described as "broken."

"I totally get it," he said. "But if you ever change your mind . . ."

I smiled and shook my head. An agent till the end. But I knew that soon he would be focusing on clients who, unlike me, were eager, even desperate, to work. I would become a distant memory—the writer, he'd tell people, who peaked too early and burned out.

"I won't. But thanks, Larry. For everything."

I hung up the phone and looked around my office. Bright sunlight was pouring in through the windows, spilling across the vintage Steelcase desk that Carl had handed down to me back in New York. Almost every script of my career was written at this desk, starting with my very first specs, back when I had no idea what was in store for me. I decided it was time to get rid of it. With a new desk, I would start over. I would find my voice again.

16

Home

One night Mike and I made love and realized, a little too late, that I was in the fertile phase of my cycle and we had forgotten to use protection. I'd been practicing a method of birth control that involved charting my temperatures and other fertility signs to determine the day I was ovulating—or, as Mike called it, "egg day."

"Uh-oh," I said, remembering my chart. "Sweetie? I think it might be egg day."

Mike held me closer. "Well, then . . . should I make an honest woman out of you?"

I looked into his face and saw that he was serious. My heart pounded against his chest.

"Are you proposing?"

We both welled up with tears. Mike jumped out of bed, ran to his office-slash-man-cave, and returned with a velvet clamshell box. He opened it, revealing a beautiful ring, a slim band of diamonds set in white platinum that was decorated with delicate etchings.

"Will you marry me?"

I said yes. Yes, yes, yes. When we first started dating, I'd had a meltdown one day, worrying that Mike might turn out to be another commitment-phobe. "I don't want to wake up in five years and still be single," I'd told him. Mike had replied, "If we're still together in five years, we'll be married." In fact, it had taken us only two.

I didn't get pregnant, but the engagement stuck. That night we stayed up late talking about our wedding. I had never fantasized about weddings the way most girls do. Other than a white pillbox hat, I had no idea what I'd like to wear, and I hadn't thought about possible venues or what the food or flowers would be like. It wasn't that I didn't want all those things—I just never let myself go there, in the event that marriage never happened for me. *Especially* when I was dating Carl, I squashed such fantasies the instant they arose. I became an expert at avoiding disappointment while my dreams were quietly being crushed.

Now I was like a kid in a candy store, overwhelmed by the myriad choices. Shortly after I got engaged, I visited my friend Melissa and she took me to see *Sex and the City: The Movie*, which had just come out and featured Carrie Bradshaw's wedding. "I figured you might need some ideas," she said. But that ostentatious affair and Vivienne Westwood gown weren't my style. Mike and I decided that we wanted to get married at Burning Man. For the last couple of years, we had been going to this weeklong festival in the Nevada desert—or, as they like to call it, an arts and self-expression event—and we were already planning to go again that summer. Many of our friends would be there anyway.

To keep our parents from disowning us, we decided to have a second, more traditional wedding in San Francisco, just for family. We planned to tell them about the engagement on Mother's Day—the same holiday that Mike had first met my family two years before. Mike flew up to visit his mom and I went to my parents' house, where my mom was preparing one of her feasts. While she flitted around the kitchen, cooking and chatting with relatives, I arranged garnishes on the serving platters, with my engagement ring squarely in her line of sight. But the hostess with the mostest was too in the zone to notice.

The suspense was killing me. When she was no longer wielding any sharp objects, I sidled up to her at the counter. "Hey, Mom!" I said, wagging my finger in her face.

She stared for a moment, then exclaimed, "Oh my God!"

The cilantro she'd been holding fell from her grip and she threw her arms around me. This was what she'd been waiting for my whole life. After Carl, when she was worried about me ending up an "old maid," I had told my parents, "I want you guys to be prepared for the possibility that I may never get married. I want to—I really do. But if I don't meet Mr. Right, I hope you'll try to accept the life I have."

"Of course we will," she said. "We love you no matter what."

Hearing this had made all the difference. I finally knew that her desire for me to get married wasn't all about checking off a box or showing off to her friends. Sure, that was part of it, too. But she also sincerely wanted me to be happy, whatever that turned out to look like.

The rest of the day was a blur as my dad, brother, sister-in-law, aunties, and uncles congratulated me and peppered me with questions. My mom was so verklempt that she forgot to serve a bunch of the dishes she'd made, not that anyone would notice amid the bountiful piles of food. Mike called and we put our moms on the phone together so they could share their joy. From that day on, they were friends and confidantes—or, as Mike and I liked to say, "in cahoots."

When we told them about the Burning Man wedding, my mom was confused, since she didn't quite get what Burning Man was. Mike's mom was horrified—she thought it was a noisy rave full of unwashed hippies.

"Why would you want to get married with all those weird people around?"

"Mom," said Mike, "we *are* those weird people."

Indeed, it was the Burning Man wedding that truly reflected our tastes and personalities. Mike, having grown up Catholic, had an idea to build a church out of Costco carports, in which we would hold the ceremony. We named it the Cathedral of Blessed Debauchery. His friends made faux stained-glass windows from colored vinyl, depicting the seven deadly sins; the one for gluttony heavily featured bacon. Instead of a cross, we topped the church with a big question mark outlined by the purple glow of EL wire.

I wore a strapless white lace dress, and Mike wore a sixties vintage black tuxedo. We were the most normal-looking people there. My best friend from college played "Rainbow Connection" on the viola as we walked down the aisle, which of course made us weep profusely. Jill, my middle school friend who had introduced me to Mike, officiated the ceremony. After she said, "You may now kiss," she added, "May the Force be with you." Then she sang Pink Floyd's "The Great Gig in the Sky," accompanied by our other musician friends. I still can't listen to that song without crying.

That night Mike and I rode around on an art car, exploring the playa, and slept in the 1968 Airstream trailer we bought with the money we'd received in lieu of wedding gifts. We didn't have a Williams Sonoma registry because, as thirty-six-year-olds who already lived together, the last thing we needed was more plates.

This was not the wedding I would've imagined as a little girl. It was so much better.

Most people have heard about the ritualistic burning of the Man, a gigantic effigy that gave Burning Man its name. But there is also the Temple Burn. The Temple is a majestic several-story structure made of intricately carved wood. Each year a different Temple is erected, and inside it, people leave remembrances of dead loved ones or tokens of things they want to let go of. Then, on the last night, the structure is destroyed in a spectacular fire.

A few days before our wedding, I had biked out to the Temple and put Carl's letter inside—the twelve-page plea he'd written on pink floral stationery, in which he begged me to take him back. I had read the letter only once, that day at *Desperate Housewives*, but for years I'd felt an emotional and psychological drag on me whenever I thought about it stashed away in my file cabinet. Yet I couldn't bring myself to get rid of it—until now.

I laid the letter on the dusty ground and anchored it with a rock. Seeing it surrounded by other notes, pictures, and random objects, took away some of its power. Everybody had a letter like this, or something like it. I wandered around the Temple, soaking it all in, before climbing on my bike and heading back to our camp. On Sunday night, I didn't even bother to watch the Temple Burn. Just knowing the letter was in there, turning to ash, was cathartic. It made me feel even freer from my past and ready to start a new life with my husband.

When I was with Carl, his first answer to everything was no. Mike's first answer to everything was yes. When I wanted to plant a garden, he went to the nursery with me to buy plants, loaded them into the back of his convertible, and got down on his hands and knees to dig holes in the dirt. When I started to tell him about a rescue dog that needed a home, he picked out a name before I even finished my sentence. At first I hesitated to run ideas by him, because I'd been shot down so many times by Carl. But no matter what my request, Mike welcomed it with an open mind and childlike enthusiasm.

For the first time, I could share my love of domesticity with my partner. Like my mom, I had always taken pleasure in making a home and nesting in it. For most of my adult life, I'd been shopping for food alone, with no one to share either the burden or the joy. Mike came with me to Ralphs every Saturday, holding the produce bags open for me and running around looking for weird new snacks. He made it fun.

He makes everything fun.

It didn't matter that I couldn't afford to go on lavish vacations anymore, because being at home with Mike was enough. I thought of the five-star hotels, spas, and infinity pools of my past the same way I remembered the party-all-night, shit-faced romps of my early twenties: with fondness, but no desire to go back. Just like when I was a child, home was now my happy place.

There was nothing better than hanging out in the yard, grilling chicken wings, while Mike made cocktails and rubbed our dog's belly. Sometimes we'd cuddle on the bed in our guest room and listen to prog rock records on an old turntable. On Sunday mornings we'd make pancakes, bacon, and a pot of strong coffee, then sit side by side at the kitchen table and do the crossword, like on our very first date.

Before living with Mike, the last party I had thrown was in 1997, back in New York. I didn't realize how much I had missed having parties until Mike and I began inviting friends over. The parties we threw were a natural outgrowth of the fun we had as a couple, as well as a creative outlet. We had a party to celebrate the thirtieth anniversary of *The Empire Strikes Back*, where we projected the movie in our backyard and served Lando Kale-rissian salad, Wookiee cookies, and s'mores made of Imperial March-mallows. For our eighties-themed party, our friends came dressed as preppies, punks, and New Wave dandies. We had Cool Ranch Doritos, quiche, Cherry Coke, and wine coolers. On the bathroom counter, we put out a giant tub of Dep hair gel, a mangled box of Tylenol, and a hand mirror with a mound of cornstarch on it. A small disclaimer read PROP COKE! DO NOT SNORT!

Our first Christmas together, we bought a tree and went nuts with decorations. I'd grown up celebrating Christmas, but it's different when you're an adult because you can make up your own traditions. Over the years Mike and I started many, like our Christmas Eve ritual of reading all the Christmas cards we'd received and burning them in the fireplace to see what cool colors they emitted when they burst into flames. We put a wooden Advent calendar on our mantel, and instead of filling each day's compartment with gifts or chocolate, we'd write a cherished memory from the year on a piece of paper. Then, every night in December up to the 25th, we'd open one of the little doors and read a memory aloud—a tasty meal, something funny one of us had said, or an unexpected adventure after the GPS had sent us on a strange detour.

A year after I quit television, I started writing this book as a therapeutic exercise, a way to process my experiences and get back into writing, which was now more difficult than ever. I had become not only rusty but frightened. When I sat down to write, I would get a panicky feeling from head to toe, like when you're climbing to the top of a roller coaster and you know that terrifying drop is coming and you can't get off.

So I created rituals to guide myself through the fear. Every day before sitting down at my desk, I would first sit on my cushion and meditate, to calm my nervous system and quiet my mind. While writing, I'd keep a notebook next to my computer in which I would jot down any negative self-talk. At a meditation retreat I attended, this was our assignment for the week; when I read over my list, I couldn't believe how much self-hatred was there. Putting those thoughts on paper gave me an arm's length from them, making it easier to see that they weren't helpful. If a person told me, "Your writing sucks and no one wants to read it," would I trust them? Would I think they were looking out for me? No, I would ignore them and keep going.

After each writing session, I would get down on my cushion and meditate again, like a palate cleanser. Then I'd fill out a questionnaire that I had designed to bring awareness to my writing process. It had questions like "What sensations do you feel in your body?" I often noticed that my shoulders were hunched, for instance, or my stomach was in knots. I'd breathe into these areas, letting the tension dissolve. Then I would look at the negative self-talk in my notebook and counter it with things that were positive and specific. For example, the antidote to "You didn't get enough done today" would be to celebrate a sentence or phrase I was proud of, something I'd been struggling with and had finally mastered.

After a while, with enough self-encouragement, I got to the point where I actually liked what I wrote a lot of the time.

But I kept the focus on process rather than results. Instead of saying, "I'm going to finish this chapter," I'd say, "I'm going to write for two hours." It was far easier to meet process goals and feel successful—and, ultimately, I couldn't control the results anyway. The chapter would be done when it was done. All I could do was keep plugging away at it until then, cheering myself on along the way. "You did it! You showed up!" Showing up was more than half the battle. My book became a *practice*, instead of a stressful sprint toward a finish line.

There were no more marathon writing sessions. I took plenty of breaks. I'd cook, do laundry, exercise, work on other projects. I would write in the morning and sew in the afternoons. Sometimes I'd feel the old pull to keep writing until I was exhausted, but I would make myself switch gears so that I could nourish different parts of myself. The link between stress and success that was forged when I pulled my first all-nighter in high school was finally broken. I discovered that I didn't need to be miserable to write well.

A few months after Mike and I got married, we started trying to get pregnant. But both of us had reservations. We had watched some of our friends' lives get overtaken by babies and toddlers.

Even though I always assumed I'd have kids, to be honest, babies seemed foreign to me, even after my nephew was born. I didn't feel compelled to pick them up, kiss them, and coo over them the way I did with dogs. If I saw someone walking a raggedy-ass mutt, I had to restrain myself from fawning all over the good little boy or girl. Not so much with human children.

Mike and I tried to imagine our life with kids, but it wasn't easy. People told us, "Having kids is great because you get to be a kid again!" Well, we didn't need that—we already felt like kids. One weekday we walked to the neighborhood 7-Eleven in our bathrobes, just for fun. When the cashier asked why, I said, "It's bathrobe day at the office," and he said, "I want to work where *you* work."

I wondered if I could have a baby and still write. When I brought it up with a life coach, she said, "What makes you think you can't do both? My mom raised two kids while she worked full-time *and* started a nonprofit." But I didn't have role models like that. And most of these "having it all" stories glossed over the hidden supports undergirding them: generational wealth, racial privilege, nannies, and extended families that were available and willing to help.

Despite my ambivalence, I was brainwashed into thinking my fertility was an urgent matter. My periods had become erratic and I'd been having some midcycle spotting, so I went to my gynecologist and she talked me into seeing a fertility specialist to get myself checked out.

"You're no spring chicken," she said, as if I were sixty rather than thirty-seven. "If there's any chance you'll want to have children, you need to get on it *now*. Trust me, you'll regret it if you wait."

She stuck a business card in my hand. With the fear of God in me, I obeyed and made an appointment at the upscale fertility clinic she recommended, wondering if she would get a commission for the referral.

Walking into the huge, sleek waiting area, Mike and I were taken aback. It seemed more like a Botox spa than a medical facility, right down to the New Age music. The fertility specialist was an ageless man with a waxy complexion, his hair neatly parted and combed like a Brylcreem ad. As he asked me questions about my health, his demeanor was oddly stilted, as if he were a robot attempting to imitate human behavior. He seemed unconcerned that my spotting might indicate a serious illness. All he cared about was getting me pregnant.

"How long have you two been trying to conceive?"

I glanced at Mike. "About a year?"

The doctor looked up from his notes. "That long? No birth control at all?"

I shook my head. "I chart my cycles using the Fertility Awareness Method. So I know exactly when I'm ovulating, and we always have sex around that time. But I have noticed that my luteal phase is unusually short—maybe ten, eleven days—and I know that can make it hard for the egg to implant."

"That's true. But if we do artificial insemination or IVF, I can make your luteal phase longer," he said with a confident smile, then added, ". . . if you'll let me."

After that creepy interaction, we turned to alternative methods to boost our chances. But they all seemed ridiculous, from chanting in

Sanskrit to having sex at a Point Reyes inn where women allegedly got pregnant in droves. A friend gave me a book about fertility-boosting yoga, but I couldn't bring myself to read it, let alone do the poses. After seeing an article about a fertility trend called V-steaming, where you squat over a bucket of hot water infused with mugwort and wormwood, we decided there would be no more trying. If we happened to get pregnant, great. If not, that would be perfectly fine.

Turned out the spotting I'd originally gone to the doctor for was being caused by a uterine polyp, which my new doctor estimated had been growing for at least two years. It was benign, but I had to get it surgically removed. When I awoke in the recovery room, Mike was next to my bed, holding my hand. I turned my head to find our Winnie the Pooh on one side of my pillow and, on the other, a stuffed felt uterus named Flo that we'd gotten at a craft fair. He helped steady me as I got dressed, still woozy from the anesthesia, and held a bowl for me to puke into when I became nauseated.

Though the surgery should've made it easier to get pregnant, we still weren't able to conceive. The acceptance of our childless-ness came with far less drama than I'd imagined. I had once envied women who knew for sure that they wanted to be mothers, as well as those who vehemently did not. But the desire to have children is not always black or white—it's a continuum, like sexuality and so many other things that our society frames in extremes. Mike and I saw ourselves as a family, even without human babies. We had our furry ones and, of course, each other.

A lot of upsetting stuff came up while I was writing the book. I worried that people would be mad at me for sharing my story. I had dreams where Carl would be yelling at me, chasing me through the streets, his face red with rage. I would process all this with my therapist week after week, trying to believe her when she said, "You don't owe him anything." She helped me reframe the terrible experiences I'd had in my TV jobs so that I no longer blamed myself for being treated badly.

Writing a memoir is like reliving all the worst parts of your life— voluntarily. I often asked myself why I was putting myself through that when I could've just shoved those memories away and never talked about them again. But that's what it is to be a writer: you write because you can't help it.

In October 2016, I finished the first draft. I still had a lot of work to do, but I wanted to celebrate this milestone. Mike and I threw a party at our house. The invitation had a picture of me smiling behind my laptop, its cover adorned with a bumper sticker with *The Big Lebowski* quote, "I'm unemployed." I made a dress for the occasion from fabric that had cute pastel typewriters on it. We hung out with friends around the firepit, drank tiki cocktails, and ate way too many cupcakes.

Three days later, my mother had a stroke.

Her health had always been good, other than high blood pressure. She was taking medication for it, but her constant worrying didn't help; in modern parlance this would've been called an anxiety disorder. In 2015 she had suffered a minor stroke that affected only her eyesight, after which she vowed to "try to relax more." But she never sought therapy or stress management and remained as busy as ever, going out of her way to take care of friends and relatives and worrying about them needlessly. And a year later, she had a massive brain hemorrhage in the middle of the night. After my dad awoke and called for an ambulance, she was rushed to the hospital and underwent a four-hour surgery.

When I walked into her post-op recovery room, the sight of her made my stomach drop. Her short, permed hair was shaved on one side and covered with a big bandage. Her face—still beautiful and wrinkle-free at seventy-five—was now swollen and sallow. She struggled to open her eyes and saw me staring at her, frightened.

In a slurred, hoarse voice, she said, "Don't worry about me."

Ironic advice from a woman who'd spent her whole life worrying about me and everyone else she loved. Soon she was unconscious again and her body began to shiver, seizure-like, from head to toe. I was crying so hard that my dad dragged me from the room and banished me to the lobby.

My mom was paralyzed on her entire left side. She could no longer stand or walk; she could barely even keep her head upright. Since she had trouble chewing and swallowing, a feeding tube was surgically implanted into her stomach. She was incontinent and had to wear diapers, which is an indignity for any adult but even more unspeakable for someone as fastidious as my mother.

The worst part was that her brain function was decimated, her personality erased. She had almost no understanding of what was happening around her. When the nurses came by to give her neuro checks, asking her a series of simple questions, she failed most of them. One time a nurse asked her where I was born. My mom turned to look at me, her face blank.

"Mrs. Lin?" the nurse repeated. "Do you know where your daughter was born?"

After a long pause, she said, "California."

I winced and wiped my eyes. The stroke had erased my childhood from her memory.

Her most lucid moment happened in early November, the day after the presidential election, when I switched on CNN in her hospital room. Images of Donald Trump's gloating orange face flashed across the screen. I pulled up a plastic chair next to my mom's bed, pointed to the news coverage, and told her, "Trump won."

"How did this happen?" she asked in her halting speech.

She was never that clearheaded again. Lying motionless in her hospital bed, she had no interest in reading, watching TV, or listening to music. I loaded up her iPad with audiobooks, but she wouldn't even touch it anymore. All she did was stare into space. When I showed her the get-well cards people had sent, she had no reaction. I became convinced she was no longer capable of reading. Once a gifted writer, and now words were inaccessible to her.

She spent three months in a skilled nursing facility, where a beefy physical therapist worked with her to no avail. When it became clear that rehabilitation wasn't possible, my mom was allowed to return home, taking up residence in what used to be the den on the first floor. Mike set up the small room with a huge flat-screen TV, even though she never watched it, and built a bed inside the closet so that my dad could sleep next to her hospital bed and still leave enough space to maneuver her wheelchair.

For the next few months, I drove out to Azusa two or three times a week to help out. I'd read the newspaper to my mom or paint her nails bright red, her favorite color. I'd help her with her PT exercises, telling myself she was getting stronger even as her head drooped from her neck like a broken flower stem.

Mike and I convinced my dad to hire a part-time nurse, but he still spent all his time caring for her, trying to create a semblance of normalcy. After months of figuring out the logistics of getting her to the mall, he took her to the Din Tai Fung next to Nordstrom, hoping that her cherished ritual of eating soup dumplings and shopping would spark something in her. But when I asked him later how it went, he said, "It was okay." And in those three words, I could sense the sadness that he would probably never be able to articulate.

One morning in the summer of 2017, he couldn't get my mom to wake up. She was rushed to the hospital again and found to have had another massive brain hemorrhage, this one so severe that the doctors wouldn't even operate. Best-case scenario, she'd be a vegetable; worst case, she'd die on the table.

My dad chose to bring her home for hospice care and we started wrapping up her affairs. She died a week later, with Mike on one side of her bed and me on the other, cradling her freshly manicured hand. My dad had just gone to get something from the kitchen. It's hard not to believe that on some level she knew this and waited until he left the room to spare him.

Her death was tragic, of course, but, to be honest, also a relief. She had no quality of life after the stroke. I had essentially lost her that night in October 2016 and had been saying goodbye ever since. That nine-month period before her death was heart-wrenching, but not in the way it might have been if there were important things left unsaid between us. I was so grateful for the hard work we had done on our relationship, the painful conversations we braved, and the growing calm after the storms. Though I was sad to lose her, I didn't have regrets.

Over the next few months, I helped sort through my mom's things, giving away clothes to her sisters, tossing expired cosmetics, shredding paperwork. When I was a kid, my mom had compulsively thrown stuff out; I'd often search for something all over the house only to learn she had disposed of it long ago. But going through her dresser drawers after her death, I found the white crocheted cape that she used to dress me in when I was a baby, the one her neighbor had made after I'd come home from the hospital. My mom had kept it for forty-six years

I clutched the cape to my face and sobbed into it. She may not have been an effusive American mother who said "I love you" all the time, but there was no doubt she did, maybe more than I could even fathom.

When I was in my twenties, I had a vivid dream one night that I was lying on the couch in the house I grew up in, my hands folded atop my big swollen belly. I was pregnant and filled with the deepest joy and contentment I'd ever felt. Though it never translated into a burning desire to have children in my waking life, the dream stuck with me for many years and was part of my long-held assumption that I would have kids one day.

Now I look back and wonder if this dream was about me or about my mom.

The thing about trauma is that it never goes away completely. Even after years of processing my showbiz experiences, I would occasionally get triggered—like when I'd see one of my former bad bosses being lauded in a newspaper article. I kept working on this with Bonnie and even did some EMDR (Eye Movement Desensitization and Reprocessing), a type of therapy designed to treat PTSD. Even though my situation was nothing compared to that of, say, soldiers or victims of physical abuse, I felt so stuck in some areas of my life that I was willing to try anything.

The therapy unlocked something in me, and I began doing things without the usual fear or inhibitions. I confronted someone who'd been using me for my screenwriting connections. I apologized to a childhood friend for ostracizing her in the fifth grade. I started getting up onstage at The Moth, an open-mic storytelling competition, and working part-time as a TV and film extra—after insisting for years that I was not a performer. Though I had never liked talking to strangers, I made, for Burning Man, a life-sized replica of Lucy's "Psychiatric Help" booth from the Peanuts cartoon, where I gave free advice to dozens of people who wandered by. I had amazing conversations at the Lucy Booth, because it allowed me to bypass the small talk and get right to the good stuff.

A guy I met at the booth leaned forward on his stool after I'd given him advice. He rested his elbows on the wooden plank between us and clasped his hands.

"Now, what do *you* need help with?" he asked.

This happened a lot. People would turn the tables on me, which I loved because, like Lucy, I was not uniquely qualified to give advice. Or qualified at all! The beauty of the booth was that anyone could be either therapist or client.

"I've been working on a book for ten years," I said, ashamed of what I thought was an unreasonable pace. "It's pretty much done, but I'm afraid to put it out there."

This was my big secret. I had been revising my manuscript over and over, trying to make it perfect and un-rejectable, as if that were even possible. I wanted to share my story, not hide it away. But I was afraid to put it out into the world because everything in my gut was warning me this was dangerous.

"Put it out there, girl!" The guy slapped the booth with his palm. "It's *your* book. If someone doesn't like it, they can go suck a lemon."

These words from a stranger in a sparkly orange vest and moose-knuckle shorts rang in my head for days. His pep talk, along with my EMDR-fueled courage, propelled me to write query letters to agents and email them my manuscript.

While my book was on submission to publishers, we were in the midst of a global pandemic. I talked with my therapist every week on the phone, holed up in the Airstream for privacy while Mike puttered in the house. At this turning point in my career, I felt especially vulnerable. I had fallen into the habit of judging myself by old standards, comparing myself to the conventional, showy achievements of people who were still in the rat race. Many of my conversations with Bonnie were a variation on this theme: "What have I done with my life? I've got nothing to show for the last ten years."

"You've built a wonderful life with a partner who loves and supports you," Bonnie would remind me. "You learned how to talk to your parents. You quit a career that almost no one has the courage to walk away from, and you found your creative spark again. I wouldn't call that nothing."

She was always pointing out things like that. Things that I was blind to because I'd been living with them for so long—and because I was defining success the way I used to.

For a while, I was making lavender-scented eye pillows and selling them on Etsy. But I was embarrassed by it, picturing myself like Jan on *The Office* with her Serenity by Jan candles. Though I put great craft and care into sewing, blogging, cosplaying, and making projects for Burning Man, I didn't think of these activities as legit because they weren't bringing in income. The cozy home I made with Mike, the tasty meals I'd put on our table, the fun excursions and social events I'd arranged—none of these things counted when I was taking stock of my "success." Looking at myself through this narrow lens, I was just a has-been who hadn't done anything in a decade.

But that view of myself started to change.

Seven years before my mother died, she wrote an article about their house getting broken into. She submitted it to a Taiwanese newspaper and it got published. When she showed it to me, I congratulated her and displayed it on our fridge, even though it was written in Chinese and I couldn't read it. I was hoping it was a belated start to the writing career she always should've had.

But she never published again—or even tried to, as far as I knew. This reinforced the narrative I'd been telling about my mom for ages: that she was a frustrated writer who had given up on her dreams. It wasn't until she died that I realized this story wasn't true. At Taiwanese memorial services, the eulogies are always about the person's accomplishments, their hard work and sacrifice, the honors their children have won. When I gave my mom's eulogy, I talked about her personality, what I loved about her, the moments of joy we shared. I talked about how she took care of the people she loved. How she treated Mike like a son. How she spoiled our dog with sashimi. I talked about her crispy duck, her green thumb, her shopping obsession. The after-school cupcakes and snuggling me to sleep during *Fantasy Island*. These were the things I would remember her for. These were her accomplishments.

My mother wasn't a frustrated writer. She wasn't bitter about having to take care of us—she chose to take care of us. She lived a beautiful, fulfilling life. She was a success.

When I eventually got my book deal, I celebrated with Mike over dinner at our favorite Indian restaurant, where we ordered almost everything on the menu. I rolled home that night and called my dad to tell him the news. My stomach, bloated with lamb vindaloo, tightened as I waited for him to pick up, because part of me was worried he'd have the wrong reaction. Would he understand what a big deal this was?

"Hey, Dad."

"Is everything okay?" He always says this when I call.

"Yeah, I just wanted to tell you the good news. I sold my book!"

Then I heard a noise that was the closest thing to a squeal that has ever come from my dad. He didn't ask questions, just congratulated me and said he'd take us out to celebrate. Figuring he'd want to know, I started to tell him about the advance.

"It's not about the money," he interrupted. "It's the sense of accomplishment."

His reaction was perfect. As I hung up the phone, I was struck by the memory of my dad saying, "You've had enough fun," when I begged him to let me go to that Culture Club concert. Now I remembered that not only had he let me go to their concert the year before, but he drove me and my friend Jill there and stood with us through the entire show, next to a giant amp that probably gave him early hearing loss.

That was the kind of dad he was. And still is.

A couple of weeks before the book deal came through, I was sitting in the Airstream, having a phone session with Bonnie, and talking about how each rejection I received stung a little less than the one before. It was an unusually cold January night, and I was bundled up in my gingham pajamas and wrapped in a fleece blanket, with my legs tucked under me and my dog curled up by my side.

"For so many years while I was writing this book, I couldn't even *think* about the possibility that it might not get published. But now it looks like it might not . . . and I'm okay with that."

My definition of success had evolved, slowly but surely. That night as Mike and I lay in bed, I asked him, "Would you be okay if I never wrote anything again and just worked as an extra the rest of my life?"

"Of course." He put his arms around me and kissed me. "I don't love you because you're a writer. I love you because you're you."

Everything after that was gravy.

Acknowledgments

Writing the acknowledgments for this memoir is a daunting task because there are so many people who have helped, influenced, and shepherded me throughout my life. If I were to include them all, this section would go on longer than the end credits of a Marvel movie. I hope my gratitude for them is evident in the pages you just read. On *this* page, I would like to thank all the people who specifically helped make this book possible.

My agent, Jon Michael Darga, believed in this manuscript from the beginning and enthusiastically took on the uphill battle of getting it published. His intuitive suggestion to add more of my personal life to the story brought it closer to my original vision and that of my eventual publisher. He held my hand through a few freakouts and patiently answered my newbie questions about the publishing world. Thanks also to Todd Shuster for his insightful notes, and the rest of the Aevitas team who touched my book: Kate Mack, Deirdre Smerillo, Maggie Cooper, Arlie Johansen, and Catherine Bai.

Huge thanks to my editorial team, especially Pamela Cannon, who saw the big picture and urged me to go deeper than I thought I was capable of. Like all great editors, she refused to let me look bad, no matter how much I insisted. Kathleen Harris oversaw the editorial process with aplomb and kept many trains running on time while also keeping it casual. Terry Deal checked my facts and made sure my commas were in the right place.

Much gratitude to my publisher, Zibby Owens, a force of nature with boundless energy, generosity, and ingenuity. She created a fun, collaborative experience that a first-time author could only dream of. Leigh Newman had faith in my "writerly chops" and told me I was funny when I needed to hear it. Thanks to Anne Messitte, Bridie Loverro, Madeline Woda, Sherri Puzey, Diana Tramontano, Sierra Grazia, Chelsea Grogan, Lindsay Quackenbush, and everyone else on the Zibby Books team who worked tirelessly to make my book a success. And a shout-out to the Zibby Books authors—all talented and very cool women—for their camaraderie and cheerleading, sans pom-poms.

Every writer needs friends and readers. Melissa Miscione Dart read early drafts of these chapters before I even knew they were a book. Suzanne Casamento, Aadip Desai, Leah Breuer, Cat Crimins, Brooke Michael Smith, and Dan Smith gave notes and/or encouragement. Andrew Durkin gifted me with his editorial assistance and wise guidance. Thanks to Jill Knapp for reconnecting us, and for her advice about social media (and eye shadow).

Is it totally L.A. to thank your therapist in the acknowledgments? Bonnie Sicher helped me process and recover from the experiences I've written about in this book. Without her insights, I would not have been able to tell this story.

Finally, I'd like to thank my family—especially my dad—for not asking, "When are you going to get a real job?" during the twelve years I was working on this thing. And there's no credit sequence long enough to thank my husband, Mike Carter, for his unflagging love, support, and compassionate feedback. He knew how much I needed to write this book and he never let me quit. It truly would not exist without him.

About the Author

Patty Lin is a former TV writer and producer whose credits include *Freaks and Geeks*, *Friends*, *Desperate Housewives*, and *Breaking Bad*. She has also written pilots for Fox, CBS, and Nickelodeon. Her *Breaking Bad* episode, "Gray Matter," was nominated for a Writers Guild Award for Outstanding Script of 2008 in the Episodic Drama category. She retired from television writing to pursue other interests and occasionally appears in background acting roles. She lives in Los Angeles with her husband.

@virtualpattylin
www.pattylin.com